Key Concepts in Chinese Thought and Culture

Published in partnership between FLTRP and Palgrave Macmillan, the Key Concepts in Chinese Thought and Culture offer a unique insight into Chinese culture, defining and contextualizing some of China's most fundamental and at times complex philosophical concepts. In a concise and reader-friendly manner, these works define a variety of quintessentially Chinese terms such as harmony (hé/和) or association (xīng/兴) – and examine how they first appeared and developed in Chinese culture, the impact they had on Chinese thought and why they continue to have significant meaning in China today. At a time when the understanding of different histories, languages and cultures globally is at a premium, this series provides a valuable roadmap to the concepts which underpin 21st century Chinese society.

Hao Fan

Lunli and Confucian Moral Theory

外语教学与研究出版社
FOREIGN LANGUAGE TEACHING AND RESEARCH PRESS

palgrave
macmillan

Hao Fan
Nanjing, China

Translated by
Yanan Shao
Foreign Languages School
Tianjin Chengjian University
Tianjin, China

ISSN 2524-8464   ISSN 2524-8472 (electronic)
Key Concepts in Chinese Thought and Culture
ISBN 978-981-99-9104-4   ISBN 978-981-99-9105-1 (eBook)
https://doi.org/10.1007/978-981-99-9105-1

Jointly published with Foreign Language Teaching and Research Publishing Co., Ltd
The print edition is not for sale in China (Mainland). Customers from China (Mainland) please order the print book from: Foreign Language Teaching and Research Publishing Co., Ltd.

© Foreign Language Teaching and Research Publishing Co., Ltd 2024

This Palgrave Macmillan imprint is published by the registered company Springer Nature Singapore Pte Ltd.
The registered company address is: 152 Beach Road, #21-01/04 Gateway East, Singapore 189721, Singapore

If disposing of this product, please recycle the paper.

Publisher's Note to "Key Concepts in Chinese Thought and Culture Series" (English Edition)

In the course of human history, Chinese civilization has always been known for its long history and remarkable breadth and depth. In a unique geographical environment and thanks to a fascinating historical development, the Chinese nation has nurtured academic traditions, humanistic spirits, values, a way of thinking, ethics and customs unfound elsewhere in the world. All of this was expounded and sublimated by Confucius, Mozi, Laozi, Zhuangzi, Mencius, Xunzi and other ancient sages and philosophers, and encapsulated into thousands of highly concise and profound key concepts underpinning the brilliant and rich Chinese culture. Reflective of the supreme wisdom and rational thinking of the Chinese nation, the concepts have come to be known as "key concepts in Chinese thought and culture." They are the brainchild fostered by the Chinese nation engaged for thousands of years in independently exploring and rationally thinking about the universe, the world, social norms and ethics, ways of thinking and values. They represent the unique and most significant hallmark of Chinese thought and civilization produced by the Chinese nation. They are the greatest intellectual legacy left by ancient Chinese philosophers to the contemporary Chinese and the most valuable intellectual wealth contributed by the Chinese nation to world civilization.

The past four decades of reform and opening up have witnessed continued growth of the Chinese economy and its comprehensive strength. As an active participant and contributor to globalization, China has been increasingly admired in the international community for its national conditions, history, thoughts and culture. On the other hand, its basic research has fallen behind with the development of the times. So far there exists no comprehensive and systematic collation and interpretation of the concepts that reflect its thought and culture, for introduction to overseas readers. There is no unified comprehension and interpretation of many terms, especially those reflective of the unique Chinese philosophy, humanism, values, and ways of thinking. It is even more regrettable that the lack of unified norms for the translation of such terms into foreign languages has frequently led to deviations from their actual meaning, and consequently confusion and even misunderstanding on the part of overseas readers may result. To ameliorate the above circumstances, we officially launched in 2014 the "Key Concepts in Chinese Thought and Culture Project." Drawing on the excellent history of traditional Chinese thought and culture, the Project has focused on key concepts encapsulating Chinese philosophy, humanistic spirits, values, ways of thinking, and cultural characteristics, especially those with implications for the development of contemporary world civilization and in line with the common values of the human race. Those concepts were then interpreted in objective and concise Chinese and translated into English and other languages, for overseas readers to better understand the connotations and essence of Chinese thought and culture, and consequently to promote equal dialogue and exchanges between Chinese civilization and other civilizations of the world, so as to jointly build a community and shared future of mankind. So far, over 600 terms have been collated, interpreted and translated by Project experts and published by the Foreign Language Teaching and Research Press (FLTRP) in six volumes in Chinese and English under the serial title of "Key Concepts in Chinese Thought and Culture." However, due to style and volume restrictions, the historical context, semantic context, origin and evolution, academic influence and the underlying humanistic spirit, values, and modern implications haven't been fully elaborated for some of them. To give overseas audiences a more comprehensive and in-depth understanding of them, FLTRP and Springer Nature have jointly planned the new "Key Concepts in Chinese Thought and Culture Series" (English Edition).

Each volume of this series will be centered on one concept only or a couple of closely related concepts. The authors are required to examine in detail the historical context, semantic context, origin and evolution, and academic influence, based on the research findings on ancient Chinese literature. They are expected to unfold their elaboration around important figures in the development of Chinese thought and culture, as well as their works, theories and academic viewpoints. The series thus features comprehensive and original academic contributions offering relevant theoretical approaches and insights based on independent research by the respective authors. Integrating professional studies with popular interest, it emphasizes integration of corroboration and exposition and equal emphasis on Oriental and Occidental scholarship. All authors selected are young and middle-aged scholars accomplished in the study of Chinese thought and culture. It is believed that the publication of this series will make it possible for overseas readers to have a more systematic understanding of the philosophy, humanistic values, academic perspectives and theoretical viewpoints underlying the key concepts of Chinese thought and culture, and a clearer understanding of the ways of thinking, the values and cultural characteristics of the intellectual world of the Chinese nation and overseas Chinese.

We are grateful to Harmen van Paradijs, Vice President of Springer Nature Group, and Myriam Poort, Editorial Director, Humanities and Social Sciences, Springer Nature for their generous support in planning and publishing this series.

Foreign Language Teaching and Research Press
August 2018

CONTENTS

CHAPTER 1

Introduction: How to Enjoy the Cultural Elements of *Lunli*?

1 Big Ears for Einsteinian Gravitational Waves

Every nation has some basic discourses that carry its own codes of life. These discourses are the meta-concepts or meta-ideas of the discourse and value systems and serve as the root of the nation's culture. They shape or help shape the cultural genes of the nation, and are the important chromosome of its civilization. Because of their genetic significance in creating life, they are often expressed and interpreted in a cultural instinctive way as the habitus of mind and are used day by day knowingly; because of the cruel power of their genetic reproduction logic, in the long evolution of civilization history, emerging adolescent cultural elements always try to detach themselves from their original culture in some determined way to declare their independence, but time and time again, their inescapable destiny always makes them ultimately aware and dependent of their original culture.

The diversity of the world requires civilizations to find a reference to move forward through dialogue and gain vitality for growth, but there is always a potential misalignment and risk in the dialogue between civilizations: on the one hand, civilizations are in a constant search for a similar discourse or a so-called soulmate among different cultures for mutual justification; on the other hand, even if the civilizations look similar, their

© Foreign Language Teaching and Research Publishing Co., Ltd 2024
H. Fan, Lunli *and Confucian Moral Theory*, Key Concepts
in Chinese Thought and Culture,
https://doi.org/10.1007/978-981-99-9105-1_1

cultural meanings are diametrically different due to their different positions in the cultural system, which leads to a terrible and sad dislocation of meanings and alienation of values in the dialogue between civilizations.

Based on these basic concepts, humans must evolve big ears to detect Einsteinian gravitational waves,[1] so as to find out the following:

- the cultural elements from local, global, traditional and modern civilizations;
- the original signs of life derived from the national spirit at the roots of civilization and the depths of culture;
- these signs of life in the main forms of life that currently carry them during their long journey of civilization through time and space;
- the mutual interaction between different cultures;
- the best of exotic flavors and the cultural symphony between them and the domestic signs of life, and thus the common heartbeat of modern civilizations.

Of course, to have these big ears, one must have an open and confident mind and wisdom as well to see the error of a thousand miles that may be caused by the slightest difference in similar concepts in the realm of the invisible and the inaudible.

In the context of both the dialogue and the clash of civilizations, perhaps no academic effort is more important and urgent than the mutual listening and understanding of these fundamental discourses, whose significance is by no means limited to the reconstruction of indigenous discourses. Within a civilization, it has the original significance that knowing thyself answers the ultimate questions: Where do we come from? Where are we going? In the dialogue between civilizations, it is the philosophical prerequisite for genuine understanding of cultures and reconciliation of civilizations.

Lunli is one of the most important basic discourses in Chinese culture. One can hardly deny its genetic significance in Chinese culture, and its status in the history of civilization has been revealed by five thousand years of Chinese cultural tradition as well as by outstanding researches

---

[1] In 1916, Albert Einstein predicted the existence of gravitational waves based on the theory of general relativity. In the last decade or so, scientists from all over the world have built many gravitational wave detectors that have successfully captured the sound of distant stars from distant times, and these detectors have been compared to big ears.

in China and elsewhere and in ancient and modern times, but the new challenge is how to enjoy the cultural elements of *lunli*.

Obviously, Hans-Georg Gadamer's hermeneutics has been stretched to the limit in terms of interpreting fundamental discourses such as *lunli*. Neither original intended meaning nor meaning and neither interpretation nor understanding can reveal the far-reaching and incessant genetic significance of *lunli* in Chinese culture, and grasp the chromosomal status of *lunli* in Chinese culture in the dialogue between civilizations. To understand *lunli*, or more broadly, to understand the signs of life derived from those meta-concepts or meta-ideas of any culture, one must use the great philosophical wisdom that Laozi discussed to start his *Daodejing*: "The *dao* that can be told of is not the absolute *dao*; the names that can be given are not absolute names." Because they are the cultural genes of national life, these concepts can be told of or named, but once they are told of or named, they no longer are the *dao* or the name they are intended to be. They are absolute in that they are the roots or in a position of the meta. According to the *Daodejing*, "The nameless is the origin of all things while the named is their mother."

Lunli is an important cultural chromosome of the Chinese nation. It participated in the historic creation of the cultural life of the Chinese nation in its primitive state of namelessness. While being named, i.e. during the *lunli* awareness of Chinese culture and the world's cultural awareness of China, it has started and developed the 5,000-year civilizational history of *lunli* culture. In Chinese culture, the *lunli* that can be told of is the absolute *dao* of *lunli* in the general sense; the *lunli* that can be named and acquired the name as such is not the *lunli* in the everyday sense, much less in the Western sense.

The *lunli* that can be told of is not the absolute *dao* and the *lunli* that can be named is not the absolute name. In listening for the cultural flavor of *lunli*, it is imperative to philosophically examine Chinese cultural tradition, cross-cultural dialogue, and the history of civilization, so as to both hear the Chinese voice of *lunli* and see its universal significance in the history of civilization.

2   WHAT IS THE SUPREME
CONCEPT OF CHINESE CULTURE?

The conclusion of the philosophical examination of the local cultural roots of China is that *lun* is the supreme concept of Chinese culture that *lun* and *dao* are chromosomes in the genes of Chinese culture.

The German existentialist philosopher Karl Theodor Jaspers (1883–1969) proposed the Axial Period, and Jin Yuelin carried on this concept, stating that the most important contribution of the Axial Period was to put forward some supreme concepts. However, both the Axial Period and the supreme concepts have encountered serious logical and historical challenges.

Jaspers stated that, "It would seem that this axis of history is to be found in the spiritual process that occurred between 800 and 200 B.C. It is there that we meet with the most deep-cut dividing line in history. Man, as we know him today, came into being. For short we may style this the 'Axial Period'."[2] The Axial Period was the time when the foundation of human spirituality was laid, and the common awakening to the belief that humans could spiritually elevate themselves to the same level as the universe arose almost simultaneously in different regions such as China, Greece, Hebrews, and India, giving birth to such prophets of thought as Laozi, Confucius, Socrates, Plato, and Buddha.

Jin Yuelin went further to point out that this spiritual foundation was marked by the creation of some "supreme concepts." The enlightenment of the Axial Period has the status as the root of civilizational history. "Humanity has always lived by everything that was thought and created in the Axial Period, and every new leap recalls this period and is ignited by it."[3] The renaissance discourse, which is widely popular in the world today, points to the Axial Period in a significant sense.

The concept of the Axial Period is highly expressive and influential, but it has been the subject of intense academic controversy since its inception. Many scholars argue that it has a clear Western-centric tendency,

---

[2] Cited by Peter Watson, Ideas: A History of Thought and Invention, from Fire to Freud, New York: HarperCollins, 2005.

[3] Karl Theodor Jaspers, *The Origin and Goal of History*, Beijing: Huaxia Publishing House, 1989, p. 14.

cutting the entire history of civilization in half.[4] It is an obvious fact that, according to the theory of the Axial Period, Chinese civilization is only 2,000 years old, starting from Laozi and Confucius, and the 3,000-odd years as the root cause are meaningless, thus reducing the 5,000-year history of Chinese civilization to only 2,000 years. As some scholars have criticized that the idea of the Axial Period came from Hegel, who believed that, "All history goes toward and comes from Christ. The appearance of the Son of God is the axis of world history."[5] The Axial Period is only a theoretical assumption of Western thinkers, not a real concept; it is only an explanatory concept, not a factual one.[6]

However, no matter how deep the controversy over the Axial Period may be, it is undeniably a concept that has had a great impact. To suspend this cross-cultural controversy, another question needs to be asked: assuming that an Axial Period really existed, was the supreme concept put forward by Chinese civilization in this period what Jin Yuelin called *dao*?

In his *On dao*, Jin Yuelin discovered that each cultural region has its central idea, and each central idea has its supreme concept, which is the basic driving force. China has the *dao* based on Confucianism, Daoism and Mohism, India has Brahman or Nirvana, Greece has the Logos, and Hebrews has God. However, the facts of spiritual history show that the most significant awareness of Chinese civilization in the Axial Period was not only *dao*, but also *lun*, they constitute the two supreme concepts of Chinese culture which supplement and interact with each other in the so-called Axial Period, and they are chromosomes of Chinese civilization.

---

[4] As Cho-yun Hsu (1930–) said, the theory of the Axial Period is suspicious of highlighting ancient Greece but denying its status as the origin of civilization, and "Several major early cultures—the Two Rivers, Egypt, China and the Indus Valley—all had their written languages. Yet Jaspers did not acknowledge the existence of an axial culture in the Two Rivers and Egypt. His problem lies in his failure to recognize that the ancient cultures of the Two Rivers and Egypt were in fact the sources of the Persian, Greek and Israelite cultures." Cho-yun Hsu, "On the Background of Karl Theodor Jaspers's Axial Period," *Chinese and World Culture*, Guiyang: Guizhou People's Publishing House, 1991; Yu Guoliang, "A Review of the Discussion on Axial Civilization," *Twenty-First Century*, 2000, no. 2.

[5] Karl Jaspers, *The Origin and Goal of History*, New Haven, CT: Yale University Press, 1953, p. 1. 60.

[6] Zhang Rulun (1953–), "The Concept of the Axial Period and the Birth of Chinese Philosophy," *Philosophical Trends*, 2017, no. 5.

It seems that there is not much controversy about *dao* as the supreme concept contributed by Chinese culture to world civilization in the Axial Period, but *dao* alone is not sufficient to explain the cultural genes of Chinese civilization and the Chinese nation. The most systematic discussion of *dao* is found in Laozi's *Daodejing*, but neither the *dao* nor the *de* in the *Daodejing* is what is called the absolute *dao* or the absolute *de*, or moral metaphysics, but rather the philosophical metaphysics of the universe and life. *dao* reveals the ontology of the formal world, and beyond the formal ontology there is the totality of the world of life, and the concept of this totality is called *lun*.

This can be justified in the following three ways.

First, on the surface, the core term of both the *Daodejing* and *The Analects of Confucius*, which are respectively the classics of Daoism and Confucianism, is *daode*. In the *Daodejing*, *dao* is used 77 times, *de*, 45 times, and *lun* and *li*, nil. In *The Analects of Confucius*, *dao* is used 89 times, *de*, 40 times, *lun*, only twice, and *li*, nil. However, this does not prove that *daode* is superior to *lunli*.

In fact, the discussion of *dao* and *daode* in both the *Daodejing* and *The Analects of Confucius* is based on and points to the human relations in society. Moreover, there are other conceptual formulations of *lunli* and *daode*, which are *li* and *ren*, respectively. In the *Daodejing*, *li* is used five times and *ren*, eight times. In *The Analects of Confucius*, *li* is used 75 times and *ren*, 110 times. Divided into the *Dejing* and the *Daojing*, the *Daodejing* is themed to derive the *dao* and *shi* of humanity from the *dao* of Heaven, and the so-called *dao* and *shi* of humanity are human relations. The theme of *The Analects of Confucius* is that "subduing one's self and return to *li* (propriety) is perfect *lun* (virtue)" and that the *lunli* of *li* is higher than the *daode* of *ren*. Although the term *lun* is not used or rarely used in *The Analects of Confucius*, this is not a sufficient basis for asserting that its cultural status is inferior to that of *dao*.

Second, in Chinese culture, the concepts of *lun* and *lunli* probably emerged earlier than the concepts of *dao* and *daode*, or they were created at least at about the same time. The terms *dao* and *lun* can already be found in both *The Book of Poetry* and *The Book of History*. In his *On lun*, Chinese sociologist Pan Guangdan (1899–1967), based on the research made by Chinese exegetist Liu Xi (believed to be born around the year 160) in his *Interpretation of Names,* stated that:

- The Chinese characters for *lun,* which share仑, such as 伦, 沦, 论, 纶, and 抡, are interchangeable;
- 论 means the same thing as 伦, i.e. *Lunli* (ethics);
- 沦 means the same as 伦, i.e. *Lunli* (orderly ripples on water);
- 纶 (guan) is also written as 伦, which means twisted silk.

The use of *lun* or *lunli* to describe other characters sharing 仑 indicates that *lun* and *lunli* were created earlier than them.

Third, the most classic explanation of the relationship between *dao* and *lun* is provided by the famous statement in "Teng Wen Gong I" from *Mencius*: "People possess *dao*; and if they are well fed, warmly clad, and comfortably lodged, without being taught at the same time, they become almost like the beasts. This was a subject of anxious solicitude to the sage Shun, and he appointed Xie to be the Minister of Instruction, to teach human relations." It is *dao* that makes humans human, but the success of adhering to or rescuing it relies on *lun*. "People possess *dao*, so they should be taught human relations," which is the fundamental logic and awareness of Chinese culture. This cultural logic is consistent with Confucius' proposition that "subduing one's self and return to *li* (propriety) is perfect *lun* (virtue)." This shows that in the *dao* of Confucius and Mencius, the mainstream of traditional Chinese culture, *dao* and *lun* are a pair of chromosome-like supreme awareness.

Both China and the West have different philosophical traditions in terms of the construction of the Axial Period and the recognition of the supreme concept by later generations. Greek and Hebrew cultures searched for a single arche or creator and thus had a logos or God. Following the law that "Near at hand, in his own person, he found things for consideration, and the same at a distance, in things in general," as revealed in *The Book Changes*, Chinese culture takes the syndrome differentiation of *yin* and *yang* as the root of the world and believes that the successive movement of *yin* and *yang* operations constitutes what is called the course of things and that the life of the world and of culture is like a human being's life gene, which is differentiated as *yin* and *yang* chromosomes. *Lun* and *dao*, or *lunli* and *daode*, are the Chinese cultural life, the Chinese people's moral strength, and a pair of cultural chromosomes of the Chinese awareness of the Axial Period.

Unfortunately, when it comes to understanding and explaining this, the Chinese people tend to accept the Western arche or ontological thinking and only identify *dao* as the supreme concept. As a result, at most, they only pursue the ontology of the physical world while leaving out and deconstructing the totality of the real-life world. According to the same logic, when understanding *daode*, the Chinese people grasp *dao* at the expense of *de*, and when understanding *lunli*, they grasp *lun* at the expense of *li*. As a result, their interpretation of the history of civilization and their grasp of the world are inevitably fragmented, and they find it difficult to understand and interpret the history of civilization and the history of culture as they are.

3   *Lunli* = Ethic?

This is a philosophical argument in cross-cultural dialogue, and the answer is: *lunli* ≠ ethic.

In modern Chinese academic interpretation of the concept of *lunli*, from doctoral dissertations to professorial lectures, one perception and expression has become a paradigm: *lunli* is ethics in English. The common practice is to find the ancient Greek origin of this English concept to prove that the two terms are both identical and harmonious with each other. Undoubtedly, in the current era of globalization and dialogue between civilizations, the interpretation of any basic concept needs to find a corresponding reference in another culture in order to make the dialogue possible, just as passengers in a high-speed train car always perceive the movement and speed of the train with a stationary reference outside the window, and it is often difficult for people to visualize the speed of an airplane in cloudless skies.

However, the biggest limitation of this interpretation is that it can only help look for foreign references without making it possible to find a real soulmate among foreign cultures. This is because any concept, especially the supreme concepts, always grows from a single cell to a primate in its native motherland, and it can find foreign cultures with similar appearances, but not "a true twin." A simple interpretation of discourses is likely to risk the loss of information, distortion of meaning, and even alienation of values.

It can be said that simply analogizing *lunli* to ethics and even equaling them are the most common and profound misunderstanding in the understanding and dialogue of the concept of *lunli*.

First, according to the transplantation theory of humanities and social sciences, humanities and social sciences follow a completely different law of dialogue from natural sciences.[7] Natural sciences are global in nature, and the so-called Chinese mathematics and Chinese physics imply the development of mathematics and physics in China, while Chinese *lunli* and Chinese philosophy must be the *lunli* and philosophy of Chinese people and are *lunli* concepts and philosophical theories grown in Chinese culture. The distinction between the Chinese terms "Chinese *lunli* "and "Chinese mathematics," if expressed in English, is "Chinese ethic" and "mathematics in China." The humanities and social sciences follow the law of transplantation, and the difference between culture from one's own homeland and that from a foreign land can be as vast as that between true oranges and trifoliate oranges.[8]

Second, in the broad view of civilization, the concepts of *lun* and *lunli* in Chinese culture may be hundreds or even thousands of years older than the ethical concept in ancient Greece. The ancient ethical concept was not formally introduced and a systematic theory was not constructed until Aristotle in the classic *The Nicomachean Ethics*; whereas the terms "*lun*" or "*lunli*" were already found in *The Book of Songs* and *The Book of History* in China. In *The Rites of Zhou,* there was the phrase "split the arm of a bow along with its *lun* (meaning "wooden grain"). *The Analects of Confucius* can be regarded as a systematic treatise on the human relations or *lunli,* and it can even be said that *The Analects of Confucius* (论语) means Confucius on *lun* (伦语). Even if we compare *The Analects of Confucius* with *The Nicomachean Ethics*, Confucius preceded Aristotle by more than two hundred years, so it is obvious that there is a historical misalignment in interpreting an earlier cultural concept with a later concept.

---

[7] Cf. To Cho Yee (ed.), *Transplantation and Application of Western Social Sciences Theories*, The Chinese University of Hong Kong Press, 1993.

[8] This is derived from a story in *Yanzi Chunqiu*. The story goes like this: As the prime minister of Qi, Yanzi was on his mission to Chu. The King of Chu planned to humiliate him. Then the king had a man bound with ropes as a thieve, telling Yanzi that the man was from Qi. The king asked why men of Qi were born to be adept thieves. In response, Yanzi quoted a proverb about the difference between true oranges and trifoliate oranges due to the different geographical locations where the oranges grow. The oranges grown in the south of the Huai River are true oranges; once transplanted to the north of the river, they become trifoliate oranges. Although they resemble in the shape of leaves, yet they differ widely in taste. Yanzi ironically concluded that people born in Qi were incapable of theft, but once in Chu they committed this crime due to the ethics and practices of Chu.

Third, the status of *lunli* and ethics in their respective civilizations and their fate in the history of civilization are very different. The word "ethic" was born in ancient Greece, but later in the process of Latinization in ancient Rome, it was converted into the English word "moral" by Marcus Tullius Cicero. As Hegel said, Kantian concepts are only about morality, but not ethics and even expressly destroy it.[9] It was not until the appearance of Hegel's *The Phenomenology of Spirit* that the position of ethnic was restored in spiritual philosophy.

In China, on the other hand, not only were ethnic and morality born at almost the same time, but also the human relations were often more specific and given greater priority than morality. The Mencian paradigm, marked by the statement that "humans are called human solely because they can be taught to behave in the human relations," clearly shows the cultural and philosophical linkage between *lun* and *dao*. Moreover, *lunli* was born as an independent discipline. Although *lunli* seems to be a study of moral issues, as some textbooks loosely put it,[10] in the modern West ethics is often called moral philosophy or moral science. It can be seen that not only was the cultural status of *lunli* and ethics in Chinese and Western civilizations not equal, but also their historical fate was quite different. Using the latter to explain and describe the former would seem rather irrelevant.

Fourth, *lunli* in Chinese culture carries many cultural messages that ethics does not have, the core message being the consistency between human relations and natural laws and between human relations and human ways. *Lunli* is the concept of ultimate and fundamental significance in China's culture that emphasizes being engaged with society. Without it, China's culture which emphasizes being engaged with society would not have taken shape and endured till today, for the metaphysical ontologeticality of *dao,* unlike the totality of *lun,* provides no home-land or ultimate solace for the real-life world. This has been proved by Daoism becoming an applied doctrine. In Western culture, however,

---

[9] "Kantian usage prefers the expression morality, as indeed the practical principles of Kant's philosophy are confined throughout to this concept, even rendering the point of view of ethics impossible and in fact expressly infringing and destroying it." Georg Wilhelm Friedrich Hegel: *Elements of the Philosophy of Right.*

[10] I don't agree with this view, because the study of moral issues should be directly called "moral science," and "ethics" is the study of *lun* and *li.*

ethics presupposes the existence of God or some other divine beings—
a value system alleged to have existed as an ultimate substance. The fact
even more meaningful to the history of civilization is that the law of *lunli,*
as a supreme concept that integrates the family and state with the former
coming before the latter down a cultured path, or a state-family cultural
notion, is that the human relations are pivotal to natural laws and the law
of humans is rooted in the divine law of family blood relations.

In view of the above four aspects, when *lunli* is interpreted by ethics
or *lunli* is taken as ethics, the inevitable result is the loss of information
and the alienation of values. Undoubtedly, to conduct dialogue between
cultures, it is essential to find their same concepts, but it is important to
keep in mind the fact that these concepts are only similar to each other
and therefore cannot be used as an alternative for each other.

4   Is *Lunli* an Ideology, or a Model
of Culture or Civilization?

This is a philosophical argument from the history of civilization.

Today, the concept of *lunli* is generally only discussed and understood
in the sense that it corresponds to *daode* and is treated as a model of
consciousness or spirit. This may be rational for the Western concept of
ethic. However, in Chinese culture, this has seriously narrowed or even
distorted the connotation of the concept of *lunli* and its civilizational
meaning.

Historically, Chinese culture has been called *lunli* culture, which indicates not only that *lunli* is a model of consciousness, but also that it is a
cultural paradigm. Its status is so important that it has created a culture,
namely, *lunli* culture, and a civilization, namely, *lunli* civilization.

Liang Shuming revealed the special status of *lunli* in Chinese culture
with several famous propositions: "China is a *lunli* -based society"; "*lunli*
is religious"; China "organizes its society with *lunli.*"[11] Liang found that
Western society has the group and the individual as its two components
without the family, "but the Chinese family relations bring into play
and organize society with 1 *lunli* without the individual and the group
serving as two components." He did not believe it was appropriate and

[11] Liang Shuming, *Essentials of Chinese Culture,* Beijing: Academia Press, 2000, pp. 77,
85, 113.

convincing to identify Chinese civilization as family-based on the grounds that *lunli* starts from the family, and the family is the natural foundation of *lunli*, so "*lunli* is derived from and goes beyond the family."[12] However, the family serves not only as a root but also a paradigm in Chinese culture. The notion that "*lunli* is religious" means that "China lacks religion and *lunli* in family life is used in lieu of it. But if we say that there is religion in China, it is in the form of ancestor worship and sacrifice to Heaven." He called this religion "*lunli* religion."[13] Liang found that since Confucius proposed the rectification of names, Chinese culture began its long-term institution building by consciously carrying out the cultural design and course of organizing society with *lunli*. Confucius' idea of rectifying names is both a personality ideal and an organizational order, and his greatest gift to future generations is the outline of a *lunli* order.[14]

Many Western scholars have also discovered the *lunli* temperament of Chinese culture. Hegel stated in "The Eastern World: China" of his *The Philosophy of History* that China was built entirely on a moral union, and that the identification substance of the state was objective family piety. The Chinese translation of this statement may be faulty, but according to his *The Phenomenology of Mind* and *Elements of the Philosophy of Right*, it may be more accurate to translate it as China was entirely built on a *lunli* union instead of a moral union.

One might argue that *lunli* culture can more convincingly explain only traditional societies which differed vastly from modern China. However, the concepts and ideas of *lunli* should be explored more thoroughly in the broader Chinese cultural context to seek out its genetic significance. *Lunli* is not only rooted in Chinese tradition, but it more convincingly explains and describes millennia-long traditional Chinese society and the historical development of Chinese cultural traditions as well. In addition, facts show that modern Chinese culture remains a *lunli* culture.

According to the information of the three national surveys we have conducted since 2007, although modern Chinese society, especially in the 40 years of reform and opening up, has undergone fundamental changes, the genes of *lunli* culture has remained unchanged. There are two specific

[12] Ibid., pp. 78, 79.
[13] Ibid., p. 87.
[14] Ibid., p. 121.

manifestations. First, religion has not become the mainstream of Chinese people's cultural-ethical life, with less than 10% of the population being religious; second, the *lunli* path is still the first choice for regulating interpersonal relationships. This shows that even today, prizing *lunli* and abandoning religion is still the temperament and style of Chinese culture. Neither traditional nor modern Chinese society has chosen to pursue the religious path even when facing a choice between religion and *lunli*. This is fundamentally due to the actual existence of *lunli*. The courage of rejecting religion lies in support from *lunli*. There is an apparent causal relationship between prizing *lunli* and abandoning religion.[15]

In short, the *lunli* concept in Chinese culture carries rich and wide implications. It is not only a model of mind but also a paradigmatic model of culture and serves as a model of culture and civilization with profound significance in the history of civilization. To grasp the *lunli* concept, one should not indulge in abstract, oversimplified conceptual analysis of *lunli* or willful linguistic matchmaking about it. Instead, one must understand the world ecologically and deepen one's understanding of life from the perspectives of the history of global and Chinese civilization. Approaching *lunli* with Western interpretive methods, including modernist deconstruction, will only lead to the disintegration and misinterpretation of *lunli*.

Through an in-depth exploration of Chinese culture, a cross-cultural dialogue with Western culture, and an attempt to return to the historical panorama of civilization and to pursue the philosophical significance of life, three philosophical perceptions about *lunli* can accordingly be established: The first is that *lun*, the supreme highest concept of Chinese culture, together with *li*, form a pair of chromosomes of Chinese culture. The second is that *lunli* is not equivalent to ethic. The third is that *lunli* is not only a model of mind but a model of culture and civilization. Only thus can a person enjoy the cultural elements of *lunli*.

---

[15] For an argument that modern Chinese culture remains a *lunli* culture and the relationship between prizing *lunli* and abandoning religion, see Fan Hao, "Cultural Consensus on the Development of Ethics and Morality in Chinese Society: An Analysis Based on Data from the Continuous Survey of 40 Years of Reform and Opening Up," *Social Sciences in China*, 2019, vol. 8.

5   THE CULTURAL ELEMENTS OF *LUNLI*

How to enjoy the cultural elements of *lunli*? The methodological dialogue between Laozi, Hegel and Hans-Georg Gadame might provide a "big ear" to listen to the gravitational waves of *lunli*. At the beginning of his *Elements of the Philosophy of Right*, Hegel stated that philosophy has to do with ideas and therefore not with what are commonly described as mere concepts. Thus the existence of the concept is its body, just as the latter obeys the soul which produced it. "The concept and its existence are two aspects of the same thing, separate and united, like soul and body.... The unity of existence and the concept, of body and soul, is the idea."[16] In fact, the basic discourse in any civilization is not just concepts, but ideas, which are not only information symbols, but also express and convey attitudes toward the world.

The Chinese *lunli* discourse is an idea, not a concept. It is not an abstract discursive tool, but a living national spirit and *lunli* life, and therefore cannot be limited to abstract conceptual analysis. It must be analyzed by looking into life and gaining an understanding of the ecology based on the panorama and historical process of the nation's *lunli* spirit and life.

Hegel's idea gives an important philosophical insight: enjoying the cultural elements of *lunli* contains two inseparable dimensions. One is the so-called "soul," namely the discoursal structure of " *lunli.*" The other is the "body," namely the national ethical spirit and life expressed and constructed by that structure. Gadamer's hermeneutic differentiation of "meaning" and "what its author originally intended" also provides a source of modern theoretical reference for that dichotomy. The "soul" of discourse is "authorial intention," whereas the national spirit and ethical life it constructs is "meaning."[17] "Authorial intention" carries messages about its creator's life incapable of being perceived by the reader. "Meaning" is the vitality of the subject who carries and inherits it, forming a harmonious melody in its construction and continuation. However, since

---

[16] G. W. E. Hegel, *Elements of the Philosophy of Right*, Chinese version by Fang Yang and Zhang Qitai, Beijing: The Commercial Press, 1996, p. 1.

[17] According to Gadamer's hermeneutics, one's explanation cannot truly grasp what "its author originally intended," but can only grasp the "meaning," which is constructed in the relationship between the subject and the text.

it is a basic discourse, with the temperament of being interpretable but not being interpreted, but having to be interpreted.

In the final analysis, it boils down to the philosophical context that Laozi described: "The *dao* that can be told of is not the absolute *dao*." Whether it is the soul or the body, or whether it is the discoursal structure or the national spirit, it should be told of. However, it is also necessary to look into and grasp its absolute *dao*.

Enjoying the cultural elements of *lunli* entails another question: How to conduct a dialogue between Chinese and Western culture? Dialogue between civilizations or between cultures is the sole access to a thorough understanding of *lunli*. The basic discourse constitutes the genetic cells of cultural traditions and life. Dialogue must be about every aspect of life. Any casual approach to the myriad theories of academic history may trap the dialogue in chance and lead to serious misinterpretations. A feasible tactic would be to use Hegelian philosophy, especially his *The Phenomenology of Mind* and *Elements of the Philosophy of Right*, as the texts for dialogue with the Chinese *lunli* discourse.

First, narrating against the backdrop of the entire Western civilizational and spiritual history, *The Phenomenology of Mind* is a spiritual phenomenon in the history of Western civilization. Targeted at Western experience and its cultural spirit is a systematic structuring of the "objective spirit," namely spiritual self-actualization, in Hegel's "philosophy of mind."

Second, these works are also philosophical classics which inquire into issues of ethics and morality. To some extent, therefore, their cross-cultural dialogue with the Chinese *lunli* discourse is the mutual interpretation and interaction between Chinese and Western cultural traditions and lives.

In order to reveal the cultural code of *lunli,* three kinds of discursive strategies can be adopted on the basis of knowledge archaeology and theoretical analysis.

The first is the cultural dialogue, especially between Chinese and Western classics, focusing on the historical development of the spirit of Chinese *lunli* and the systematic Hegelian philosophy of mind.

The second is the *lunli* decoding of some significant cultural events in civilizational history, such as Confucius' visit to various states, Laozi's disappearance at Hangu Pass, the death of Socrates, and the Wrath of God in the Axial Period.

The third is the analysis of the *lunli* underpinnings of major Chinese traditional festivals, especially the four major national festivals of Spring Festival, Qingming Festival, Dragon Boat Festival, and Mid-Autumn Festival.

The analytical and discoursal strategies mentioned above will perhaps help enjoy the cultural music elements of *lunli*.

PART I

The Discourse Structure of *Lunli* and Its Chinese Code

Chinese culture's *lunli* is a discourse formed by four structures: *lun, li,* establishing *lun* based on *li,* and the *lunli* world. Specifically, the *lun* substance, the conscience of li, and the law governing the practice of establishing *lun* based on li, the *lunli* worldview and the *lunli* world it creates. This discourse is the concept of *lunli* and the soul of the *lunli* discourse.

CHAPTER 2

Lun: The Lunli Substance of State-Family Civilization

1 Lun and the Ethical Substance

In Chinese discourse, *lun* is one of the basic concepts that are explained but left unexplained, and it is difficult to find its exact counterpart in heterogeneous cultures. If it must be expressed in English, the most sensible strategy is to transliterate it as "*lun*." However, although it is "absolute *dao*," it can and must be told of. In a nutshell, *lun* is a transcendent substance of ultimate concern which emphasizes being engaged with society; it is a Chinese discourse for the ethical substance in the civilizational state-family path and system.

Lun is a Chinese discourse for the ethical substance. In his *The Phenomenology of Spirit*, Hegel proposed the concept of ethical substance and argued about the relationship between ethics, substance, nation, and spirit, which is summarized in one sentence: nation is the substance and spirit of ethics. He argued that the essence of ethical substance is spirit, "but spirit is ethical actuality." Spirit carries the meaning of home for individuals. He stated that, "Spirit is the substance and the universal persisting essence in-parity-with-itself—it is the unshakable and undissolved ground and point of origin for the activity of each and all."[1] The actualization of spirit is the ethical substance, which becomes an ethical substance

---

[1] G. W. E. Hegel, Phänomenologie des Geistes: *The Phenomenology of Spirit*, Chinese version by He Lin and Wang Jiuxing, Beijing: The Commercial Press, 1996, vol. II, p. 2.

© Foreign Language Teaching and Research Publishing Co., Ltd 2024　　19
H. Fan, Lunli *and Confucian Moral Theory*, Key Concepts
in Chinese Thought and Culture,
https://doi.org/10.1007/978-981-99-9105-1_2

when the spirit realizes itself and creates a real spiritual world. "Spirit is the ethical life of a people insofar as it is the immediate truth; it is the individual who is a world."[2]

The Western wisdom and its philosophical enlightenment offered by Hegel's too complicated exposition is that ethics is a substance or public essence of humans, which is a spirit and has the capacity to actualize itself; that the difference between substance and spirit is that substance is a public essence that is not conscious of itself, while spirit is a human public essence that is conscious of and realizes itself; that the ethical substance is both spirit in all its forms and realizes itself as the world in all its form, and its direct form is the ethical life of the nation. Hegel's concept of ethical substance provides an exotic reference for understanding *lun*, but it is difficult to express the Chinese gene and therefore does not give a convincing explanation.

Compared with the concept of ethical substance in Western culture, *lun* also has the meaning of substance and is closely related to the concepts of ethics, family, nation, and spirit, but it is more structural and realistic, pointing not only to spiritual and real substances with ultimate meaning, but also to the divine root and structural relations of these substances.

2   Substances that have the Meaning of Ultimate Social Concern, and are Social and Transcendent

A. Substances of integration and division

There are three ways to interpret *lun,* namely, knowledge archaeology, meaning tracing, and theoretical metaphorization. Since it is a fundamental discourse, its true cultural meaning can be grasped only through a combination of all these three approaches.

In Chinese culture, derived from 人 and 侖, *lun* (伦or 倫) is both a phonographic and an associative character, and also a meaning character. *Explanation of Script and Elucidation of Characters* says, "Derived from 스 and 冊, 仑 (侖) means thought (思). Pan Guangdan, a famous sociologist, interpreted *lun* in the way of textual archaeology: thoughts need to be organized with 冊 dividing thoughts and 스 integrating them. In

---

[2] Ibid.

fact, the character "思," referred to in *Explanation of Script and Eluci-dation of Characters* may mean more than thought. Mencius said, "To the mind belongs the office of thinking." 思 means thought as well as spirit as Hegel defined. By the same token, the character "侖" may also mean more than order, but reveals the two fundamental laws—division and integration—of the human world, including the spiritual world and the world of life. To be precise, as the substance of human world and human spirit, the philosophical essence of *lun* is neither integration nor division, but the substance of 侖 which is constituted by the integration of the 合 and the division of 冊. The substance of spirits is the unity of spirits and the division of spirits. In other words, order and distinction constitute the philosophical essence of *lun*.

This derivation may be suspected of overinterpretation, but its cultural code has been shown in the Chinese tradition. Expressed with Daoist philosophy, the wisdom of the integration and division of *lun* is to "secure uniformity in irregularity," that is, to ensure that the uniformity of the social order of the group is based on irregularity; in the Confucian moral discourse, it is called "benevolence and righteousness."

In the Chinese tradition, not only do *lunli* and *daode* correspond to each other, but also benevolence and righteousness correspond to and can even replace *dao* and *de*, so benevolence and righteousness and *dao* and *de* are considered one and the same. Han Yu said in his "The Origin of *dao*," "Benevolence and righteousness are nouns with definite meanings, and *dao* and *de* are nouns with indefinite meanings." That is, benevolence and righteousness are the real content of *dao* and *de*, and *dao* and *de* are the formal expression of benevolence and righteousness. What is the *lunli* essence of benevolence and righteousness? Benevolence is meant to promote harmony while righteousness is designed to define differences.

The value of benevolence is sameness based on uniformity, and is designed to sublate the individuality and abstraction of humans through love or love for others, so that the world becomes one family and all things become one. This is why benevolent people love others and benev-olence is integrated with all other things under Heaven and on earth. The essence of the notion that "the benevolent has no enemy" is that when the state of benevolence, in which the world becomes one family and all things become one, is reached, there will be only the Hegelian abso-lute spiritual benevolence in the world, and there will be no other things in opposition to it. As such, the benevolent has no enemy, that is, it is opposed by nothing. This gives benevolence an ontological meaning.

The value of righteousness is that it is different based on differences, that is, in the substance of sameness based on uniformity, the precedence between superiors and inferiors and between elders and youngers is observed so as to determine the reasonableness and legitimacy of individual behavior. According to *Mencius*, the sameness of benevolence based on uniformity is the spiritual home, that is, "Benevolence is the quiet home in which humans should dwell." The notion that righteousness is different based on its differences is the right road to benevolence, that is, "Righteousness is the straight path."

It is evident that the integration and division of 侖, as well as 倫 that follows, are both pictorial and metaphorical manifestations of the truth of *lunli* and its substance, and they also contain the Chinese philosophical wisdom and Chinese cultural codes about *lunli* and its substance.

Chinese scholars have been accustomed to using *bei* (輩) to explain *lun* in knowledge archaeology. Written by Xu Shen in the Eastern Han Dynasty, *Explanation of Script and Elucidation of Characters* says, "*Lun* means *bei*." In his note to this, Duan Yucai of the Qing Dynasty said, "One hundred carriages are called a *bei* of carriages. By extension, the generation of peers is called *bei*. So *lun* is *bei* or *lei*. What is the essence of using *bei* to explain *lun*? The character for generation in daily life helps to explain it.

The basic meaning of generation refers to the natural *lunli* status of an individual in a blood relationship, and generation is the rhythm of life of a generation of people, and the basic unit of the tree of life. The same generation of people is in the same *lunli* position and has different power and obligation relationships with different generations of blood groups. The blood relationship and blood status between people of the same generation is generation, and the resulting power and obligation is called "*fen*," and *bei* and *fen* are also called *lun* and *li*.

The substantial meaning of *lun* is directly and deeply reflected in the culture of name. In any culture, the relationship between surname and given name may be about the substance of *lun* and the relationship between the individual and the substance of *lun*, but the name in Chinese tradition has a different *lunli* implication from that of the West.

A name generally consists of two parts—surname and first name, but anyone who knows anything about the Chinese tradition in and before the twentieth century knows that the name in Chinese culture consists of three parts—surname, generation, and first name. The first character is surname, which is the common symbol of the family lineage substance;

the second character is generation, which indicates the individual's position in the history of the large and complex family lineage. The third character is given name, the unique symbol possessed by the individual.

The most important thing is that as the common blood symbol of the natural ethical substance of the family, surname comes before first name, which is the other way round in the West. This quite significantly represents the different status of blood relations in culture and the different ethical orientations of individuality and substance, and is therefore a result of the development of the two civilizational traditions. Putting surname before first name is obviously substance-oriented and the opposite is individual-oriented. The symbol of the blood community, surname is the most important for the Chinese.

Each person's name has a representative of the common *lunli* status of people of the same generation, that is, generation, which is, generally speaking, is the middle name. For example, Mao Zedong's generation symbol is "ze," so in the Mao family, whose who share the middle name of ze are of the same generation. This thus determines the relationship between these people and those of the upper and lower generations. Mao Zedong's father called Mao Yichang, so in the Mao family, those who shared the middle name of yi were his uncles or aunts. Wherever you are, with surnames and generations, you can easily understood what *lunli* relationships are.

The last character of the name of a Chinese person is his or her unique symbol in the real sense. This not only gives the individual the home of the family blood substance, but also clearly shows his or her position in the history of the family. Stressing the generation of individuals means being identified with *lunli*. The family name and generation clearly express and present the position of the individual in the family community both vertically and horizontally, forming an ethical substance of integration and division. This tradition began to decline in the second half of the twentieth century and largely disappeared in the one-child era.

As a result, using integration and division to explain *lun* and using *bei* to interpret *lun* gives *lun* the meaning of life and community of life, and thus brings it closer to what Hegel called ethical substance, but makes it more meaningful in terms of the community of life and blood.

Later on, the meaning of *bei* (generation) was extended from blood relations to other social relations, resulting in the phenomenon of stressing seniority. Seniority means the seniority of an individual in a community, which is related to age and the length of time one has been in the community. Although it has the disadvantage of stifling the vitality of individuals, it is also related to the Chinese tradition of stressing seniority. It is a cultural extension of the natural ethical substance to the social ethical substance. The so-called sequence of seniority in Japanese society, especially in Japanese companies, is related to similar traditions, and many phenomena in Chinese social life today can also be explained by it. For example, the system governing government employees' use of vehicles carries the cultural gene of grading carriages. In ancient China, not only were carriages divided into grades, but their owners were also graded. Ancient Chinese people rode carriages and they were graded in terms of social status by the carriages they rode. Their symbol of social status is similar to government officials' use of vehicles today. Thus, the use of *bei* to interpret *lun* is not only about inherent natural blood relations, but is also extended be about social relations, the so-called natural relations and human relations. In both natural and human relations, the concept of *lun* is an ethical substance that includes blood relations and social relations.

B. The ultimate concern without God, and the *dao* and Logos with temperature

In Chinese culture, the greatest charm of *lun* lies in the fact that it is not only a human substance, but also the ultimate substance; it is not only the ultimate substance, but also the ultimate secular substance; it is not only the ultimate social substance, but also the ultimate concern, and it is the ultimate substance and ultimate concern that is both social and transcendent.

Hegel believed that "the ethical is the universal in itself."[3] *lun* is the Chinese expression of what Hegel called the communal essence of the individual or the human substance. In the substance of *lun,* individuals attain what Hegel called "the commandment of right": "be a person and respect others as persons,"[4] that is, the so-called mutual recognition.

---

[3] G. W. E. Hegel, Phänomenologie des Geistes: *The Phenomenology of Spirit*, Chinese version by He Lin and Wang Jiuxing, Beijing: The Commercial Press, 1996, vol. II, p. 8.

[4] G. W. E. Hegel, *Elements of the Philosophy of Right*, Chinese version by Fan Yang and Zhang Qitai, Beijing: The Commercial Press, 1996, p. 46.

Lun is not the ancient Greek Logos, but it has the force of necessity of the Logos, which is the unshakable starting point and ground of individual behavior.

Lun is not the God in Hebrew culture, but it has the sense of ultimate concern inherent in God. The family and its extension—the clan—are the natural substance of *lun* or the natural community of humans. However, unlike Western culture, this natural community is the ultimate social concern. Many of the *lunli* imperatives in Chinese culture, such as filial piety and compassion, have a transcendent sense of ultimate concern.

The *lun* is not the *dao* in Chinese culture, but the *lun* has a more substantial temperature than the *dao*. In the Chinese people's philosophical intuition and cultural perception, *dao* exists on the other shore, just like Logos, while *lun* exists on this shore, whether it is about natural relations or human relations. In the world of daily life, it can be touched, experienced and confirmed.

In short, *lun* has the necessity of Logos and *dao* but carries the temperature of life and living; *lun* has the ultimate concern of God but exists on this shore, "social and transcendent substance" is the Chinese code of *lun* and its universal civilizational meaning.

Some people once metaphorically referred to *lun* as the ripples formed by a stone thrown into the water. This philosophical imagination may be closer to the cultural nature of *lunli*, and also has some academic basis.

The Book of Songs says, "Whose waters flow clear in rippling circles." Liu Xi of the Eastern Han Dynasty explained in his *Interpretation of Names*, saying: "*Lun* (伦) means orderly ripples on water." *lun* (沦) is interchangeable with *lun* (伦), so 沦 means orderly ripples on water (*lunli*). *Lunli* therefore means ripples.

How do ripples interpret *lunli*? The ripples formed by the stone thrown into the water are the root of life or the bloodline of life. The whole ripple is called *lun*, which in daily life is the surname as the symbol of family. The relationship between each drop of water and the whole ripple is the relationship of *lun*. The relationship of *lun* is not just the relationship between drops of water which are connected to each other, or even not its relationship with the root of the ripple, but is its relationship with the entire ripple as a solid substance. Only in the ripple can each drop of water find its place, the so-called *lunli* status or generation, and only in the whole ripple can it have vitality, and from such ripples can it cautiously return home and to the substance, gaining the ultimate concern of substance.

In this sense, it can be said that *lun* is the impersonal God who exists in the world on this shore; *lun* is the *dao* and Logos that are the necessary relationship between humans and their own communal nature and carry the body temperature of life. Chinese people tend to look for concern in the world of life and spirituality first in the family and clan, and second in the social relations with family ties serving as paradigms. The ultimate concern exists on this shore of the world, not on the other shore of the ultimate substance of religion, and is therefore the substance of the ultimate social concern. In the solid relationship between integration and division defined by surname and generation, the individual also completes the transcendence from natural existence to ethical existence and from natural person to ethical person. In the relationship of substance between integration and division defined by surname and generation, the individual also completes the transcendence from natural existence to ethical existence and from natural person to ethical person. This transcendence is accomplished in the social ethical substance rather than in the relationship of ultimate substance between humans and God, and is therefore social and transcendent.

This also proves Liang Shuming's assertion that *lunli* is religious; it also explains his other proposition that "*daode* can replace religion." In Chinese culture, both *lunli* and *daode* have the cultural significance of religion substituting culture, but what is the difference between them? *Lunli* is more social than *daode*, or rather, it is in *lunli* that one finds a cultural sense of meeting the God of ultimate concern; the Chinese call this *lun* and the Westerners personify it as God. *Lun* is on this shore and God is on the other shore.

C. Human relations and interpersonal relations, and *qunxue* without interpersonality

Pan Guangdan believed that sociology can also be called *lunli* or the science of *lunli*. He said with regret that if scholars engaged in moral studies had not already translated ethics as the science of *lunli* when sociology was introduced to China, sociology would be better translated as the science of *lunli*. Although Pan's proposition can be a bridge between sociology and ethics, there are profound differences between Chinese ethics and Western sociology, the root of which lies first in *lun*.

As Pan said, a Chinese concept that is closer to Western sociology is *qunxue* or *qunlixue*. Yan Fu translated Herbert Spencer's *The Study of Sociology* as *On Qunxue*. *Shehuixue*, the Chinese translation for sociology, was borrowed from the Japanese translation for sociology. Sociology and the study of *lunli* are both about *qun* (group) in a sense, but the object of sociology is interpersonal relations and that of *lunli* is human relations. The subtle difference between the two is that interpersonal relations presuppose interpersonality, while human relations are the commonality relations between individual persons and the *lun* of substance, just like the relations between a drop of water and the whole ripple.

One sentence that could best summarize the difference between *lunli* and sociology is that *lunli* has no interpersonality. What *lunli* studies and constructs is the substance of humans, the relationship of substance of home, and therefore there must be another condition for the existence of *lunli* substances, which is spirit rather than the so-called reason. This will be discussed below. Sociology, however, focuses on revealing social facts. The difference between *lunli* and sociology is as fundamental as the difference between value and fact and between transcendence and reality.

3 THE UNIQUE DISCOURSE AND TRADITION OF STATE-FAMILY CIVILIZATION

The key to understanding the discourses of *lun* and *lunli* and the most criticized aspect of the Chinese concept of *lun* and *lunli* tradition is the relationship between family and *lun* and *lunli*. It can be said that without the family, it is impossible to truly understand the Chinese cultural discourse and tradition of *lun* and *lunli*. The key to accurately grasp this issue is that *lun* and *lunli* are the unique discourses and special traditions of the nation-family civilization.

Born in a special cultural ecology, the basic discourse of any cultural tradition interacts with the civilizational history of the nation and is the basic structure of the nation's discourse. It is not necessary to look closely to see that *lunli* and ethics have a completely different status at the beginning of Chinese and Western civilizations, although they are both related to virtue or *daode*.

Aristotle started his *The Nicomachean Ethics* by stating that, "There are two kinds of virtue: intellectual and moral." He repeatedly discussed whether the intellectual virtue is superior to the moral virtue. In Western culture, ethics was originally a custom and later extended to those qualities that were spontaneously generated by individuals in communal life, which were not subject to intellectual reflection and thus were neither universal and unconditional rationality. In Mencius, however, advocated teaching human relations and constructing *lunli* is the only way to transcend the notion that humans are almost like the beasts if they are not taught human relations. Human relations and *lunli* have an ultimate meaning similar to that of salvation in Christian culture.

This explains why, from ancient Greece and Rome to the modern West, the ethical discourse has always come and gone, while in the Chinese discourse and world of life, *lunli* has always had a fundamental position, and the loss of human decency and incest have been a more irredeemable original sin than any moral problem. The root cause of this is that at the beginning of civilization, China and the West had diametrically different civilizational paths. *Lunli* and ethics are two different discourses in two different civilizational paths and civilizational systems.

Cultural anthropology shows that although the genetic code of civilization was conceived in ancient times, the greatest secret was hidden in the different paths in the first and most important transition in the history of civilization, that is, the transition from primitive to civilized society. Primitive society is so far the longest model of civilization in which humanity found it most difficult to know themselves and made the most profound influence on the history of civilization. The history of the development of human society and the history of civilization should be consistent with the history of the development of human life.

Human ignorance of primitive civilization may be like the individual's ignorance of everything in his or her mother, but the impact of this unknowable history on civilization is as genetically inescapable as the impact of the mother in which the individual is conceived on the whole of human life; likewise, psychologists have found that individuals are born with a lack of memory of everything they have experienced until about three years of age. Human societies also lack a clear collective memory of what happened to them as they emerged from the primitive state, and although archaeology and mythology can activate some fragmentary and eisegenic recollections, they are mostly present-day interpretations or even imaginations.

Nevertheless, humans always have as exact a memory of how they came from primitive societies as individuals have of their parents' identification substance, and say that there is no doubt about the natural and social

genetic significance it has for them. Thus, the paths and ways of transition from primitive to civilized societies of different peoples are genetically
inherited for the development of later civilizations, while what is accu-
mulated by later experiences is often only some acquired heredity. *Lun*
and *lunli* are the unique genetic expression and cultural discourse of the
path of the Chinese nation's state-family civilization, or more accurately,
family-state civilization.

The transition of ancient Greek city-states from primitive society to
civilized society was a path of separation of family and state. One of
the core issues of the three major reforms—the Theseus reform, Solon
reform, and Cleisthenes reform—was the breaking away from of blood
ties and the division of citizens by geography. The most powerful city-
state in ancient Greece, Sparta, was even more radical, as children were
separated from their families at birth and grew up knowing only the city-
state but not the family. This was the so-called state civilization, on the
basis of which the modern sense of country grew.

In contrast, China took another path through the Western Zhou
reform, forming a state-family civilization that integrates the family and
state with the former coming before the latter. The state-family civilization successfully preserved and creatively transformed the blood heritage
of humanity formed in the longest society—primitive society, transformed
blood relations into family *lunli* substances, and used it as a model to
construct the state, forming the state-family civilization. This is the historical achievement of the Western Zhou reform. This is why it is said that
although Zhou was an old state, its mission was to innovate. The reform
formed different models of civilization that complemented the country.

Country is a concept with a strong *lunli* temperament, conveying three
lunli messages: the precise expression of state-family civilization is the
family-state civilization, the essence of which is that the family and the
state are integrated rather than the Western-style separation of the family
and the state; the family prevails in the relationship between the family
and the state, so the family comes before the state rather than the other
way round; not only that, its highest ideal is to turn the state into the
family.

Sociologists refer to Chinese society as a gemeinschaft society and
Western society as a gesellschaft society. The typical model of a gesellschaft
society is that Europe and the United States form countries in the modern
sense by uniting states, that is, the so-called "*guojia*" in the Chinese
discourse. The United States and Britain are alike in that they are both

united states, but different in that Britain consists of institutionally united states with a kingdom as their supreme and final spiritual command and is a spiritual kingdom. However, in any case, country cannot be directly equated with country in the Chinese discourse, because the family cannot be found in it, let alone its principal and paradigmatic status in the country. Translating *"guojia"* as "country" is like translating *"lunli"* as "ethic," which may inherently lose a lot of consciousness and alienate values.

Lun is a special discourse and a special cultural phenomenon of the civilizational path and civilizational system of state-family. The Western Zhou reform only institutionally or structurally chose the civilizational path of integrating the family and the state with the former coming before the latter and established corresponding political systems. The Duke of Zhou developed the rites and produced music, trying to accomplish this historical task culturally and spiritually, but he did not establish a systematic and mature theory.

Confucianism, represented by Confucius, accomplished this task brilliantly by creating a theory that matched the state-family civilization. *Lunli* and *daode* are the core of this theory, and *lun* and *dao,* and *lunli* and *daode* are the core discourses and values that embody the laws and cultural requirements of the state-family civilization.

In this sense, Confucianism has become the mainstream and authentic aspect of Chinese culture because they have brilliantly accomplished the most important and fundamental task of Chinese civilization and Chinese culture to blaze the civilizational path that integrates the family and the state with the former coming before the latter and the theory that matches that path, and completed the project the first and most important state-family civilization in the history of China.

The reason why *lun* or *lunli* has become a substance of the ultimate social concern and social transcendence lies in its *lunli* law integrating the family and the state with the former contribution the latter, and the structural discourses of this *lunli* law are the so-called natural relations and human relations. Natural relations are the blood *lunli* substance with the family as the core, and human relations are the social *lunli* substance expanded therefrom. However, what is most important as Chinese discourse and Chinese theory is not yet these two concepts, but the *lunli* law of their relationship: human relations are established based on natural relations.

One of Mencius' greatest contributions to Chinese culture is the Five Cardinal Relationships, the essence of which is not the five cardinal *lunli* relationships between ruler and subject, father and son, husband and wife, older and younger brothers, and friends, but the significance of the five *lunli* relationships for Chinese *lunli* and Chinese society as a paradigm and the basic *lunli* laws of Chinese society and culture revealed by the five *lunli* relationships. Among the five *lunli* relationships, those between father and son and between older and younger brothers are natural relationships, those between ruler and subject and between friends are human relationships, while that between husband and wife comes between natural and human relationships and are the intermediary of their mutual transformation.

The cardinal relationship between father and son is the paradigm of all the relationships between ruler and subject, between elders and youngers and between superiors and inferiors. There is the so-called optimistic tension between them, the typical expression of which is all within the four seas are brothers. However, the relationship between husband and wife cannot be the paradigm of all relationships between men and women, as Confucianism holds that, "That male and female should dwell together, is the greatest of human relations." The relationship between a man and a woman and between husband and wife is a matter of the continuity of the human race and the progress or decline of civilization, so Chinese *lunli* has always been highly vigilant and nervous about it, and even preferred to push it to the extreme, advocating that, "Males and females shall not allow their hands to touch in giving or receiving anything."

The essence and nature of the Five Cardinal Relationships is that human relations are established based on natural relations and social *lunli* relations are modeled on family *lunli* relations, which is the cultural expression and *lunli* construction of the civilizational path and system that integrates the family and state with the former coming before the latter.

In Western ethics, such as Hegel's, although there are also expressions about family *lunli* relations and social *lunli* relations, natural relations and human relations in Hegel's *The Phenomenology of Spirit* are the so-called human and divine laws, which are culturally compatible with each other. However, on the one hand, Hegel treated the two laws as the two ethical forces in the ethical world, and focused on revealing the tension and conflict between them, with one law suppressing the other and the most just being the most unjust. On the other hand, he described the two laws as the law of darkness and the daylight's law, which already indicates his philosophical attitude toward the two ethical laws. In Hegel's discourse on the ethical world, the divine law and the law of darkness are in no way as sacred as the natural relations in Chinese discourse and do not have the cultural coherence and ethical affinity of natural and human relations evident in the civilizational system integrating the family and the state. What Hegel had is a discourse and philosophical tradition of the civilizational tradition of the country which separates the family and the state.

The *Li* of *Lun*

1 THE *LI* OF *LUNLI* AS THE *LI* OF *LUN*

In the Chinese discourse, *lunli* should rather be interpreted as a compound concept with a subject-predicate structure consisting of two links: *lun* and *li*. *Lun* is the substance that is the same as the public essence of a person or an individual, and *li* is the principle, rule, and natural law of *lun* or its substance and is also about how the conscience and ability, which is acquired by the individual from *lun*, act on *lun*. In the words of Hegel's philosophy, *lunli* is self-being, and *li* is self-doing, and the combination of the two is the *lunli* and its substance that is both self-being and self-doing. The *li* of *lun* is not only the Chinese discourse of *li*, but also the Chinese gene and Chinese cultural code of *lunli*.

The semantics of the *li* of *lun* contains two meanings in the narrow sense and the broad sense. The *li* of *lun* in the narrow sense is and is nothing but the principle and law of *lun*, as well as the consciousness of and action on *lunli*, and its problem awareness and cultural reference are the so-called reason of Western moral philosophy. The *li* of *lunli* is not the discursive, priori universal *li*, but the *li* rooted in the substance of *lunli* and derived from the specific *lunli* situation and experience. It is also the natural *li* because of its *lun* substantial premise and its life nature.

The *li* of *lun* in a broad sense means that the *li* of Chinese culture has its own special tradition, which was not only originally but also has its roots in the *li* of *lun* in terms of language. In other words, the *li of*

© Foreign Language Teaching and Research Publishing Co., Ltd 2024   33
H. Fan, *Lunli and Confucian Moral Theory*, Key Concepts
in Chinese Thought and Culture,
https://doi.org/10.1007/978-981-99-9105-1_3

Chinese culture first referred to or was only the *li* of *lun* or the *li* of *lunli* from the beginning, rather than the *li* of *wuli* based on the Western scientific tradition. The *li* of *lunli* and the *li* of *wuli* represent the two traditions and their different genes of the *li* in *lunli* and scientific cultures.

The discourse of *li* of *lun* is based on the special Chinese philosophical tradition. The Chinese philosophical view of the universe and life is what *The Book of Changes* says: "Heaven and Earth existing, all material things then got their existence. All material things having existence, afterwards there came male and female. From the existence of male and female there came afterwards husband and wife. From husband and wife there came father and son. From father and son there came ruler and minister. From ruler and minister there came high and low. When the distinction of high and low had existence, afterwards came the arrangements of propriety and righteousness." All things under Heaven and on Earth and the natural and human relations eventually gave rise to *lunli*. The way to grasp of the world is, as *The Book of Changes* puts it, "Near at hand, in his own person, he found things for consideration, and the same at a distance, in things in general." "Anciently, when Baoxi had come to the rule of all under Heaven, looking up, he contemplated the brilliant forms exhibited in the sky, and looking down he surveyed the patterns shown on the earth. He contemplated the ornamental appearances of birds and beasts and the different suitabilities of the soil. Near at hand, in his own person, he found things for consideration, and the same at a distance, in things in general. On this he devised the eight trigrams, to show fully the attributes of the spirit-like and intelligent operations working secretly, and to classify the qualities of the myriads of things." The notion that "Near at hand, in his own person, he found things for consideration, and the same at a distance, in things in general" is a way of thinking that advocates judging others by what is nigh in ourselves. First, it must be "Near at hand, in his own person," and then "he found things for consideration, and the same at a distance, in things in general." In other words, one should know the nature of things based on the nature of humans, and then move on to know the nature of the universe based on the nature of things.

Based on the above three aspects, the *li* of *lun* or the *li* of *lunli* is both a reflection based on *lunli* or *lun* but also a special paradigm of philosophical thinking. As a kind of reflection based on *lunli*, it is *li* or a way of thinking based on *lun*, rooted in *lun*, and taking *lun* as realistic and rational. As a philosophical paradigm, it is based on the presupposition that Heaven and Earth appear before all things which come into existence before men and women, and that if you look up, you will see the image in the sky, and if you look down, you will see the image in the earth. Based on the notion that "Near at hand, in his own person, he found things for consideration, and the same at a distance, in things in general," it is a philosophical paradigm that advocates harmony between nature and humans, aiming at using the integrated, divine virtue to praise the nurturing of Heaven and Earth and compare the situation of all things. This philosophical paradigm advocates harmony between humans and nature in terms of metaphysics but harmony between nature and humans in terms of reality. It tries to realize harmony between nature and humans by ensuring that people give full play to their own good nature in order to do the same to the good nature of others and all things. The essence of harmony between nature and humans is a reflection based on *lunli*, a *lunli* worldview, and the philosophical paradigm of *lunli* culture.

Thus, to understand the concept of *lunli* in Chinese culture, it is essential to first grasp the subject-predicate relationship between *lun* and *li*, and it is not in the tradition of Chinese *lunli* culture to seek the so-called *li* in isolation of *lun*; it is a tradition of Western rationalism. In addition, it is necessary to grasp the position of *lunli* as the meta-concept and meta-idea in the context of the discourse and theoretical system of the Chinese philosophical tradition. This is integral to deciphering the Chinese cultural code of *lunli*.

2   The Cultural Message of *li* Explained by Extracting Jade from Rocks

The most important cultural decoding of the knowledge archaeology of *li* is why it is interpreted as extracting jade from rocks; what kind of righteous information it conveys that fits with the Chinese *lunli* tradition; and how it became a kind of concept devoted exclusively to *lun* and was later expanded be the universal *li*?

The most cited explanation of *li* (理) in Chinese scholarship is *"li* is to extract jade from rocks. It is derived from *yu* (玉) and pronounced based on *li* (里)" from *Explanation of Script and Elucidation of Characters*. How is 理 associated with 玉? *Stratagems of the Warring States* says, "The Zheng people call rocks with jade in them that have not been cut gemstones. The King had a jeweler polish up the gemstone and got the treasure out at last." (*Hanfeizi*).

The stone containing jade is called gemstone. To get the jade from the gemstone, one must cut it. Gemstone is stone with jade in it that has not been cut, so 理 means to cut (治) and separate. According to *Guangyun*, "理 means to cut." 理 and 治 are interchangeable and later on, they were given the meaning of *lunli* and politics. 治 means to govern the country and cultivate oneself and is exchangeable with both *li* and *lun*. According to *Zhuangzi*, "You, Sir, govern (治) the kingdom." Cheng Xuanying had a note to this, stating, "治 means 理."[1] According to *The Book of Rites*, "He superintended their instruction in all they had to learn and the art of self-government." Kong Yingda explained, "治 means self-cultivation."[2] *Supreme Mystery* says, "The great *lun* of people is called self-cultivation."[3] How did 理 evolve from 治 to 伦 (*lun*)? This was explained through the archaeology of knowledge.[4]

As an extension of the interpretation, an important aspect of knowledge archaeology is that it about the relationship between using *zhiyu* (治玉, cutting jade) to interpret 理 and the Chinese *lunli* tradition. 理 means to extract jade from gemstone. To cut jade, it is necessary to follow the 理 (law). 治 means to follow.

This raises a philosophical question: what kind of cultural message does the *li* in the discourse of *lunli* convey, as it is connected to jade at its source?

Is it possible for an individual to transcend his or her individuality to reach a public essence, i.e. *Lunli* universality since *lunli* is by nature something universal? How is it possible? The belief of Chinese culture is that humans at their birth are naturally good. In the history of Chinese *lunli*, there was a debate on whether humans are naturally good. After Mencius proposed the theory that humans' natures are naturally good at their birth, the theory has become the mainstream of Chinese *lunli*. In fact, the most classical expression of Chinese *lunli* about where humans

---

[1] Guo Qingfan, *Interpreting Zhuangzi*, vol. I (1), punctuated and collated by Wang Xiaoyu, Beijing: Zhonghua Book Company, 1961, p. 24.

[2] "Correct Meaning of *The Book of Changes*," vol. 62, with notes by Zheng Xuan and explanations by Kong Yingda, *Notes and Explanations of The Thirteen Classics*, verified by Ruan Yuan, p. 1690.

[3] Yang Xiong, *Notes on Supreme Mystery*, vol. 9, annotated by Sima Guang, Beijing: Zhonghua Book Company, 1998, p. 208.

[4] For the relationship between 理 and 治, see Zhang Jiang, "Discerning 理 and 性," *Social Sciences in China*, 2018, no. 9.

are naturally good is Confucius' statement that, "Humans' natures are much the same; their habits become widely different." In the development of Chinese tradition, the notion that humans' natures are much the same evolved into Mencius' theory that humans' natures at their birth are naturally good; Xunzi's theory that characterizes human nature as bad was derived from the notion that humans' habits are widely different. Both schools of thought evolved from Confucius' theory. In Song-Ming neo-Confucianism, Cheng Yi, Cheng Hao and Zhu Xi put forward the doctrines of nature endowed by Heaven and nature endowed by *qi*, which ended the 2,000-year-long debate over human nature. As Song Confucians said, if this doctrine had been put forward earlier, there would not have been a debate over whether human nature is good.

What is the main point of the human nature theory of Confucius and Song-Ming neo-Confucianism? It is hidden in the interpretation of 理 with 治玉. Humans are gemstone at their birth, and the good human nature is the jade in the gemstone, which must be obtained through cutting. Interpreting 理 with 治玉 reveals two potential Chinese codes. One is the respect for and trust of human nature. The theory of good human nature is not so much a cognition as an identification; it is not so much a knowledge as a belief. Unlike Western ethics, Chinese *lunli* and its tradition are based on the respect for and trust of human nature. The other Chinese code is that human nature is gemstone, which has only the seeds and possibilities of a good nature, and gemstone must be cut to get jade. So Chinese *lunli* was extended from cutting jade to cultivating oneself and to governing the state.

Humans are not angels, so they need *daode* to govern their behavior; they are not devils, so they may have *daode*, which provides the metaphysical basis for explaining 理 with cutting jade. The need to cultivate oneself became what *The Great Learning* teaches. In other words, the core of traditional Chinese philosophy's construction of *lunli* substances and moral subjects is self-cultivation.

3   CONSCIOUS REASON

Lun is associated with *li* is because it is *li*. *li* is easily interpreted as the so-called "reason" in modern discourse. For Chinese culture, however, reason is an entirely foreign product, and it is not known when it made its way to China and gradually prevailed, but it is certain that modern civilization has been impregnated with reason. Although the human world has suffered much from reason, reason and rationalism are still marching forward without turning back.

The Western tradition has taken ethics and morality as reason, from Socrates' statement that virtue is knowledge to Aristotle's distinction between ethical virtue and rational virtue, the ethical foundation was laid for rationalism. The ethical tone of rationalism has been established. In classical German philosophy, although Kant had no concept of ethics at all, it did not prevent him from attributing morality to reason and calling it practical reason. Although Hegel discussed ethics and morality in the general discourse of absolute spirit and in the system of philosophy of spirit, the so-called *The Phenomenology of Spirit* is, in the final analysis, reason. As he said, reason is the dwelling place of spirit, where spirit reveals itself. To explore the Chinese code of the *li* of *lun*, it is necessary to first distinguish *li* from reason.

However, since reason has established its discursive and value dominance in modern civilization, and is significant as a coordinate in the discourse and value system, the interpretation of the *li* of *lun* seems to be inseparable from the reference of reason. So, if we must say that *li* is some kind of reason, we can only say that it is a kind of conscious reason. Coined by Tu Wei-ming, conscious reason is a discourse and a thesis that has had a significant impact. It is not only used to interpret Chinese *lunli,* but also Chinese philosophy and Chinese tradition, and can be said to be one of the general discourses on the modern interpretation of Chinese *lunli,* Chinese philosophy and even Chinese culture. The main point is to distinguish Chinese conscious *li* from Western cognitive reason, and thus to conduct a civilizational dialogue between the two traditions.

A careful consideration reveals that in its dialogue and exchange with the Western culture, the discourse of conscious reason carries a certain Daoist style of compromise and even submissiveness characterized by the statement that, "They know that there is no alternative to their acting as they do, and rest in it as what is appointed." It connects conscience, which is the signature discourse of the Chinese *lunli* tradition, with the mainstream concept of reason of Western culture, trying to ensure they interact with and interpret each other, so that the Chinese tradition becomes a concept that Western culture can understand and accept. However, conscious reason is an attributive structure with reason at the center, but conscience is used to mean that it is a special kind of reason. Thus, under the strong discourse of reason in the West, conscience can only be subordinated to a position of being explained and interpreted.

Under these circumstances, not only the Chinese style of the discourse system, but also the Chinese flavor of the theoretical system and cultural tradition may be lost or at least diluted. However, in the dual contexts of globalization and modernization, finding it necessary to transform itself and positioned to be transformed by others, conscious reason is a necessary and valuable effort in terms of cultural strategy and tactics, and its international impact has shown that it has achieved a certain degree of success.

In fact, the interpretation of the *li* of *lun* can be expressed directly as conscience as indicated in conscious reason, leaving behind the crutch of the Western reason discourse. Conscience is not only a Chinese discourse, but also a Chinese tradition as it has always been. From Mencius' intuitive knowledge and intuitive ability to Wang Yangming's "to conscience," conscience's discourse and theory have been used throughout the historical development of Chinese philosophy and Chinese *lunli,* and in modern civilization conscience is still used as a habit of the mind and has become a deep-seated part of Chinese culture. In modern civilization, conscience is still a habit of the mind and a deep structure of Chinese culture. Conscience can most convincingly explain and express the *li* of *lun.* Mencius says, "The ability possessed by men without having been acquired by learning is intuitive ability, and the knowledge possessed by them without the exercise of thought is their intuitive knowledge. Children carried in the arms all know to love their parents, and when they are grown a little, they all know to love their elder brothers." This shows that intuitive knowledge is the knowledge possessed without having been acquired by learning and is knowledge of *lun* that encourages people to love their parents and their brothers.

Mencius explains this knowledge of this *lun* with the feeling of commiseration for a child about to fall into a well. "Even nowadays, if men suddenly see a child about to fall into a well, they will without exception experience a feeling of alarm and distress. They will feel so, not as a ground on which they may gain the favor of the child's parents, nor as a ground on which they may seek the praise of their neighbors and friends, nor from a dislike to the reputation of having been unmoved by such a thing. From this case we may perceive that the feeling of commiseration is essential to man...."

When people see a child about to fall into a well, why they will without exception experience a feeling of alarm and distress? Mencius ruled out many rational choices including, for example, they will feel so, not as a ground on which they may gain the favor of the child's parents, nor as a ground on which they may seek the praise of their neighbors and friends. The choice that they will feel so not from a dislike to the reputation of having been unmoved by such a thing is most obviously different from Western rationalism. The difference is most obvious. In explaining why we should help the poor, Feuerbach said that we should help the poor because we want to be happier and if the poor moan around us, it will affect our feeling of happiness. Mencius here categorically excluded this rational option, affirming that the feeling of commiseration for a child about to fall into a well is the intuitive knowledge possessed without the exercise of thought.

Conscience is a kind of *lun* knowledge or *lunli* knowledge, which has nothing to do with reason. Wang Yangming further theorized about this kind of conscience in his *Instruction for Practical Life*, "Knowledge is native to the mind; the mind naturally is able to know. When it perceives the parents it naturally knows what filial piety is; when it perceives the elder brother it naturally knows what respectfulness is; when it sees a child fall into a well it naturally knows what commiseration is. This is intuitive knowledge which is not attained through external investigation."[5] Innate knowledge is natural in the *lunli* situation of perceiving the parents and the elder brother and seeing the child fall into a well, or the instinctive knowledge that comes from the experience of the ethical substance with the parents, the elder brother, and the child.

The *li* of *lun* is the knowledge of natural conscience from *lun*. It is the natural knowledge of *lun*, and thus the knowledge possessed without the exercise of thought. In the Chinese discourse, intuitive has various meanings such as natural and good, and the intuitive knowledge referred to by Mencius and Wang Yangming is the knowledge that comes from the natural instinct of *lun* and the natural conscience of *lun*. This is the *li* of *lun*. The *li* of *lun* is from the instinct of *lun* and the natural goodness of *lun*, and thus is possessed without the exercise of thought.

Therefore, the *li* of *lun* is not only not reason in a significant sense, but also fundamentally rejects reason, as Mencius said, it fundamentally rejects reason because if the *li* of *lun* is mixed with rational calculations or trade-offs, it is not the intuitive knowledge of the *li* of *lun*, but the reason

---

[5] Wang Yangming, *Instruction for Practical Life.*

of Western-style utilitarianism. The *li* of *lun* is intuitive knowledge, must be intuitive knowledge, and is nothing but intuitive knowledge.

4 EMOTIONALISM

The intuitive knowledge of the *li* of *lun* is neither Western rationalism nor Western emotionalism, and if it must be attributed to some theoretical form, it is Chinese emotionalism.

The history of Western ethics has long been marked by a debate between rationalism and emotionalism. Rationalism is the unshakable mainstream, and the modern classical form is the dominant rationalist ethics of Kant and Hegel, but emotionalism has never been absent. Hume's *A Treatise on Human Nature* and *An Enquiry Concerning the Principles of Morals* set the tone of modern Western emotionalist ethics. In the 1930s, emotionalism used to be the most popular meta-ethic in Britain, typified by Ludwig Wittgenstein and C. L. Stevenson, advocated ethics as the expression of human emotions and denied its scientific nature, but they eventually moved toward relativism. The Chinese *lunli* tradition, from the pre-Qin period to the Song-Ming neo-Confucianism and even to the modern era, has generated and continued a tradition of emotionalism, and the *li* of *lunli* and *lun* is the discourse of the emotionalist tradition and its theoretical form.

Sociologists have long found that Chinese culture has chosen the path of emotion from the beginning, refusing to move in the direction of pure reason. This is true with both philosophy and poetry.[6] In fact, this path of China is closely related to the background of a *lunli* culture under the path of state-family civilization, and it is not pure sentimentalism that China has followed, but emotionalism. The key point of emotionalism is to make sense out of emotion, and the so-called emotion has the double meaning of actuality and emotion.[7] Confucius' argument of three years of mourning for parents is typical of sentimentalism.

The idea of three years of mourning for parents has been one of the most important *lunli* customs and institutions in China since time immemorial. According to *The Analects of Confucius*, Confucius' student

---

[6] See Chang Te-sheng, *Confucian Ethics and the Order Complex*, Juliu Book Co., Taiwan, 1989.

[7] Li Zehou and Yang Guorong, "Ethical Issues and Beyond," *Social Science*, 2014, no. 9.

Zai Yu questioned this idea, stating that, "The three years of mourning for parents are too long." Confucius responded, "This shows Yu's want of virtue. It is not till a child is three years old that it is allowed to leave the arms of its parents. And the three years' mourning is universally observed throughout the country. Did Yu enjoy the three years' love of his parents?".

In Confucius' case, "the want of virtue" was not a general rebuke, but a very severe criticism, because benevolence is the distinguishing characteristic of persons. *Mencius* says, "Benevolence is the distinguishing characteristic of persons. As embodied in persons' conduct, it is called the path of duty." A person's want of virtue means he or she has to develop his or her characteristic as a person and acquire the correct path of duty.

How did Confucius justify the idea of three years of mourning for parents? He did it by appealing to the reasoning of life and living that, "It is not till a child is three years old that it is allowed to leave the arms of its parents." After the birth of a child, the parents have him or her in their arms for three years, and after the death of the parents, their child must mourn for them for three years. This is the reward for parents and therefore the three years' mourning "is universally observed throughout the country."

Chinese *lunli*, especially the Song-Ming neo-Confucianism, advocates the need to ensure that heavenly principles are constantly preserved and human desires disappear. Some people dismiss this as being typical of "ruthlessness" or even "stifling" or "extinction of love." In fact, the love that Chinese *lunli* wants to sublate is the so-called human desires which do not refer to human need or lust in general, but rather to "excessive desires," i.e. "extravagant desires" and "wrong desires." On the contrary, reasonable human desires are considered to be heavenly principles. Zhu Xi made a famous proposition or slogan, "Within heavenly principles, human desires are the most important." Emotionalism is a Chinese form and Chinese temperament that is different from Western rationalism and emotionalism, and the human conscience that arises from emotionalism is the so-called *li* of *lun*. Chinese *lunli* conscience or the so-called *li* always exists based on the existence of *lun* and is the *li* in the concrete substance of *lun* and the *lunli* situation. It is therefore the *li* of *lunli*.

In the Chinese tradition, Daoism is considered to be rationalistic because of the metaphysical temperament of its doctrine, that is, "persons of virtue do not harm themselves with excessive likes or dislikes." In fact, Daoism superficially rejects emotion, but the philosophical paradigm

of the *Daodejing* is that "the laws of nature are also those of humanity" and the emotion of humans is the destination of its philosophy. In
the *Daodejing*, the *daojing* is the heavenly *dao*, and the *dejing* is the *shi*
of humanity. The heavenly *dao* is *li* and the *dao* of humanity is emotion.
They combine to form the *Daodejing* which is also essentially reason, and
is meant to derive the reason or *lunli* for daily life from the heavenly *dao*.

This philosophical paradigm is exemplified by the way Laozi argued
about water. He first discussed the formal nature of water, from which
he deduces the *lunli* proposition of taking softness as the fundamental
virtue of humans, and then from the heavenly way of water, he introduced the *shi* of humanity, i.e. the reason of life, based on the principle
that the soft overcomes the hard. He said, "There is nothing in the world
more soft and weak than water, and yet for attacking things that are firm
and strong there is nothing that can take precedence of it;—for there is
nothing (so effectual) for which it can be changed. Everyone in the world
knows that the soft overcomes the hard, and the weak the strong, but no
one is able to carry it out in practice." According to the *Daodejing*, "The
softest thing in the world dashes against and overcomes the hardest." This
kind of interpretation of the philosophical nature of water becomes even
clearer when compared to ancient Greek philosophy. The first philosophical discovery in ancient Greece was Thales' notion that "Water is the
best," which is only an ontological proposition. Laozi, however, deduced
from the nature of water the sentiment of softness overcoming strength
and the *lunli* proposition of taking softness as the fundamental virtue
of humans. This shows that there are profound differences between the
Chinese and Western traditions even at the ontological level.

To this day, the Chinese value is always a trinity of emotion, reason,
and law in that order, with emotion and propriety being brought to
bear before the law is brought to bear. This sentimentalist orientation is
systematically expressed in Xunzi's arguments about propriety. The status
of propriety in pre-Qin Confucian *lunli* underwent a dialectical development process. Confucius made it the overarching discourse of the ethical
substance, the highest concept of the *lunli* system. The so-called ethical
substance of Western philosophy was expressed in the Chinese tradition
as the so-called propriety. Mencius internalized propriety as one of the
Four Virtues of benevolence, righteousness, propriety and wisdom. Xunzi
not only restored the supremacy of propriety but also institutionalized it.
This is what Tu Wei-ming called the landmark of the transformation from
spiritual Confucianism to institutionalized Confucianism.

However, Xunzi's argument for propriety is not based only on institutions but also on the three-dimensional integration of emotion, reason, and law. According to *Xunzi*, first of all, propriety is a natural principle of living in communities and being one. "They are not as strong as oxen or as fast as horses, but oxen and horses are used by them. How is this so? I say it is because humans are able to form communities while the animals cannot. Why are humans able to form communities? I say it is because of social divisions. How can social divisions be put into practice? I say it is because of *yi*." Community, division, and *yi* constitute the heavenly logic of propriety. Humans not only live in communities in the reality, but also are one in spirit. Living in communities is the ethical substance of objectivity, as Hegel called it. Being one is the spiritual consciousness of the ethical substance and its identification with it, so that the *lunli* existence of living in communities reaches the spirit of being one. This is the heavenly principle.

Xunzi also interpreted propriety as human feelings in the theory of using propriety to nourish feelings. According to *Xunzi*, "From what did propriety arise? I say: Humans are born having desires. When they have desires but do not get the objects of their desire, then they cannot but seek some means of satisfaction. If there is no measure or limit to their seeking, then they cannot help but struggle with each other. If they struggle with each other then there will be chaos, and if there is chaos then they will be impoverished. The former kings hated such chaos, and so they established propriety and *yi* in order to divide things among people, to nurture their desires, and to satisfy their seeking. They caused desires never to exhaust material goods, and material goods never to be depleted by desires, so that the two support each other and prosper. This is how propriety arose. Thus, propriety is a means of nurture."

Lust is the nature of humans, but acting in accordance with lust, it is bound to be a struggle, so we should develop propriety to regulate it to prevent people's pursuit of material desire from becoming excessive. This is called regulating lust to ensure that it is both satisfied and stays within limits.

Finally, propriety is also the law. It is fundamental for self-cultivation and national governance. *Xunzi* says, "Hence, if their lives are without propriety, then people cannot survive. If affairs are without propriety, in them success does not thrive. If state and clan are without propriety, for them peace does not arrive. Propriety is the height of good order and proper distinction. It is the fundamental point for making the state strong. It is the way to inspire awe pervasively. It is the crucial element for gaining accomplishments and fame." Mencius advocated rule by benevolence, and Xunzi advocated rule by propriety, so he regarded propriety as the highest principle of *daode*. Xunzi said, "Propriety is the great division in the model for things. Outlines of things' proper classes are in the property found. And so, learning comes to propriety and then stops, for this is called the ultimate point in pursuit of the Way and virtue." Thus, propriety is the unity of the heavenly principle, human feelings, and the law of the state, that is, the unity of emotion, reason, and law.

How is the *li* of *lun* generated and expressed? What is the reason and reality of rationalism? The classical Chinese discourse and paradigm is the reflection based on *lunli*.

In his *The Analects*, Confucius said, "My doctrine is that of an all-pervading unity." In the same book, his students interpreted this doctrine as follows: "The doctrine of our master is to be true to the principles of our nature and the benevolent exercise of them to others, this and nothing more."

Being true to the principles of our nature and the benevolent exercise of them to others are at the core of Confucius' doctrine, and their philosophical essence is that one should do as one would be done by others: Being true to the principles of our nature means to treating others with sincerity; the benevolent exercise of these principles to others means that one should do as one would be done by others. The specific content is the golden rule that, "Now the person of perfect virtue, wishing to be established himself, seeks also to establish others; wishing to be enlarged himself, he seeks also to enlarge others. Do not do to others as you would not wish done to yourself." Doing as one would be done by others is a kind of *daode*, and its *lunli* expression is considering others in one's own place. Mencius said, "Treat with the reverence due to age the elders in your own family, so that the elders in the families of others shall be similarly treated; treat with the kindness due to youth the young in your own family, so that the young in the families of others shall be similarly treated."

Neither doing as one would be done by others nor considering others in one's own place means that one establishes and enlarges himself before one does this to others; neither of them means one treats with the reverence due to age the elders in one's own family before similarly treats the elders in the families of others, or treats with the kindness due to youth the young in one's own family before similarly treating the young in the families of others. Rather, it is a *lunli* situation designed to place *li* in the specific context of *lun*, and gain conscience through the experience of *lunli* empathy, that is, the so-called *li* of *lun*. Thus, rational *lunli* calculations and abstract *lunli* teachings are applied to concrete life situations, so that *li* has the foundation of *lun* and *li* becomes the natural conscience of *lun*.

Emotion itself is not only knowledge, but also action, just as Hegel said, emotion is the subjective form of will, which has the ability to act directly. Mencius' four feelings of commiseration; shame and dislike; modesty and complaisance; and approving and disapproving are people's intuitive conscience and ability and represent benevolence, righteousness, propriety and wisdom. The first three of the four feelings are about emotion and only the last one is about *li*. In this sense, the structure of Chinese human nature is a structure of emotion and reason primarily based on emotion. Different from the Western "reason + the will" human nature structure, it does not require the intermediary of reason to reach the so-called categorical imperative, but through the *lunli* experience of empathy, it makes moral behavior directly reflect intuitive conscience and ability.

What needs to be further discussed and explained is that both Mencius' knowledge possessed by people without the exercise of thought and Wang Yangming's natural knowledge are a kind of knowledge of *lun* and knowledge of *lunli* and in the final analysis, *lunli* emotion. "The *lunli* relationship is a relationship of friendship, which is also a relationship of obligation in a mutual relationship. Based on emotion and righteousness, the *li* of *lunli* better reflects mutual affection and emphasizes emotion and righteousness."[8] *Lun* is the foundation and prerequisite of goodness, which makes it possible for people to possess knowledge without the exercise of thought and show filial piety toward their father naturally. The *li* of *lun* is intuitive conscience, *lun* is intuitive, and *li* is knowledge. Whether it is the *li* of *lun* or intuitive knowledge, they are both the discourses and theories of the Chinese form of sentimentalism, as well as the Chinese cultural code of potential sentimentalism.

---

[8] Liang Shuming, *Essentials of Chinese Culture*, Beijing: Academia Press, 2000, p. 80.

CHAPTER 4

Taking *Lun* as Home and *Li* as the Intuitive Knowledge and Heavenly Principle

Lun is the substance and home, *li* is the law of *lun* and the intuitive conscience of *lun*. How is *lunli* formed by the combination of *lun* and *li*, or what is the principle of the relationship between *lun* and *li*? In a nutshell, it is necessary to take *lun* as home and *li* as the intuitive knowledge and heavenly principle.

1 STAYING TRUE TO *LUN* AND DOING ONE'S PART

The *lunli* in Chinese cultural discourse is not an abstract code of conduct, nor is it just the so-called ethics and *lunli* order in the general sense. It has a lot of cultural information that is not contained in Western ethics and morality. *Lun* refers to the order of human relationships, especially the paradigm constructed by human order, namely, the so-called heavenly principle. It is also a metaphor for the fact that this human order is not a requirement external to humans, but a home of *lun* generated by the unity of the individual with his own public essence and his identification with it. The so-called "*li*" is the law that lies within *lun*, which is a metaphor for the essence and sanctity of *lun* as the home of humans. Therefore, the *li* of *lun* is not only the truth, but also the heavenly principle; it is not only the knowledge of *lun*, but also the intuitive conscience. The *lunli* formed by the unity of *lun* and *li* represents the individual's

© Foreign Language Teaching and Research Publishing Co., Ltd 2024   47
H. Fan, Lunli *and Confucian Moral Theory*, Key Concepts
in Chinese Thought and Culture,
https://doi.org/10.1007/978-981-99-9105-1_4

identification with and return to his or her own home, as well as the laws and intuitive knowledge embedded in *lun*.

Unlike *daode*, *lunli* does not require the individual to obey the rules. The rational premise of obeying the rules is to reflect on the reason and validity of the rules, and obeying the rules may be done for many complicated reasons such as utilitarianism and obligation. Therefore, there have been arguments between deontology and utilitarianism, and between the theory of motive and the theory of effect. The basic requirement of *lunli* for individuals is what Hegel called doing what one knows within his situation in an ethical community, which is expressed in the Chinese language as "staying to *lun* and do one's part."

In the everyday discourse of traditional Chinese society, there is a saying that goes like this: be content with one's lot and live within *lunli*. However, nobody knows when people began to use it as a positive term. In the process of moving toward modernity, it has become increasingly forgotten or even dead not only in the discourse but also in the collective memory, because it seems to imply some kind of *lunli* conservatism. In fact, this is also a discursive representation of the loss of tradition and a rupture of values.

Being content with one's lot and living within *lunli* is the wisdom of a *lunli* culture that integrates *lunli* and *daode* and gives priority to the former. It is different from the abstract adherence to *daode* rules, and its discursive premise and behavioral basis is *lunli* identification, because both being content with one's lot and living within *lunli* can only be possible in a *lunli* substance. Being content with one's lot is the power and obligation of the individual in the *lunli* substance and the *lunli* order, while living within *lunli* is the position or status of the individual in the *lunli* substance, which indicates that humans have reality only in the concrete *lunli* substance.

As Hegel said, to designate an individual as a legal person is an expression of contempt. The difference between individual and individuality is that the individual has a body, and this body is the reality in the ethical substance, and the atomic individual who leaves the ethical substance is only the non-actual shadow.

If we are looking for some kind of linguistic mirroring between everyday speech and academic expression, "stay true to *lun* and do one's part" is the expression that corresponds to "be content with one's lot and live within *lunli*" and is better able to convey cultural information about *lunli*, particularly the Chinese cultural code that integrates *lunli* and *daode*. "Stay true to *lun*" refers to recognize *lunli* and "do one's part" refers to pursue *daode* freedom. "Stay true to *lun* and do one's part" not only means the unity of recognizing *lunli* and pursuing *daode* freedom, but also conveys a strong message that *lunli* takes precedence in its relationship with *daode*, "stay true to *lun*" is a prerequisite for "do one's part," and without *lun* serving as a prerequisite, it is impossible to clarify *lun*, stay true to it, and do one's part. The essence of staying true to *lun* is to be self-restraint, that is, to conform to one's own *lunli* responsibilities or duties, while the essence of doing one's part is to live within *lunli*, that is, to fulfill one's own rights and obligations within a *lunli* substance. Stay true to *lun* and be self-restraint is to take *lun* as home while do one's part and keep to oneself is to take *li* as the intuitive knowledge and heavenly principle.

The Chinese discourse conveyed by taking *lun* as home and *li* as the intuitive knowledge and heavenly principle is the journey taken by the individual by starting from the home of *lun*, taking *li* as the intuitive knowledge and heavenly principle, i.e. obeying the laws of *lun*, and following the path of spiritual and realistic identification chartered by the knowledge possessed without the exercise of thought. In this way, "*lunli*," which is generated by "*lun*" and "*li*" and "taking *lun* as home and *li* as the intuitive knowledge and heavenly principle," not only presupposes but also inevitably requires the unity of *lunli* and *daode*. In this unity, *lunli* has unquestionable philosophical priority, yet both *lunli* and *daode* are distinct from each other and cannot be separated from or substituted for each other.

"Take *lun* as home and *li* as the intuitive knowledge and heavenly principle" is the philosophical expression of the everyday discourse of "stay true to *lun* and be self-restraint" and the academic discourse of "stay true to *lun* and do one's part." The meaning of the everyday discourse is that it has become a living tradition, that is, it has developed into a habitual mindset of the cultural subject that carries it. This habitual mindset is often already classically expressed in the traditional canon and nurtured by it. However, because it is already a traditional discourse, it is likely to be misinterpreted in the reflection on the tradition because of the critical cleansing that it has encountered, and it is thus not only silenced in the current discourse, but is also rejected in the value system. So it expects mistakes be rectified. In the Chinese tradition, the classical expression of "take *lun* as home and *li* as the intuitive knowledge and heavenly principle" is what Confucius called "rectifying names."

In the doctrine of Confucius and his discourse, propriety is the so-called *lunli* substance of the modern philosophical discourse, and benevolence is the so-called *daode* subject. The transformation of the *lunli* substance of propriety into the *lunli* subject of benevolence needs an important spiritual link, namely, *lunli* identification, which is not the superficial adherence to the forms of rituals, but the respect for the *lunli* order it constructs. China's Spring and Autumn Period, during which the policy of "letting a hundred flowers bloom and a hundred schools of thought contend" was implemented, is a period in which, as Nietzsche put it, "everything is permitted." It is also a time when "the people do not know how to move hand or foot," a time of misconduct and disorder. Sociologists have found that it is this childhood memory of cultural misconduct and disorder that has given birth to the order complex of Chinese people.

The focus of Confucius' cultural strategy to rebuild *lunli* substances and *lunli* order is the so-called rectification of names. According to *The Analects of Confucius*, when Zilu asked about government, Confucius replied, "What is necessary is to rectify names.... If names be not correct, language is not in accordance with the truth of things. If language be not in accordance with the truth of things, affairs cannot be carried on to success. When affairs cannot be carried on to success, proprieties and music will not flourish. When proprieties and music do not flourish, punishments will not be properly awarded. When punishments are not properly awarded, the people do not know how to move hand or foot." After this deduction, the serious consequence of incorrect names is that the people do not know how to move hand or foot, that is, there is misconduct and disorder.

What caused a greater misinterpretation of the theory of name rectification and of the nature of Confucius' entire doctrine was the famous Confucius' answer to Duke Jing of Qi's question about government: "Let the ruler be a ruler, the minister a minister, the father a father, and the son a son." (*The Analects of Confucius*) Thus Confucius' doctrine is believed to be a conservative theory that upholds the patriarchal hierarchical order.

In fact, to correctly interpret Confucius' theories of rectifying names and letting the ruler be a ruler, the minister a minister, the father a father, and the son a son, they must be understood not only by what they are targeted but also in philosophical terms. Feng Youlan found that, "The loyal ministers and filial sons of China through the ages were not loyal or filial to individuals, but were devoted to the concept of ruler and father.

The objects of their loyalty and filial piety 'were not in the world of concrete objects but in the world of Forms or Ideas of Plato."[1] According to this interpretation, what Confucius meant by letting the ruler be a ruler, the minister a minister, the father a father, and the son a son is not a specific person, but a conceptual world, i.e. the kind of *lun* that is represented, and thus is essentially a recognition of and identification with *lun*.

Another counter-evidence is Mencius' famous defense of King Wu's strike against King Zhou of Shang. He separated Zhou from the kingship, stating that, " I have heard of the execution of a man named Zhou, but not of regicide." Since the target of execution was not the king but only a man, there was no crime against *lunli*. Although Feng Youlan's abstract method of inheritance has been questioned and criticized, it does provide a different way of interpreting the tradition, in which the most important message is the attitude toward the tradition and the cultural realm achieved.

From this point of view, Confucius' theories rectifying names and letting the ruler be a ruler, the minister a minister, the father a father, and the son a son affirm *lun* and safeguard *lunli*, and are identified with and return to the *lunli* substance and *lunli* order. In philosophical terms, they take *lun* as home and *li* as the intuitive knowledge and heavenly principle.

Taking *lun* as home and *li* as the intuitive knowledge and heavenly principle is not only about the concepts of *lun* and *li*, but also the different cultural laws of *lun* and *li* and their cultural attitudes. *Lun* is the substance, the home, in which the individual can live; *li*'s essential meaning is to obtain intuitive knowledge and ability from taking *lun* as home. When *lun* is taken as home, the moral requirements of benevolence, righteousness, propriety, and wisdom are, as Mencius said, "are not infused into us from without. We are certainly furnished with them.... All things are already complete in us."

Related to the concept of taking *lun* as home and *li* as the intuitive knowledge and heavenly principle are the concepts of staying true to *lun* and doing one's part and of being content with one's lot and living within *lunli*. *Lun* refers to the *lunli* substance and *lunli* order that should be identified with, that is, one should place oneself in the *lunli* substance.

---

[1] Chen Lai, "Feng Youlan's 'Ethical Concept'," *Journal of Tsinghua University, Humanities and Social Sciences,* 2016, no. 2.

Doing one's part represents one's rights and obligations within the *lunli* substance, which need to be performed. Do one's part means to perform the *lunli* rights and obligations for *lunli* identification, and one means the one derived therefrom who lives within *daode*.

In Hegel's words, the philosophical meaning of taking *lun* as home and *li* as the intuitive knowledge and heavenly principle is as follows: "Virtue consists rather in ethical virtuosity.... In an ethical community, it is easy to say what someone must do and what the duties are which he has to fulfil in order to be virtuous. He must simply do what is prescribed, expressly stated, and known to him within his situation. Rectitude is the universal quality which may be required of him, partly by right and partly by ethics."[2] Taking *lun* as home means to place the individual in the *lunli* community, and taking *li* as the intuitive knowledge and heavenly principle is the universal rectitude which may be required of him by *lunli*. The essence of taking *lun* as home and *li* as the intuitive knowledge and heavenly principle is the *lunli* attainment.

2   CULTIVATING ONESELF TO GIVE REST TO OTHERS

In the Chinese discourse and tradition, the cultural meaning of taking *lun* as home and *li* as the intuitive knowledge and heavenly principle lies in the requirements for taking *lunli* as home and for one, i.e. the individual, to live within *lunli*. While *lun* is the dwelling and yet to be dwelt in, *li* is derived from *lun*, and taking *lun* as home is the path *li* must take. *Li* is found in *lun*; there is no *li* outside of *lun*. Seeking *li* is only like seeking fish from a tree. Taking *lun* as home and *li* as the intuitive knowledge and heavenly principle is the Chinese cultural paradigm of the relationship between *lun* and *li*, and taking *lun* as home means *lun* is the home of the individual, his starting and end point, the basis for the reason and legitimacy of his behavior in the *lunli* relationship, and is also the root motivation of the behavior.

The key meaning of taking *lun* as home is to stay true to *lun*. The term "stay true" expresses the *lunli* code of the relationship between individuals and substances in Chinese culture. Staying true to *lun* and doing one's part is the *lunli* truth, principle, and law of this relationship. Staying true to *lun* is more related to everyday life than taking *lun* as home. The

<hr>

[2] G. W. E. Hegel, *Elements of the Philosophy of Right*, Chinese version by Fan Yang and Zhang Qitai, Beijing: The Commercial Press, 1996, pp. 170, 168.

basic requirement of staying true to *lun* is to live within *lun*, that is, to be content with one's position in the *lunli* substance and fulfill one's *lunli* duties, which is what Confucius called name rectification. Name rectification requires one to act in accordance with one's status in *lunli* relationships, without exceeding limits.

From this we can understand why Confucius was so furious when the head of the Ji family had eight rows of pantomimes in his area as recorded in *The Analects of Confucius*: "If he can bear to do this, what may he not bear to do?" This is one of the few times that Confucius lost his temper, because when the head of the Ji family had eight rows of pantomimes in his area, he had overstepped the rules of etiquette by enjoying eight rows of pantomimes reserved for the Son of Heaven. By so doing he was believed to have destroyed the *lunli* order or was suspected of attempted rebellion in today's language. He was considered to have subverted the theory of taking *lun* as home or not have been content with his lot or lived within *lunli*.

If this were the only point, taking *lun* as home might be just a set of laws of the Confucian ethical code, but the ultimate basis of taking *lun* as home lies in the inherent *lunli* concern of *lun* toward the individual. The notion that taking *lun* as home is the same as staying true to *lun* means that the individuals can only stay true to *lun* within the *lunli* substances of the family, nation, and country. This makes him feel at home and fulfill his life. The substance of *lun* is not only the *lunli* home of the individual, but also his ultimate concern, conveying his identification with and devotion to the *lunli* substance. In this sense, staying true to *lun* has much cultural significance similar to the ultimate substance of being content with God in Western culture. The difference is that this kind of ultimate staying true to *lun* does not require the help of the other shore; it can be attained on this shore, and its meaning of the ultimate social concern exists not only in the ultimate end of life but also in daily life.

The Chinese concept of family is, to a great extent, the *lunli* design and *lunli* embodiment of the ultimate social concern of *lun*. As for the *lun* substance care meaning of home for the individual, staying true to *lun* and taking it as home lasts throughout the entire process of life from the nurturing in infancy, to the arrangement when entering society, to the comfort during setbacks, and even until the burial in the family tomb after death.

It is safe to say that from the leaving home and returning home of Chinese people commuting every day, to the family reunion during important festivals, especially the Spring Festival, which is marked by the large annual human migrations in the world—all these are *lunli* manifestations and developments of the ultimate social care of home. After one takes *lun* as his home, as long as one lives within *lunli*, i.e. keeps to one's *lunli* status in *lunli* substances and relationships, one can obtain the rationality and legitimacy of behavior from the *lunli* intuitive knowledge one possesses without the exercise of thought. This is the so-called "taking *li* as the intuitive knowledge and heavenly principle." Taking *li* as the intuitive knowledge and heavenly principle fundamentally means living within *lunli*. Taking *li* as the intuitive knowledge and heavenly principle is a natural result of taking *lunli* as home and intuitive knowledge possessed without the exercise of thought. It not only has rationality and legitimacy, but also has *lunli* sacredness. It of course also has the secular sacredness of the worldly culture.

"*An*" (安) is a term with strong *lunli* connotations in Chinese culture. It conveys many genes of *lunli* culture, from personal identification with *lunli* to national and social stability. If *lunli* is brought from classical and theoretical domains into daily life, many expressions related to "*an*" in Chinese culture are related to *lunli* or staying true to *lunli* and taking *lun* as home. Staying to *lunli* includes not only identification with *lunli* but also a deeper sense of being at ease. Survival and being at ease are not only *lunli* expectations and demands, but also *lunli* care and obligations.

In this way, staying true to *lun* shifts from an individual to all others, that is, it is not only the individual's identification with the *lunli* substance, but also his *lunli* care for others and his *lunli* obligation to the substance. In other words, it is not only about one's own identification with *lunli* but also about his care for others. Care for others is a *lunli* advancement from taking *lun* as home and *li* as the intuitive knowledge and heavenly principle to staying true to *lun* and doing one's part. Such advancement is expressed in the classical Confucian a *lunli* discourse with "cultivating oneself to give rest to others" and "cultivating oneself to give rest to all the people." In fact, most of the classical expressions of Confucianism about staying true to *lun* is about care for others. Care for others is not only a *lunli* concern and *lunli* sentiment, but also a *lunli* realm, because care for others must be premised on cultivating oneself. Taking *lun* as home and staying true to *lun* require cultivating oneself, which is the so-called name rectification. Care for others is both the *lunli* realm of cultivating oneself and the *lunli* fruit of cultivating oneself.

According to *The Analects of Confucius*, "Zilu asked what constituted the superior man. Confucius said, 'The cultivation of himself in reverential carefulness.' 'And is this all?' said Zilu. 'He cultivates himself so as to give rest to others,' was the reply. 'And is this all?' again asked Zilu. Confucius said, 'He cultivates himself to give rest to all the people. He cultivates himself to give rest to all the people—even Yao and Shun were still solicitous about this.'".

Here is a record of Confucius' three requirements of the superior man: cultivate himself, give rest to others, and give rest to all the people. Cultivating oneself is to become a virtuous person who meets *lunli* requirements or has *lunli* attainments. Cultivating oneself to give rest to others benefits others; cultivating oneself to give rest to all the people is about national governance for conferring benefits on the people and assisting all. The *an* here not only means peace and happiness in general, but also has the *lunli* meaning of being able to establish one's life.

According to *The Analects of Confucius*, when Confucius discussed benevolence with Yan Yuan and Zilu, Zilu said "They are, in regard to the aged, to give them rest; in regard to friends, to show them sincerity; in regard to the young, to treat them tenderly." Here *an* means peace and happiness in general, and the object of *an* is the aged, that is, others, not oneself.

Also according to *The Analects of Confucius*, "So it is. Therefore, if remoter people are not submissive, all the influences of civil culture and virtue are to be cultivated to attract them to be so; and when they have been so attracted, they must be made contented and tranquil." In the contexts of "not being submissive" and "cultivating virtue," the statement that "when they have been so attracted, they must be made contented and tranquil" includes not only peace and happiness, but also "staying true to *lun* in the *lunli* substance."

It can be seen that staying true to *lun* in the sense of giving rest to others is the higher realm of taking *lun* as home.

The core of Chinese *lunli* is a set of theories and practices for establishing one's own life, and the fundamental requirement of *lunli* is not only that the individual should be at ease in the *lunli* substance and obtain the attachment to the world of life and the world of spirit, but also that the individual has the obligation to establish and enlarge others. Establishing and enlarging others not only points to the world of life, but also, and more importantly, to the *lunli* world. As Liang Shuming said, the Chinese treat politics as a *lunli* matter, or deal with politics in a *lunli* context, so to speak.[3] The way of ruling a country is no more than about addressing three issues—*yang*, *bao* and *an*. *Yang* means the creation of material wealth; *bao* means the protection of the external security of *lunli* substance; and *an* means the internal stability of *lunli* substance. Chinese culture is characterized by addressing *yang* and *bao* as *an*.[4]

Confucius summed up his life journey, stating that, "At thirty, I stood firm." This means standing in the *lunli* substance of propriety; otherwise it is difficult to understand the preceding sentence: "At fifteen, I had my mind bent on learning." and the following sentences: "At forty, I had no doubts. At fifty, I knew the decrees of Heaven." Having one's mind bent on learning at fifteen is propriety, so is having no doubts at forty. Knowing the decrees of Heaven at fifty is to subdue one's self and return to propriety. Propriety is the *lunli* substance that Confucius identified with and tried to return to, modeled on the Western Zhou *lunli* and political systems. Thus, not only is the so-called establishing one's life taking *lun* as home in the *lunli* substance, but also the core of the so-called survival is the construction of the *lunli* world and the world of life in the context of *lunli*.

3   ROLE ETHICS OR THE PRINCIPLES OF *THE GREAT LEARNING*?

Because of its identification with *lun* and the *lunli* rule that *li* comes from *lun*, the Chinese tradition of taking *lun* as home and *li* as the intuitive knowledge and heavenly principle is considered to be similar with some modern Western ethical theories. The first is communitarianism. Another expression of communitarianism that is easily accepted and therefore misinterpreted in the Chinese discourse is neo-collectivism, which was one of the major trends in the West from the 1980s onwards, represented by Michael J. Sandel, Alasdair MacIntyre, etc. Communitarianism is about liberalism. It opposes individualism and maintains that the individual and the self are ultimately determined by the community, and therefore emphasizes the value of the family, society, and the state. It holds that harmony arises from the identification with the community, although the rules of the community are based on their intrinsic

---

[3] Liang Shuming, *Essentials of Chinese Culture*, Beijing: Academia Press, 2000, p. 184.
[4] Ibid., p. 237.

reason rather than external imposition. In emphasizing the priority of *lunli* substances such as the family and the state over the individual and the significance of the individual's identification with the community, communitarianism does have some similarities with the Chinese tradition of taking *lun* as home and *li* as the intuitive knowledge and heavenly principle. However, due to the *lunli* rule that human relations are based on natural relations in the construction of *lun* and because the *lunli* of the family holds a sacred position both in taking *lun* as home and in taking *li* as the intuitive knowledge and heavenly principle, communitarianism does not possess the inherent moral qualities of taking *lun* as home and *li* as the intuitive knowledge and heavenly principle for failing to explain the social and sacred roots recognized by community ethics. The philosophical foundation of taking *lun* as home and *li* as the intuitive knowledge and heavenly principle is fundamentally based on Western-style cognitive rationality rather than Chinese-style conscience rationality.

Situational ethics can also communicate with taking *lun* as home and *li* as the intuitive knowledge and heavenly principle in terms of the relationship between *lun* and *li*. This theory believes that the justification of everything and its behavior is ultimately determined by its ethical situation, and opposes the use of some a priori moral principles to constrain and evaluate human behavior. If *lun* is understood as a situation, then there is indeed some mutual interpretation between it and *li*, and taking *lun* as home and *li* as the intuitive knowledge and heavenly principle can be interpreted to confirm the reasonableness of behavior based on the historical situation of *lun*. However, Western situational ethics, represented by the American Christian theologian Joseph Fletcher, takes the existence of God and God's love as its fundamental premise, and without this premise, it loses its ultimate basis. In real life, situational ethics is prone to relativism and amoralism. Mencius' theory of flexibility to handle unexpected changes and challenges in various situations relating to *lunli* relations, especially his defense of the fact that "Shun married without informing his parents" and the question of whether a man should rescue his drowning sister-in-law can embody the cultural differences between the notion of taking *lun* as home and *li* as the intuitive knowledge and heavenly principle and situational ethics.

Mencius says, "There are three things which are unfilial, and to have no posterity is the greatest of them. Shun married without informing his parents because of this, lest he should have no posterity. Superior men consider that his doing so was the same as if he had informed them."

According to Confucian theory, it is unfilial for a son to marry without the consent of his parents, and this tradition still exists softly as a habit of the heart even in modern China. However, as a model of *lunli*, married without informing her parents, and this led to a controversy. Mencius' defense of this is that Shun did not want to had no posterity and his doing so was the same as if he had informed his parents. According to historical records, Shun's father was not only unkind to Shun, but also tried to get rid of him many times because of his eccentricity. In this particular *lunli* situation, Shun got married without informing his father in order to avoid being unfilial for having no posterity. According to Mencius, this should be considered to be the same as if he had informed his parents, because having no offspring was the greater form of unfilial behavior compared to not informing one's parents one his marriage.

There is another dialogue in *Mencius*, "Chunyu Kun said: 'Is it the rule that males and females shall not allow their hands to touch in giving or receiving anything?' Mencius replied, 'It is the rule.' Kun asked, 'If a man's sister-in-law be drowning, shall he rescue her with his hand?' Mencius said, 'He who would not so rescue the drowning woman is a wolf. For males and females not to allow their hands to touch in giving and receiving is the general rule; when a sister-in-law is drowning, to rescue her with the hand is a peculiar exigency'." Mencius upheld the *lunli* principle that males and females shall not allow their hands to touch in giving or receiving anything, and Chunyu gave Mencius a dilemma: should a man save his drowning sister-in-law? If he did not save her, he would be a wolf; if he did, he would violate the principle that males and females shall not allow their hands to touch in giving or receiving anything. According to Mencius, to help in this particular situation is in accordance with the theory of flexibility to handle unexpected changes and challenges in various situations. This is what situational ethics calls the position that moral decision making is contextual or dependent on a set of circumstances. Mencius said anyone who did not help under these circumstances was a wolf.

The Western theory that is most similar to the theory of taking *lun* as home and *li* as the intuitive knowledge and heavenly principle is the so-called role ethics.

Role ethics is one of the signature concepts of the Bostonian Confucianism in the United States, and is shared by such iconic figures as Roger T. Ames and Rebert C. Neville. In his book *Confucian Role Ethics: A vocabulary*, Ames explains Confucian role ethics in a systematic way, arguing that the Confucian project emphasizes the wholeness of experience and the constitutive nature of relationality that is entailed by it. He says that people are the totality of roles they live in relation to specific others, and people in social life thus determine their proper direction. According to Ames, Confucian role ethics points to how people live together in a system of roles and relationships composed of individuals, ethics that originates in the family and culminates in the construction of an ethical community of interdependence that leads to one family under Heaven. He believes that Confucian ethics based on role ethics can provide a new paradigm for the world, which is facing an approaching catastrophe. The role and the identification with it is a very expressive modern interpretation of the notion of taking *lun* as home, and there is a great deal of room for dialogue and mutual interpretation between role ethics and the notion of taking *lun* as home and *li* as the intuitive knowledge and heavenly principle.

However, in the Chinese *lunli* tradition, the individual does not assume one role in *lunli* relations and *lunli* substances, but multiple roles, and is a *lunli* person that plays multiple *lunli* roles. Assuming multiple *lunli* roles is just like what Karl Marx said, "Human nature is formed by the totality of social relations." Not only that, the individual in the ethical substance and *lunli* relationship must have a skillful *lunli* ability to switch between different *lunli* roles anytime and anywhere. This skillful switching ability is considered as a *lunli* education or *lunli* attainment. The same person is a son to his father, a father to his children, and a husband to his wife; a teacher to his students, and a student to his teachers. Assuming multiple *lunli* roles and constantly switching between them is the essence of taking *lun* as home, and the rationality of the behavior thus obtained is the so-called notion of taking *li* as the intuitive knowledge and heavenly principle.

In the Chinese tradition and even in the social life of Chinese people, taking *lun* as home and *li* as the intuitive knowledge and heavenly principle is undoubtedly a moral realm, which is the so-called the doctrine of the mean. The doctrine of the mean is regarded as the highest ethical realm in both Chinese and Western traditions. In *The Analects of Confucius*, Confucius exclaimed, "Perfect is the virtue which is according to the Mean." Only by raising one's virtuous course to its greatest height and brilliancy, can one pursue the course of the Mean. In his *The Nicomachean Ethics*, Aristotle said that rightness is the core of "mean" or "intermediate" states, i.e. to feel them at the right times, with reference to the right objects, toward the right people, with the right motive, and in the right way. This rightness is expressed in the Chinese language as "always maintaining the Mean." As a *lunli* person assuming multiple *lunli* roles, he takes *lun* as home for the purposes of reaching the mean or intermediate states.

Taking *lun* as home and *li* as the intuitive knowledge and heavenly principle is fundamentally the Chinese principles of *The Great Learning*. As the classic of Chinese *lunli*, *The Great Learning* is about how to cultivate the *lunli* and *daode* of people of virtue. It is said that, "He who nourishes the great is a great person." The principles of *The Great Learning* are to improve the *dao* of people of virtue, and its essence is to inwardly form the sage and externally the king. In *The Great Learning*, its principle takes the specific forms of the three guidelines and the eight essential principles.

The three guidelines are to illustrate illustrious virtue; to renovate the people; and to rest in the highest excellence. They are integral to becoming people of virtue and fundamental for great learning. Illustrating illustrious virtue is to illustrate the *daode* of cultivating oneself, clarifying one's *lun*, and taking *lun* as home. The individual illustrates his virtue while taking *lun* as home. Renovating the people means to improve their *lunli* by both becoming lovingly disposed to people generally and edifying them. It is to cultivate oneself to give rest to others. Resting in the highest excellence is the unification of cultivating oneself and giving rest to others and of taking *lun* as home and taking *li* as the intuitive knowledge and heavenly principle; it is fundamentally the unification of *daode* and *lunli*.

The first four of the eight essential principles are to study things, acquire knowledge, be sincere in thought, and rectify one's mind; they are designed to inwardly form the sage. The last four of them are to cultivate oneself, regulate one's family well, govern the state properly, and bring peace to all under Heaven and are designed to externally form the king. Studying things means to study *lunli* things including the invisible mind and the visible self, family, and state. Acquiring knowledge means to acquire conscience, or just as Mencius put it, "The great end of learning is nothing else but to seek for the lost mind."

To sum up, taking *lun* as home and *li* as the intuitive knowledge and heavenly principle conveys at least three Chinese features of *lunli* discourse.

1. Spiritual home. Taking *lun* as home is not only to safeguard the home of *lun*, but also to restore it. *Lun*, the *lun* substance, is the spiritual home of humans, and taking *lun* as home and *li* as the intuitive knowledge and heavenly principle is an important inspiration for solving the problem of lost home in modern civilization.

2. The social form of *lunli* and its social transcendence. In the modern civilization system, *lunli* and *daode* are mostly presupposed by the existence of ultimate substances on the other shore, such as God, Buddha and Allah, in theory and in reality. Chinese *lunli* is social *lunli*. How is social *lunli* made possible? How can it be social and transcendent? The most solid social foundation is provided by taking *lun* as home and *li* as the intuitive knowledge and heavenly principle.

3. The individual and the rationality, legitimacy and sanctity of his or her actions. How can an individual prove the reality of his or her existence? The most basic reality is the reality in the *lunli* substance, that is, the reality of taking *lun* as home. Where does the rationality and legitimacy of the individual's actions come from? From taking *lun* as home and *li* as the intuitive knowledge and heavenly principle. What makes *lunli* and *daode* sacred? It is not the ultimate substance, nor the absolute command, but the *lun* in social life, especially the heavenly *lun* as the natural *lunli* substance and the paradigm of human relations. The *lunli* sanctity does not need to be sought externally, and the *lunli* conscience and ability can be obtained by taking *lun* as home and *li* as the intuitive knowledge and heavenly principle.

CHAPTER 5

The World of *Lun* and *Li*

1 THE TWO ETHICAL WORLDS

The *lunli* world is a concept and theory common to both Chinese and Western cultures, but the connotation of the two and their status in the history of spirituality and civilization are very different.

Western culture has had a vision of the ethical world since ancient Greece, and Plato's *Republic* can be interpreted as a phenomenological description of the ethical world in a certain sense. The most complete theoretical account of the ethical world is that of Hegel. When making a phenomenological reduction of the history of human spirit in his *The Phenomenology of Spirit*, he took the ethical world as the self-contained state of spirit with ancient Greece as the historical prototype. According to him, the phenomenological picture of the ethical world is that the family and the people are the two ethical substances, and the man and the feminine are the element units that make the transition between the two ethical substances, and the man and the feminine represent the two ethical characters, and the feminine is bound to these Penates [household divinities], and the man moves toward polity life, so that the two ethical

© Foreign Language Teaching and Research Publishing Co., Ltd 2024   63
H. Fan, Lunli *and Confucian Moral Theory*, Key Concepts
in Chinese Thought and Culture,
https://doi.org/10.1007/978-981-99-9105-1_5

substances are in transition to and from each other and reach their state of rest and equilibrium.[1]

This is a discursive ethical world, but it is also a realistic ethical world whose intrinsic negativity is ethical action. The family and the people in the ethical world are both the two ethical substances of man and the two ethical powers that deduce the two ethical necessities of the divine law and the human law. Thus, in the self-consciousness there are also two ethical roles of members of the family and citizens of the nation, which are an undefiled and unpolluted indefiniteness or whole in the state of self, but because of the ethical action the ethical world is full of tension and conflict. In the ethical action, people are either members of the family or citizens of the nation, and the ethical world is constantly filled with tragic scenes or comic scenes of two ethical substances in conflict with each other, which is called pathos.

According to Hegel, the family is the natural ethical substance, and an individual, taken as belonging to the family but not the people, is merely the unreal shadow who lacks at all. In order to get the individuals out of the family and realize their substantiality, the government, as the whole individual of the nation, must from time to time shake them to their core by means of war. However, this ethical substantial consciousness is based on the so-called happy fortune, i.e. ethical contingency, so that the demise of the ethical world is its inevitable fate. The ethical world can eventually be restored as atoms only through the state of legality in a transition to the world of cultural maturation.

In fact, there are two ethical worlds in the Hegelian system. One is the ethical world in *The Phenomenology of Spirit*, which is the in-itself-stage of objective spiritual development, i.e. the ethical world in the state of rest and equilibrium consisting of the family, the people, the man and the feminine, which is the original state of spirit. The other is the ethical world in the *Elements of the Philosophy of Right* which is the in-itself and for-itself stage of the development of free will, i.e. the ethical world of

---

[1] Hegel had this phenomenological reduction of the ethical world: "Each universal ethical essence is an substance as a universal consciousness, and the substance as an individual consciousness; the various ethical essences have the people and family as universal realities, but the man and the feminine as natural selves and dynamic individualities.... The ethical realm is in this way an undefiled world in its durable existence, a world unpolluted by any division." G. W. E. Hegel, Phänomenologie des Geistes: *The Phenomenology of Spirit*, Chinese version by He Lin and Wang Jiuxing, Beijing: The Commercial Press, 1996, vol. II, pp. 17, 19.

the three ethical substances—the family, civil society, and state. The two ethical worlds have very different positions in the Hegelian system. The one depicted in *The Phenomenology of Spirit* is at the primary stage, and the other in the *Elements of the Philosophy of Right* is at the supreme position. The different status of ethics and ethical worlds in the Hegelian system raises the phenomenological question of the Philosophy of Right, but both theories have their validity and must be examined in the context of the Hegelian system as a whole.

The Phenomenology of Spirit is Hegel's first work and the *Elements of the Philosophy of Right* is his last. The former is the most original work not only for Hegel but also in the history of Western philosophy, while the latter, the symbol of Hegel's becoming an official Prussian philosopher, is conservative amidst maturity. A study of the process of writing shows that the second volume of *The Phenomenology of Spirit* was completed in a relatively hasty manner compared to the first volume, because Napoleon had already invaded the city of Jena at that time, and Hegel was forced to complete the second volume quickly due to the need for the author's remuneration while fleeing. He, therefore, wrote to Friedrich Wilhelm Joseph von Schelling, asking him not to give too strong criticism. It can be said that *The Phenomenology of Spirit* also gave the imagination of the later people to further improve it. It is safe to say that *The Phenomenology of Spirit* also leaves room for further improvement.

Accordingly, it is necessary to further advance Hegel's theory of the ethical world and the Western concept of the ethical world formed with this as an important academic resource, and to dialectically synthesize Hegel's two ethical worlds in order to conduct a cultural dialogue with the Chinese *lunli* tradition on this basis.

Hegel's theory on the ethical world has three basic features. First, the original state of his ethical world is naturally identical with the individual and the substance. Second, the ethical world is full of the tense conflict between two ethical laws and two ethical powers—the family and the people. Third, in the ethical world, the ethical role or ethical identification of the individual is either members of the family or citizens of the nation, and thus ethical actions inevitably lead to the splitting of the primary state in which the family and the people are naturally one, and the fate of the ethical world is the atomic transition to the world of cultural maturation. Hegel's phenomenological reduction of the ethical world provides insight into the universal nature of the ethical world, but he only reduced the ethical world based on the history of Western civilization or the history of Western culture or the history of Western spirituality. Whether it is the quiet balance or the tension of pathos, it is only the picture of the civilization history of states and countries. However, the *lunli* world along the path of country-family civilization is another picture featuring what Tu Wei-ming called the positive tension.

The ethical world mentioned in Hegel's *The Phenomenology of Spirit* is precisely a world of *lun* in Chinese culture. Obviously, the world of *lun* or the *lunli* world of Chinese culture is not a two-dimensional structure of the family and people as Hegel said, but a three-dimensional structure of the family, nation and all under Heaven. In the *lunli* world, the individual is always an undeniable being whose ultimate fate is not death as Hegel said, i.e. dissolution, but on the contrary, through cultivation to transcend oneself and integrate the family, the nation, and all under Heaven into a *lunli* world. The true meaning of *lunli* substances and the ethical world they construct is not just an abstract public polity or an abstract universal, but the unity of the oneness of the particular individual and the universal of the *lunli* substances of the family, the nation and all under Heaven.

The principles presented in the traditional Chinese classic *The Great Learning* depicts the *lunli* world and the state-family civilization it constructs. *The Great Learning* has eight principles of studying things, acquiring knowledge, being sincere in thought, rectifying one's mind, cultivating oneself, regulating one's family well, governing the state properly, and bringing peace to all under Heaven. Studying things is not a concept of cognitive science, but a *lunli* concept. The things to be studied include the *lunli* universals, i.e. the intangible mind, sincerity, and knowledge and the tangible oneself, family, state, and all under Heaven as mentioned in the eight principles. The principles of *The Great Learning* elevate the oneness of the free being of the individual to a universal of *lunli* being. Principles of *The Great Learning* is to elevate the individual from the single thing of natural existence to the universal thing of *lunli* existence to achieve the ethical and spiritual unity of the individual and the universal as Hegel said.

The cultural difference between the *lunli* world manifested in the principles of *The Great Learning* and the ethical world Hegel phenomenologically reduced is that the former is both the primary or natural state of the world and its ideal and ultimate state. The ultimate mission of *lunli* and the ultimate goal of civilization is the construction and realization of the *lunli* world. The *lunli* world is a world where *lunli* and *li* are united, and there are three Chinese codes for it: the all-under-Heaven structure which is beyond the family and the state or the family and the people as Hegel said; the special cultural significance of the family, state and all under Heaven; and the positive tension of the relationship between the *lunli* substances in the *lunli* world. All under Heaven is the unique Chinese construction of the *lunli* world.

2   The *Lunli* Significance of Family

The essence of the Chinese state-family civilization is not only that the family and the state are integrated, but more importantly, the family is put before the state and has a principal and paradigmatic *lunli* status in it. This status not only makes the Chinese *lunli* world very different from that of the West, but also renounces the Hegelian tension in the top-level design of culture.

The misinterpretation and criticism of traditional Chinese *lunli* by foreign and modern cultures often converge on family-state relations, as in the case of the fierce controversy in scholarship over Confucius' notion that, "The father conceals the misconduct of the son, and the son conceals the misconduct of the father." Although Liang Shuming argued that China is not a family-based society but a *lunli*-based society, the family does occupy a principal and paradigmatic position in the *lunli* world. Both Chinese and foreign philosophers do not deny the status of the family as the ethical root. Hegel believed that the family and the countryside are the two major sources of ethics, and that the family is the natural ethical polity. Liang Shuming stated that *lunli* begins with the family. The two theories share the same meaning, but the biggest difference is the special status of the family in the *lunli* world. The Chinese problem that the father conceals the misconduct of the son, and the son conceals the misconduct of the father reveals this special law in the *lunli* world.

The Analects of Confucius says, "The Duke of She informed Confucius, saying, 'Among us here there are those who may be styled upright in their conduct. If their father have stolen a sheep, they will bear witness to the fact.' Confucius said, 'Among us, in our part of the country, those who are upright are different from this. The father conceals the misconduct of the son, and the son conceals the misconduct of the father. Uprightness is to be found in this'." Uprightness is what Confucius wanted.

In accordance with the Western and modern civilization, it seems that the uprightness advocated by the Duke of She is more reasonable, and thus the rationality of *The Analects of Confucius* and Confucius' theory are challenged, followed by the philosophical question: If the father conceals the misconduct of the son, and the son conceals the misconduct of the father, what uprightness is that? What did Confucius exactly mean by this?

He meant the principal position the family has in *lunli* down the civilizational path toward the integration of the family and the state. The different uprightness in bearing witness to or concealing the fact the father has stolen a sheep represents the different choices of *lunli* uprightness or *lunli* justice and reflects the tension in the *lunli* world.

The family and the nation or state are two fundamental structures of the *lunli* world. *The Analects of Confucius* designs a *lunli* dilemma and raises a Chinese problem of the *lunli* world, that is, how to choose in the context of the *lunli* conflict between the family and the state. The Duke of She took the son bearing witness to the father's misconduct as uprightness whereas Confucius took the father and son concealing each other's misconduct as uprightness, believing uprightness is to be found in concealment. Confucius' *lunli* choice is difficult for Western and modern theories to understand and tolerate. However, a closer examination reveals that what Confucius wanted to do was actually making a *lunli* choice of protecting the father, and that the concealment is meant to maintain the principal position of the family in the Chinese civilization. If bearing witness to the misconduct of the father becomes a common *lunli* action, it is conceivable that although it maintains the law of the day of the nation, it shakes the family's principal position and may eventually subvert the entire family civilization. It is in this sense that Confucius said, "Uprightness is to be found in this."

How can the family achieve a principal or paradigmatic position in the *lunli* world? Anyone familiar with Chinese society will find that family titles in China are arguably the most complex in the world. In English, grandfather and grandmother refer to both father and mother's father and mother, and uncle means both father and mother's brother. However, in China, there are very strict distinctions.[2]

---

[2] In his *Origin of the Family,* Friedrich Engels said, "In view of the decisive part played by consanguinity in the social structure of all savage and barbarian peoples, the importance of a system so widespread cannot be dismissed with phrases.... The names of father, child, brother, sister are no mere complimentary forms of address; they involve quite definite and very serious mutual obligations which together make up an essential

The grandchildren may be closer to their mother's parents in terms of *lunli* and emotions, but their mother's parents are excluded in terms of property relations. The grandchildren do not have inheritance rights to the property of their mother's parents. In the tradition of marriage, and in the family relationship of many children, the term "mother's parents" has established the natural order of family property relations, and this is the Chinese family *lunli*, which has been extended for thousands of years, not as a custom but as a natural *lunli*.

This tradition was not really broken until the establishment of China's contemporary one-child society. In fact, it was not broken, but because only children made the distribution of property between the two families unnecessary and impossible, and in this case mother's parents were already just an honorary title without the reality of power and obligation relations. The *lunli* power of this tradition, which is still unreflectively accepted in some multi-child families, lies in the fact that although it is irrational, it still has the *lunli* significance of natural law because it is reasonable.

The term "*jia*" in Chinese discourse has the meaning of the terms "family, home, and house" in the English-speaking world. In addition, as the origin of life, it is about paying careful attention to performing the funeral rites to parents, and following them in ceremonies of sacrifice.

The family is a natural substance of blood relationships, but in the Chinese family discourse, *jia* (家, the Chinese for family) is an associative compound composed of "宀" and "豕," which means a herd of pigs under the house roof. Because pigs were the first animals trained by the Chinese in the age of barbarism and have been a symbol of wealth since time immemorial. The two parts of *jia* symbolize common cooking and common wealth, i.e. the substance of living together. *Ting* (庭, the character is combined with *jia* to be family) originally meant the place where the parents live, indicating that this substance is a blood substance, pointing to the common root of life.

Therefore, *jia* in the Chinese discourse not only symbolizes a dwelling place but also represents the starting point. *Jialess* implies not only the lack of a dwelling place but also the absence of a starting point. That's why *shangjia* (homelessness, 丧家) in Chinese culture has always been the most severe insult, implying rootlessness. In contrast, in English, "home"

part of the social constitution of the peoples in question." *Selected Works of Marx and Engels*, Beijing: People's Publishing House, 1975, vol. I, p. 24.

is an abstract noun, and "go home" means to return to one's dwelling place; "house" is just a spatial concept, referring to the physical structure. The different discourses on *jia* in Chinese and Western cultures have metaphorically conveyed its various meanings and statuses in the respective civilizations.

Against the backdrop of modernity and Western culture, there may be every reason to criticize the many social problems, ranging from familism to the corruption of officials in modern society, that have arisen from the civilizational path that integrates the family and state with the former coming before the latter. Yet it is an undeniable historical fact that Chinese civilization is the only uninterrupted civilization in the world, and this strong continuity is closely related to the strong *lunli* substance built on the family. A Japanese scholar found that the strongest Great Wall that protects the Chinese nation is the Chinese family.[3] Francis Fukuyama also found that although Chinese society has been scarred since modern times, the only thing that has remained unchanged is the Chinese family.

Any element of civilization, like the elements of human life, can only be understood ecologically. Negating some basic cultural elements often subverts the life of the civilization itself. The comprehensive wisdom of civilization is how to construct a dialectical and interactive ecology, endowing it with rationality and creative vitality. In fact, from the five thousand years of Chinese civilization to the anti-COVID efforts in 2020, the civilizational path that integrates the family and state has demonstrated its historical and realistic rationality. It is necessary to rethink and understand the *lunli* civilization of China, especially the traditional family *lunli*, from the perspective of the ecological worldview and ecological values provided by eco-civilization.

3   THE CHINESE ATMOSPHERE
OF THE NATIONAL *LUNLI* SUBSTANCE

Both the traditional and modern *lun* and *lun-li* worlds of Chinese culture carry the genetic information of the Chinese nation. This is embodied by the identification of the Chinese nation as a substance and the *lunli* relationship with the family.

---

[3] Inaba Kunyama said, "The only shield protecting the Chinese nation is its family system, which may provide stronger support than the Great Wall." Cited in Liang Shuming, *Essentials of Chinese Culture*, Beijing: Academia Press, 2000, p. 35.

Hegel defined government as "the simple soul, or as the self of the spirit of the people." According to him, "The government is actual spirit reflected into itself, the simple self of the whole ethical substance."[4] And this explains the relationship between the family, the people and the government or state in the ethical world. However, the government he referred to here is only a spiritual government or a government as an externalization of the spirit. With the belief that "what is rational is actual," he maintained that as a symbol of the national spirit, this government has already become actual. The people and their relation to the state as depicted in Hegel's ethical world is also based entirely on the Western experience of that era, i.e. the so-called nation-state. However, the national *lunli* substance of the concept of *lun* and the *lunli* world it constructs is the Chinese nation generated by multiple ethnic groups and races. The ethical substance and the *lunli* world carry a completely different Chinese flavor from the Western experience of the nation-state.

There is no need to verify when China was called as such. The clan-centered cultural genes of *lun* determined the Chinese temperament of the *lunli* world from the very beginning. As Liang Shuming said, China had its own religion from the very beginning, which was ancestor worship. In *The Book of Rites*, it is said, "All things originate from Heaven; man originates from his ancestor." In China, ancestor worship and the worship of Heaven exist, but there is no Christian-style doctrinal organization. If it must be called a religion, Liang would refer to it as "*lunli* religion." "Because of its doctrine which is nothing but this *lunli* concept, and its followers are the Chinese people. It is unknown whether this belief led to this society, or the society gave rise to this belief. In any case, the two complement each other."[5] Some people believe that because of ancestor worship, China cannot give birth to a unified monotheistic religion like Christianity, and this view is certainly biased.

In contrast to the West, Chinese national identification is not ethnic in the sense of a nation-state, but *lunli* in the sense that it grew out of ancestor worship. The essence of ancestor worship is ethics of return to the source, not a metaphysical presupposition of or a need for faith in the

---

[4] G. W. E. Hegel, Phänomenologie des Geistes: *The Phenomenology of Spirit*, Chinese version by He Lin and Wang Jiuxing, Beijing: The Commercial Press, 1996, vol. II, pp. 28, 12.

[5] Liang Shuming, *Essentials of Chinese Culture*, Beijing: Academia Press, 2000, pp. 87–88.

final root, i.e. God, but real experience based on life and an ethical sentiment of honoring ancestors. Although it seeks the ultimate origin and
ultimate substance like Western religions, this ultimate origin and ultimate substance exist in the history and reality of every individual's life and
lives. It is transcendental and social and on this shore; it has little religious
connotation. If it must be compared to religion, at least its *lunli* sentiment is much stronger and higher than the religious sentiment, which is
why Liang referred to it as *lunli* religion.

How did the clan ethics of ancestor worship transition to the national
lunli substance? Chinese culture has a tradition of worshiping Heaven and
Earth in addition to ancestors. "With Heaven and Earth, all things are
possible." The worship of Heaven and Earth allows individuals' spirits to
transcend the family-based ancestor worship and develop a consciousness
based on the clan, but also beyond the clan as a national *lunli* substance.

China is an agricultural country, and the worship of the Earth and grain
gods are two basic beliefs of agricultural people. From this emerged the
concept of the Earth and grain gods. They were so important that the
concept was juxtaposed with the state.

The term "*shehui*" (society) today was probably first used in connection with the worship of the Earth god. When each clan worshipping their
respective ancestors provided offerings to the god of Earth at a certain
appointed time, they would come together (*hui*) due to the Earth god.
Hence, the term "*shehui*" transcended the *lunli* of the clan and took on
national *lunli* significance. "*She*" is the common spiritual substance (earth
god worship) of the various clans who worshiped their ancestors. People
came together during these worship activities. Traditional Chinese temple
fairs may be related to this. This explanation may be far-fetched, but it at
least explains why Chinese culture has accepted the foreign term "society"
based on local genes.

Inherent in the Chinese *lunli* world is a spiritual gene that transcends
clans and races in the construction of a *lunli* substance. Although the
state-family civilization that integrates the family and state is based on
the family, all the fifty-six ethnic groups share the *lunli* identification
substance of the descendants of Emperors Yan and Huang in the *lunli*
spirit of honoring ancestors. The term "descendants of Emperors Yan and
Huang" is a way and discourse of expressing the *lunli* identification with
the *lunli* substance down the path of state-family civilization. It takes
the two outstanding tribal leaders of the origin of Chinese civilization,
Emperors Yan and Huang, as the common ancestors of the nation, not

the common ancestors but the personification of the ethical substance, to be precise. The expression "descendants of Emperors Yan and Huang" reflects the *lunli* characteristics of the multiethnic China; in addition, it also embodies the philosophical tradition of Yin and Yang in Chinese culture.

However, on closer reflection, the *lunli* identification substance of the children of Yanhuang is not complete, and the complete *lunli* identification and its discourse expression is the dragon, a cultural totem with ultimate nature that cannot be reflected.

All Chinese people identify themselves as the descendants of the dragon, which is an ultimate *lunli* substance constructed by philosophical wisdom.

Chinese culture has a firm belief that as stated in *The Book of History*, "Of all creatures man is the most highly endowed." Integrated with nature, humans are part of all things. Their ultimate concern is that they become almost like the beasts, and they must become the soul of all things based on *lunli* and *daode*.

Based on the concept of the soul of all things, the Chinese people have created and enriched the image of the dragon: the dragon has the head of a lion, which is the king of all animals; it has the body of a snake, which travels a hundred miles a day without legs; it has the claws of an eagle, which have the strength of a thousand pounds; it has the scales of a fish and travels freely in water in all seasons of the year. In short, the most outstanding parts of all things are found in the dragon, so it is comfortably the soul of all things.

In this sense, it is conceivable that there were not dragons in the biological sense first, such as dinosaurs. It was until after there was the idea of dragon created according to the soul of all things as the common *lunli* substance of all peoples that there were various specific biological names of dragon.

According to the *Daodejing*, "The name that can be named is not the enduring and unchanging name." The Chinese concept that man is the soul of all things corresponds to the Western cultural concept that man is the measure of all things, conveying two attitudes toward the world and two concepts of constructing ethical substances, namely, to slaughter and embrace things. The essence of Chinese *lunli* culture is to embrace things through virtue, but not to slaughter things, which is conquering and dominating.

4   ALL UNDER HEAVEN: THE
CHINESE REALM OF *LUNLI* SUBSTANCES

It is the Chinese realm of the ethical substance and the Chinese top design of the *lunli* world.

Chinese culture is based on the three talents of Heaven, Earth and humans. According to *The Book of Changes*, "Heaven, in its motion, gives the idea of strength. The superior man, in accordance with this, nerves himself to ceaseless activity. The superior man, in accordance with this, embraces things with virtue." This classic assertion reflects is the Chinese code of the relationship between Heaven and Earth and humans. Heaven and Earth are the moral roots and *lunli* paradigms of humans, giving them the two most important *lunli* qualities and *lunli* realms: Heaven urges humans to make improvement and Earth urges them to embrace things with virtue.

People often take making improvement as the essence of Chinese spirit or Chinese *lunli*, but it is actually a misinterpretation. Any nation must and should make improvement; otherwise it will not be able to survive. The major difference between Chinese *lunli* culture and other cultures, especially Western religious and scientific cultures, is that the national impulse of improvement is guided and harnessed by embracing things with virtue; otherwise, making improvement is likely to evolve into continuous colonial expansion. Patriotism may also, as Western scholars have criticized, "be the selflessness of individuals that makes nations so selfish."

The dialectical interaction of making improvement and embracing all things with virtue is the true Chinese spirit, and is also the nature of Heaven and Earth of the Chinese nation. This is an important reason why Zhang Dainian portrayed them as an overall expression of Chinese national spirit, which has been widely recognized.

Heaven in Chinese culture is a very broad concept, and I once called it a cultural black hole. Everything that is difficult to explain and must be explained can be attributed to Heaven, so can everything with ultimate meaning. Philosophically, there are at least four meanings of Heaven. There is the natural Heaven. Xunzi said, "There is a constancy to the activities of Heaven. They do not persist because of Yao. They do not perish because of Jie." There is the philosophical Heaven, or the so-called heavenly way. There is Heaven of faith. Some people believe that Heaven is the impersonal God while God is personified Heaven. However, the most important and the most realistic is *lunli* and *daode* Heaven, which is the root of *lunli* and *daode*. *The Book of History* says, "Heaven sees according as my people see; Heaven hears according as my people hear." The concept of Heaven in Chinese culture is generally *lunli* and has *lunli* underpinnings. The concept that combines all the meanings of Heaven and most completely embodies the Chinese code is the so-called heavenly principle. Why does the Song and Ming neo-Confucianists' discovery of the heavenly principle and construction of a *lunli* system with the heavenly principle as its core mark the completion of the traditional Chinese *lunli* spirit? This is because it integrates the Heaven on the other shore and the principle on this shore to attain the unity of essence and value, and of immanence and transcendence.

The concept of all under Heaven, formed by the combination of the meanings of Heaven, is of great *lunli* significance. As the name implies, all under Heaven means everything under Heaven, and is a concept of the sameness of the world, especially *lunli*. The concept of all under Heaven and above Earth and the notion that "Under the whole Heaven, every spot is the sovereign's ground; to the borders of the land, every individual is the sovereign's minister" carries the information inside the limits of the world of me.

However, since the natural Heaven is, to a large extent, a figurative form of the ontological and *lunli* Heaven, the ontology of being on the other shore and the form of meaning on this shore, all under Heaven has a cultural significance as an overarching concept. Because of the ontology and finality of Heaven, the discourse of all under Heaven carries a *lunli* temperature under the *lunli* totality, and implies a certain *lunli* sentiment.

In the historical process of civilization, all under Heaven is a unique and inevitable *lunli* discourse in the system of state-family civilization. Some scholars have pointed out that in the family-state civilizational path and structure, the family is the yin pole, the state is the yang pole, and all under Heaven is the *taiji* above yin and yang, which is the concept of the highest *lunli* substance. *Taiji* comes from *wuji*. The system that integrates the family and state with the former coming before the latter is a structure that is neither solely for the family nor solely for the state, but rather a system where the two are interconnected. The *lunli* entity formed by this system is the all-under-Heaven system which transcends the concept of the family and state. The all-under-Heaven concept is internalized and elevated as a form of value and spirit within the civilization system and social structure, and has, therefore, strong cultural significance as an ethical substance and ethical sentiment.

Chinese *lunli* culture looks at the world in a *lunli* way and gives the world a *lunli* nature. For example, Chinese *lunli* integrates the family, the people and the state into one, and gives birth to the concept of mother-land, which has been proven to be a concept unique to Chinese culture.[6] Motherland means not only that it is the land of the mother but also that the land is the mother. It conveys the belief of a *lunli* and cultural system that integrates the family and state. It not only refers to the country where the ancestors lived and the roots of life and culture but also refers to the spiritual and everyday world of individuals, as well as their ultimate concern and refuge.

It not only refers to the country where our ancestors lived, which is the root of life and culture, but also refers to it as the ultimate concern for the individual's spiritual and everyday world. Marx and Lenin treated the state as a product and a manifestation of the irreconcilability of class antago-nisms and an instrument for the exploitation of the oppressed class, which is a political interpretation of the state. There is a unique phenomenon in the history of Chinese civilization. As a unified multiethnic country, China experienced several instances where minority groups took over the country, such as during the Yuan and Qing dynasties. Although there were changes in the ruling styles, the ultimate outcome was that the minority groups accepted and continued to develop China's traditional culture, creating new historical splendor.

From this, we can understand the statement of Gu Yanwu, a thinker of the Ming Dynasty: "Everyone shares responsibility for the fate of all under Heaven." This is a statement that has had a profound impact on the history of Chinese civilization and is the most profound interpretation of the Chinese cultural code.

The ancients distinguished between the perish of the state and the perish of all under Heaven. The perish of the state is the change of rulers, that is, the change of dynasties, while the perish of all under Heaven meant that "beasts will be led on to devour men," which is the loss of *lunli* and *daode* and the fall of culture. This quote is from Gu's *Record of Daily Learning* and the full sentence reads, "The monarch and the ministers who eat the meat seek to protect the state. Every individual,

---

[6] Some also believe that similar expressions are found in Russian culture.

no matter how low his social status, must hold himself responsible for the defense if all under Heaven." The historical background is the Qing army's invasion of the rest of China and Gu's message was later defined by Liang Qichao as "Everyone shares responsibility for the fate of all under Heaven."

The essence of this definition is not to make each individual the subject of responsibility for the country's fall; otherwise it would be suspected of excusing the meat-eaters, i.e. the rulers, but to mean that everyone holds themselves responsible for the continuation of cultural traditions and the upholding of *lunli* and *daode*. The phrase "Everyone shares responsibility for the fate of all under Heaven" conveys the genetic code of *lunli* culture and is, first of all, a *lunli* discourse.

How does the notion of all under Heaven become the highest structure of the *lunli* world, and what kind of realm is it for *lunli* substances? The classic expression is all under Heaven is one family. The creation and construction of the *lunli* substance of all under Heaven follows a different cultural principle than that of the family, people and state. Principles of *The Great Learning* reveal the logic of the construction of all *lunli* substances: regulate one's family well, govern the state properly, and bring peace to all under Heaven.

The essence of constructing the family *lunli* substance lies in alignment. As Hegel said, the ethical relation among the members of the family is neither a sentimental relationship nor is it the relationship of love, and the ethical acts of members of the family bear to the whole family as substance and have only that substance for their purpose and their content. In modern language, it means that individuals within a family attain moral identity recognition through their roles as "family members," and derive the ethical reality and rationality of their acts from the family's ethical substance, which is called "alignment." The ethical identity and obligation correlated with blood relationships are recognized and fulfilled, achieving alignment among members of the family to ultimately create its aligned ethical substance. The key to the construction of the *lunli* substance of the state is the measuring square to inwardly form the sage and externally the king. This is what regulating the family well and bringing peace to all under Heaven mean.

The essence of the *lunli* substance of all under Heaven is *ping* which neither means conquer for institutional unification nor the Western concept of equality. Rather, it means ensuring that China is one person and all under Heaven is one family by promoting *lunli* communication and interaction, treating others as we would like to be treated, and pursuing loyalty and forbearance. This is what is meant by *ping* or bringing peace to all under Heaven. This is the *lunli ping* for all under Heaven as well as all under Heaven constructed by *lunli ping*. This is the highest realm of and has the ultimate meaning for bringing peace to all under Heaven.

It can be seen that both all under Heaven and bringing peace to all under Heaven are the highest realm of the *lunli* substance and world. Russell once said that, "China is much less a political entity than a civilization."[7] Liang Shuming also said that China is not an ordinary type of state, but has the characteristics of both all under Heaven and the state and that, "The content of 'peace under heaven' is that everyone benefits from *lunli* relations where the father is father, and the son is son. Everyone is safe and secure, and parents are nourished when living and obsequies are performed when dead." Liang added that in the West, the modern nation-state emerged after medieval Christianity, while in China, for more than two thousand years, it was always found between all under Heaven and the state.[8]

The point is that the Chinese civilizational path that integrates the family and state and stresses all under Heaven cannot be interpreted and forcibly explained in terms of the Western nation-state concept. There may be too many reasons to ridicule it as a utopia, but we can hardly give up our yearning for it, and we should not abandon our hope for it, because it is the Republic guided by Chinese *lunli* culture and longed for by generations of Chinese people.

5   THE FATE OF THE INDIVIDUAL IN THE *LUNLI* WORLD

One of the biggest differences between the *lunli* world constructed by the *lunli* discourse in Chinese culture and the ethical world restored in Hegel's *The Phenomenology of Spirit* is the fate of the individual in the *lunli* world. Believing the ethical is the universal in itself, Hegel described the fate of the individual in the ethical world as follows: "This universality which the individual as *such* attains is *pure being, death*; it is what has

---

[7] Liang Shuming, *Essentials of Chinese Culture*, Beijing: Academia Press, 2000, p. 19.

[8] Ibid., pp. 19, 20, 83, 218.

naturally and immediately come about and is not something *done* by a *consciousness*.... Death is the consummation and the highest work that the individual as such undertakes for the polity."[9] The death Hegel referred to here is not, of course, death in the sense of natural life, but death in the ethical sense of man as an individual being.

Hegel's *The Phenomenology of Spirit* takes the history of Western civilization as its narrative background, and the ethical world corresponds to ancient Greek civilization. As J. S. Kon said in his *On the Self: The Individual and the Individual's Sense of Self,* ancient Greece was a world without personhood and individuality. Since Hegel maintained that, "The ethical is the universal in itself," the ethical world is a spiritual world in which individuality must die and can only die.

The reality of the individual in the ethical world is either a member of the family or a citizen of the nation. However, both "members" and "citizens" imply the universality of surrendering individuality or particularity, which is necessary for the generation of two major ethical substances—the family and the people, as well as their ethical world. Death is the fate of individuals in the ethical world, which is what Hegel refers to as "pathos."

Ethical actions awaken the individuality in the ethical world and makes it follow one law against the other between the divine law of the family and the human law of the people, thus becoming the "moment of crime," i.e. the inherent negativity of the ethical world. There are three elements in the ethical world—the two ethical substances of the family and the people, and man and woman, but in the ethical world, man and woman are not two individuals or two genders, but only two ethical characters of the ethical world, which are linked to the ethical substances of the family and people respectively and make the transition between them.

Hegel's speculative view on man and woman as ethical characters in the ethical world is similar to Adam and Eve in Genesis of the Bible. Once they become aware of their individuality, including the individuality of "sex/gender," the integrity of the ethical world is dismantled. Therefore, eating the fruit of wisdom becomes an "original sin" because it leads to the division of the ethical world or the Garden of Eden. The inevitable fate is to be expelled from the Garden of Eden and embark on the cultural long march of redemption and salvation.

---

[9] G. W. E. Hegel, Phänomenologie des Geistes: *The Phenomenology of Spirit*, Chinese version by He Lin and Wang Jiuxing, Beijing: The Commercial Press, 1996, vol. II, p. 10.

A major historical event that exemplifies the pathos of the ethical world is the so-called death of Socrates. In the Greek and Hebrew civilizations, the death of Socrates and the expulsion of Adam and Eve from the Garden of Eden have the same significance in the history of civilization. Socrates was sentenced to death for two sins, one of which was asebeia (impiety) and the other was the corruption of the youth. What is of civilizational code significance are two questions. One is why these two sins made Socrates punishable by death. The other is why Socrates tried his best to defend himself, but did not flee after being sentenced to death. The fundamental reason is that the ancient Greek city-state was a substance-based ethical world, a world where there were only substances and no individuals, and any individual was only a citizen of the city-state. The ethical belief of ancient Greece was the motto on the Temple of Apollo: "Know thyself." The essence of "know thyself" is not to know one's own individuality, but to know the weakness and non-independence of the individual in front of the ultimate substance of God; otherwise, would the motto on the temple not downplay God's importance?

The essence of Socrates' sin of asebeia (impiety) is the deconstruction of the substance of God; and what exactly is corruption of the youth about? It is about awakening the youth to their own self-consciousness and to their own individuality with respect to the city-state substance. It can be said that for the ancient Greek ethical world, both sins were essentially sins of subversion of civilization, with the former deconstructing the substance of the spiritual world, and the latter deconstructing the substance of the world of life. That is why Socrates' philosophy is so important for the enlightenment of thought and civilization.

However, the problem is that in his defense, Socrates tried to prove that he was not involved in asebeia (impiety), and tried to exonerate himself as a teacher, so as to prove that he did not corrupt the youth. This shows that Socrates was still in the ethical world spiritually, and his enlightenment was only believed to be a heresy in the ethical world. His heroic death is fundamentally a Hegelian pathos. The fundamental reason for his refusal to escape was not his respect for Athenian law, but the question he repeatedly asked in his dialogue with Kriton: there could not be a better city-state in ancient Greece than Athens.

Socrates subverted the ethical world of ancient Greece, yet maintained a deep ethical identification with this world, so he had to die and could only die. His death exemplified the Hegelian concept of the individual's fate of death in the ethical world and the pathos of the ethical world.

Thus, his death became a significant event of historical importance in the development of civilization.

The ancient Greek civilization exemplified the fate of the individual in the ethical world with tragic sublimity, but in the *lunli* world of Chinese culture, the relationship between the individual and the *lunli* world is a comic affinity. In the *lunli* world, the fate of the individual is not death but cultivation. The term "cultivating oneself" already indicates the *lunli* attitude toward the individual. In Chinese culture, oneself is the concrete expression of the individual, and its counterpart is the so-called moral character. The essence of the discourse of cultivating oneself and nourishing one's moral character is that moral character is the substance of the individual, while oneself is the individuality. The essence of cultivating oneself is to transcend one's individuality to reach the *lunli* universality, and the *lunli* universality exists in the individual as the so-called moral character, the substance of the individual, i.e. the public nature of humans. Believing that men at their birth are naturally good, Chinese *lunli* conveys the belief and confidence that humans transcend their natural individuality and attain *lunli* universality.

In the Chinese *lunli* tradition, as a discourse of individuality, oneself represents the unity of human being as a natural being and a *lunli* being. As a natural being, oneself has emotions and desires, and may be confined to individuality. However, there is a good gene in human nature that allows for self-transcendence. Therefore, the so-called "oneself" is actually the amalgamation of the universality of the heavenly mandate of Song-Ming neo-Confucianism and the temperament of individuality. "Cultivating oneself" in any context does not involve the complete denial of individuality, including individual desires and emotions, but rather implies transcending individuality and leading desires with righteousness.

Therefore, in the *lunli* world of cultivating oneself, regulating one's family well, governing the state properly, and bringing peace to all under Heaven depicted by the principles of *The Great Learning*, the fate of the individual is not Hegelian death, but Chinese transcendence; it is not the tragic sublimity of the two civilizations characterized by the death of Socrates and the wrath of God, but the comic affinity of what Mencius said: "All things are already complete in us. There is no greater delight than to be conscious of sincerity on self-examination."

PART II

The Spiritual Temperament of *Lunli*

To sum up, the *lunli* discourse of Chinese culture is composed of *lun*, *li*, *lun-li*, and *lunli*. *Lun*, *li*, *lun-li*, staying true to lun and doing one's part, and the *lunli* world are a historical and philosophical system; lun, li, peace and harmony are the value system that keeps advancing. The dialectical interaction of the conceptual system, the historical and philosophical system and the value system forms the Chinese tradition of *lunli* thought and creates the *lunli* spirit of the Chinese nation and the *lunli* temperament of Chinese culture.

CHAPTER 6

The *Lunli* Discourse and the *Lunli* Spirit

In the system of the *lunli* discourse, *lun* and *li* are common elements. *Lun* is the home and the way of existence for human life and the truth of human life; *li* is the self-awareness of *lun* and of humans and the conscience and ability of humans existing as a *lun*. In the conceptual system, *lun-li* is the cultural principle and cultural law of the relationship between *lun* and *li*, the essence is taking *lun* as home and *li* as the intuitive knowledge and heavenly principle, and the priority is placing oneself in the *lunli* substance, i.e. proceeding from the home of *lun*, settling down through *li*, taking *lun* as home for a dwelling, and living by *li*. The final result is the *lunli* which is created by the *lunli* world by taking *lun* as home and *li* as the intuitive knowledge and heavenly principle, and the essence is harmony, which is the *lunli* cultural substance characterized by harmony in diversity. This distinguishes Chinese *lunli* from Western ethics and consequently, Chinese traditions can and must engage in a civilizational dialogue with Western traditions.

The German sociologist Max Weber found in *The Protestant Ethic and the Spirit of Capitalism* that the most important reason for the prosperity of capitalist civilization in Europe and the United States was the special spirituality of Protestantism after Martin Luther King's Reformation, that is, the spirit of capitalism, which formed the so-called ideal type of the Protestant ethic and the spirit of capitalism. There are three major spiritual temperaments: the grace, ethic and the legitimacy of making profits; the

© Foreign Language Teaching and Research Publishing Co., Ltd 2024   85
H. Fan, Lunli *and Confucian Moral Theory*, Key Concepts
in Chinese Thought and Culture,
https://doi.org/10.1007/978-981-99-9105-1_6

calling, ethic and the reason of making profits; and the frugality, ethic and the necessity of accumulation. These three concepts created a large number of workers who were excited and guided by the Protestant ethic, and the inevitable result was an increase in capitalist wealth. The Chinese *lunli* tradition has created a special social *lunli* that has complemented the ethics of transcendent religion. This has formed the unique *lunli* spirit of the Chinese nation and generated a particular cultural character and temperament, namely, a *lunli* culture.

The so-called *lunli* spirit is not a spirit of *lunli*, for every nation has *lunli*, and therefore has a *lunli* spirit. The spirit of the Chinese nation is a spirit with *lunli* as its core and cultural temperament. *Lunli* spirit is, in a sense, the cultural expression of the spirit of the Chinese nation and the temperamental characteristic of the spirit of the Chinese nation. What created by the *lunli* discourse and its tradition is not only the spirit of *lunli*, but also the *lunli* temperament of the Chinese nation and Chinese culture. Chinese culture is a *lunli* culture and the core of the Chinese national spirit is the *lunli* spirit.

Philosophically, *lunli* is connected to the people and to spirituality. *Lunli* is the spirit of the people, and once the people become aware of its own substance in terms of *lunli* and make it a reality, *lunli* becomes spirit. In Chinese discourse, *lunli* passions can be interpreted mutually. Lu Jiuyuan, a Song and Ming neo-Confucianist said, "Collect your spirit. Be your own master. All things are already complete in oneself." The spirit he referred to is the *lunli* spirit of the unity of oneself and the universe and the harmony between humans and nature. Wang Yangming interpreted intuitive knowledge in terms of spirit, equating *lunli* with spirit. Therefore, the so-called *lunli* spirit is at least not limited to the spirit of *lunli*, but is a spiritual temperament, the spiritual temperament of the Chinese nation.

What is the spiritual temperament of Chinese *lunli*? What kind of national spirit and cultural temperament does *lunli* give to the Chinese nation? According to the discourse system of *lunli*, there are three major spiritual qualities: reflection based on *lunli*; being a person and staying together; and having a home and keeping it. Specifically, reflection based on *lunli*: *lun*; being a person and staying together: *li*; having a home and keeping it: *lun-li*; *lunli* is the logical and historical unity of the *lunli* discourse and the *lunli* spirit of the nation. The three spiritual temperaments of *lunli* are also the three special contributions of the Chinese nation to global civilization: the cultural paradigm of reflection based on *lunli;* the human principles of being a person and staying together; and the family-state sentiment of having a home and keeping it.

In discussing the spirit of the Chinese nation, Liang Shuming declared with a resounding voice: "The Chinese people have not lived in vain for the past thousands of years, for they have a made contribution by discovering what makes humans human."[1] Discovering what the cultural wisdom and cultural form that has made humans human is *lunli. Lunli* means human principles, that is, the *li* of *lun* of what makes humans human. Liang Shuming stated categorically that *lunli* is the greatest contribution of the Chinese nation to the world, and therefore only by knowing *lunli* can we truly know Chinese culture and Chinese people.

---

[1] Liang Shuming, *Essentials of Chinese Culture*, Beijing: Academia Press, 2000, p. 132.

CHAPTER 7

Reflection Based on *Lunli*

The typical spiritual temperament of the *lunli* discourse and its tradition is reflection based on *lunli*, which is the distinctive cultural birthmark of the Chinese national spirit. Reflection based on *lunli* is *lunli*-oriented thinking, and is reflection based on *lunli* that starts from the substance.

It is generally believed that Chinese culture has a human-oriented tradition. In fact, it is better to say that it is a *lun*-based tradition. From cradle to grave, from birth to the ultimate end, the Chinese exist in the substance of *lun*, and also in the design and ethical care of *lun*. The life process of humans starts from the substance of *lun*, settles and lasts and also reaches eternity in *lun*. Some basic ethical norms in Chinese culture such as kindness, filial piety, and loyalty, are superficially moral norms, but in reality, they are *lunli* designs. The reason why they become *dao* and *de* (virtues) is fundamentally due to *lunli* wisdom and laws, which is the spiritual temperament of reflection based on *lunli*. The *lunli* tradition provides a cultural paradigm of reflection based on *lunli* and lays the foundation for a *lunli* culture.

© Foreign Language Teaching and Research Publishing Co., Ltd 2024   89
H. Fan, Lunli *and Confucian Moral Theory*, Key Concepts
in Chinese Thought and Culture,
https://doi.org/10.1007/978-981-99-9105-1_7

1   THE CULTURAL PARADIGM
OF REFLECTION BASED ON LUNLI

Lunli is the core discourse of Chinese *lunli* culture which exemplifies the national spirit and temperament of reflection based on *lunli*. Different from reflection based on *lunli* and theory, reflection based on *lunli* may be only ideas and theories about *lunli*, while reflection based on *lunli* is the value orientation of the whole nation. Also different from thinking based on *lunli*, reflection is not only thought but also action; it is what Hegel called thinking as the drive to give itself existence; it is not only the privilege of thinkers, but also the habit of mind of all people.

Reflection based on *lunli* is a way of knowing and doing that takes *lunli* as its base; it not only carries *lunli* concerns, but is also thinking with *lunli* as its base and orientation. As an adverb of reflect, based on *lunli* points to two dimensions of awareness. One is economic and political reflection in the world of life, highlighting the priority value of *lunli;* the other is religious and moral reflection in the spiritual world, highlighting the cultural temperament of *lunli* as distinct from them.

Chinese culture is a *lunli* culture, in a sense, because the Chinese people have the spiritual temperament of reflection based on *lunli*. The significance of using reflection based on *lunli* to interpret the discourse of *lunli* is to highlight the principal position of *lunli* in the world of life and the spiritual world and its special spirituality. The *lunli* discourse and its traditions exemplify the spiritual habit of reflection based on *lunli*, and reflection based on *lunli* is the core of *lunli* culture. Thus, in the world civilization, *lunli* has a different cultural character from ethic.

What is the Chinese tradition of reflection based on *lunli*? The four structural elements of the *lunli* discourse have already presented the cultural rules of reflection based on *lunli*: starting from the substance of *lun*, following the cultural rules of *li*, safeguarding the spiritual home of *lunli*, and constructing the real world of *lunli*. The basic rule of reflection based on *lunli* is to take *lun* as home and *li* as the intuitive knowledge and heavenly principle; start from the substance of *lunli* is the basic rule of reflection based on *lunli*. The cultural essence of reflection based on *lunli* is starting from the substance of *lun*.

What kind of civilizational paradigm of reflection based on *lunli* is provided by the discourse of *lunli*? Why is it thinking based on *lunli* rather than on religion or *daode*? The unique contribution of the *lunli* discourse tradition in the world civilization system is that it explores and constructs a transcendent national spirit based on social *lunli*, elevates the *lunli* of human daily use to a heavenly principle with divine roots and ultimate care, and creates a Chinese form of *lunli* culture. The true meaning of reflection based on *lunli* is, in the words of Liang Shuming, the *lunli* orientation, and reflection based on *lunli* is fundamentally a reflection based on *lun*, a reflection rooted in *lun* and starting from the substance of *lun*.

The *lunli* orientation and the notion that *lunli* begins in the family but is more than the family are the two main points of reflection based on *lunli*. The former declares the centrality of *lunli* in the cultural system, while the latter shows that reflection based on *lunli* is fundamentally reflection based on lun. What is reflection based on *lunli*? How does the discursive tradition of *lunli* exemplify reflection based on *lunli*?

The birth and transcendence of human *lun*, the construction of the *lun* in the world of humans, and the three major *lunli* principles of kindness, filial piety, and filial piety-based loyalty all demonstrate the cultural paradigm of reflection based on *lunli* from three dimensions. The cultural law can be summarized as follows: human principles are subject to heavenly principles and human relations are based on natural relations. Therefore, the reflection derived from *lun* is distinguished from the religious reflection derived from the ultimate substance on the other shore and the *daode* thinking derived from *dao*. Chinese *lunli* is thus distinguished from ethics in terms of discourse form.

Reflection based on *lunli* is a cultural gene carried by humans from the birth of humans and individual beings, and Chinese civilization has made it flourish, creating the civilizational paradigm of reflection based on *lunli* and the civilizational atmosphere of *lunli* culture. Many people in the world today have discovered that China is not traditionally a country, but a civilization, and that what China is trying to revive with its rise is not just a country, but a civilization. In fact, this view has been held since time immemorial. As early as the early twentieth century, when Russell spoke in China, he lamented that "China is much less a political entity than a civilization" and that reflection based on *lunli* has made China a different type of civilization from the West.

In today's world, people have learned to think economically, but although economic globalization has made the globe a village, this system of needs has become a battleground for national interests, and it is difficult to become a community with a shared future even when faced with the worldwide threat of the COVID-19 pandemic. In the spiritual world,

Western culture after ancient Greece taught people to think morally and tried to construct so-called universal ethics based on freedom of will. However, not only is it difficult to construct universal ethics, but free will has become a deconstructive force for common action in the face of the need to impose COVID-19 quarantine. In this sense, it is not so much that humans encountered the threat of COVID-19 in 2020, but rather that COVID-19 revealed the virus that civilization carries with itself, especially the virus of "a lack of *lunli*" and "reflection without *lunli*."

Han Fei, a pre-Qin thinker, described the evolutionary trajectory of history in his essay "Five Vermin" as follows: "In the ancient times, we competed in *daode*; in wisdom and strategy in the middle ages; and in strength today." Perhaps it partially restores the traces of humans coming out from the original state, but it is also the history of alienation and even fall of human spirit. Factual judgment cannot replace value judgment; otherwise humanity will lose its cultural ideal. In this sense, it is more accurate to say that Han Fei was issuing a cultural warning to history rather than providing a historical basis for Legalism.

In the grand history of civilization, it can be said that in the ancient times we competed for *lunli* and in the modern times for economic and technological development. However, ecological crises, intelligent humans, and gene technology have pushed history toward the limit of civilization. If we cannot control the recklessness of the economy and technology, the post-primitive era or post-human era will soon come. Perhaps the 2020 COVID-19 pandemic is a messenger of civilization's profound crisis encountered by humanity. Redemption or destruction, learning to reflect based on *lunli* has unprecedented significance.

The *lunli* discourse and its tradition provide a cultural paradigm for reflection based on *lunli* that has universal civilizational significance. Reflection based on *lunli* has three philosophical implications: the sense of *lun* or thinking based on lun from the substance; the *li* wisdom of staying together based on harmony in diversity; the *lunli* sentiment of taking *lun* as home and *li* as the intuitive knowledge and heavenly principle.

2   LUN AND GOD: THE LUN BIRTH OF HUMANS

The primary significance of *lun* to humans and civilization is that people are born from *lun* and have *lun* nature and character.

The difference between *lun* and *dao* in Chinese discourse is that *lun* is not only the root of humans, but also their home. *Dao* is the essence of everything in the universe, and Laozi's *Daodejing* demonstrates that the laws of nature are also those of humanity. *Dao* gives people a sense of the root of the physical world, but hardly a sense of belonging to the world of life. The Western term similar to *lun* is God, and both *lun* and God can be taken as the root and destination of humans in the context of Chinese and Western cultures respectively. The difference between the two is not only the difference between this shore and the other shore, but also the different relationship between humans and them and the civilization created by therefrom.

The different relationship of *lun* and God to humans is, in a word, birth and creation. The whole basis of man's conversion and obedience to God is that God is the Creator of the world and humans are God's creation. According to the biblical account of Genesis, God created Adam from a handful of loam and Eve from Adam's rib, thus creating human society. Thus, the relationship between God and human beings is the relationship between the Creator and His creation, and humans created by God and must be converted to Him.

However, the relationship between *lun* and humans is different. Humans are born within the larger system of *lun* which includes "Heaven and Earth, all things, men and women, and husband and wife." From this system, *lunli* relationships such as between "father and son, ruler and subject, and superior and inferior" are formed, as well as the *li* of *lun* in the principles of rituals and propriety. Humans are born within *lun*, originating from it. "Born" here does not mean "created," as the mother of birth is not some ultimate supreme personality, but rather the *lun* created in the relationships of Heaven and Earth, all things, men and women, and husband and wife.

Birth and creation represent two different relationships between *lun* and God. Because humans were produced or created, they entered into a relationship with God that is serious and stern. God is the Lord, or the Creator, and going against His will is considered a sin. Therefore, Adam and Eve's destiny of eating the fruit of knowledge led to their expulsion from the Garden of Eden, which is known as the "guilt culture" according to Benedict. In the culture of *lun*, the *lun* relationship expressed by *lun* is the relationship between life and the mother, and between the individual and the substance.

Strictly speaking, human life is born not from the mother but from the *lun* of the couple. In the Chinese cultural tradition, the relationship between men and women is not only the *lun* but also what Mencius called the great relations among humans, because they give birth to humans and, by extension, to everything else. Bear is a non-continuous verb, which carries the history of human development from single cell to primate. It is not only the process of creating something from nothing, but also the birth of one life from another. To be precise, it is the process of giving birth to life from *lun*. There are men and women, and then there is a couple. The mother is the one who conceives and gives birth, but the root of the process is the *lun* of the couple.

The *lunli* of kindness can interpret this *lunli* aspect of humans based on birth. In any culture, parents have an inherent nature of kindness and care for their children, and many countries have laws and obligations regarding the upbringing of children. However, few parents in other countries show the same selfless, intense, and enduring level of kindness and care for their children as Chinese parents do. Even in the modern era where traditional norms have been deconstructed in China, the obligation toward children still seems to be an "unlimited liability company," reflecting the unique cultural characteristics of the *lun* tradition.

Kindness is the emotional attachment of the source of life to the life it has given birth to. Under the consciousness of *lun*, human life is not just the creation of the mother, but a joint creation of a man and a woman who abandon their individuality and construct a shared personality, namely the personality of marriage. The objectification of children as the shared personality of the marital relationship is endowed with the meaning of *lun*, and in modern Chinese discourse, it is often described as the "crystallization of love." As Hegel said, the relationship between husband and wife is realized not in themselves, but in their children. However, he also believed that children are something other than themselves whereas in the cultural consciousness of *lun*, children are the shared living body of parents, and the love of parents for their children is an infinite and continuous kindness.

The essence of kindness is fundamentally a love for fellow beings, a love that parents have for their children as fellow beings. In a sense, it carries the nature of self-love. However, because children are the common creation of parents, kindness goes beyond the self-love of either the father or the mother and carries the meaning of *lun*. Kindness is a natural emotion that parents have toward their children as fellow human beings. Therefore, in Chinese culture, kindness always has the meaning of unconditional selflessness, because in kindness, parents find themselves by losing themselves, and thus achieve the shared personality of *lun* between parents.

Indeed, God's creation of humans also implies that humans must stay together with God, but what God creates is a different kind of ethical relationship. The relationship between God and the created multitude of sentient beings is more objectified, and can only be achieved through calling and conversion, while the relationship between the *lun* and the individual born from it always carries the *lunli* warmth that arises from being fellow beings. In addition, the created lacks the structural ethics of birth. All sentient beings are creations of God, so the relationship between sentient beings is both equal and atomistic. This explains why the Renaissance era of freedom and equality emerged from the darkest and most rigid hierarchical relationships of the Middle Ages. Once the Renaissance shook the absolute position of God, and freed sentient beings from God's domination, they became equal to each other. However, once the position of the ultimate substance is shaken, social life becomes atomized.

3   LUN AND US COEXIST: HUMANS' LUN TRANSCENDENCE

Every culture has families, and the birth of children is a natural event for the continuation of families. However, no culture attributes such a strong and solemn *lunli* meaning to human birth as Chinese culture does. Humans are born from *lun*, and human transcendence and ultimate care are also realized within *lun*.

There are two different discursive traditions for ultimate care. The Christian discourse is that God will be with you, while the expression in Chinese culture is that *lun* will be with you. The difference is that the care of *lun* for humans extends from daily life to the ultimate. When encountering any difficulties in daily life, Chinese people first seek help from their family *lun*. When facing major setbacks in life, such as failures in career, the family serves as the final foundation for living. The saying goes, "With children, everything is enough; without an official position, one is carefree." *Lun* in this secular world prepares for ultimate care and transcendence for humans.

As Liang Shuming once said, without death, there would be no religion. The most important cultural function of religion is to guide people toward eternal immortality, and it is realized in the heavenly kingdom on the other shore. *Lun* has bestowed on humans the cultural genes of achieving social transcendence toward eternity from the moment of birth, and its cultural enlightenment and cultural self-consciousness are condensed in the *lunli* awareness of filial piety. Undoubtedly, filial piety is a major characteristic of Chinese culture, one of the earliest cultural awakenings and *lunli* concepts that emerged from the Age of Barbarism. Filial piety is the self-consciousness of *lun* toward human life, and it can be said that without filial piety, there would be no Chinese *lunli* culture.

In social life, people often have serious misconceptions about the cultural significance of filial piety, thinking of it merely as the *daode* obligation of children toward their parents, and the virtues that arise from it without considering its *lunli* connotation. Chinese culture associates filial piety with *dao* and names it *xiaodao*. How is filial piety related to Dao? What is this Dao? In simple terms, filial piety is the *dao* of *lun* that has reached the ultimate care for eternal life.

Kindness and filial piety are two fundamental life *lunli*. Benevolence is the life *lunli* concerning the birth and growth of humans, while filial piety is the life *lunli* concerning ultimate care. The difference is that benevolence largely has an instinctive or natural nature, while filial piety requires *lunli* enlightenment and awakening of life. Hegel believed that filial piety is a different ethical emotion from kindness, stating that, "But conversely the devotion of children toward their parents is affected by the emotion of their coming-to-be, that is, having their own in itself in an other who is vanishing, and in achieving being-for-itself and their own self-consciousness only through separation from their origin—a separation in which the origin recedes."[1] Hegel insightfully grasped the significance of filial piety, but lacked sufficient explanatory power for Chinese culture.

Confucius believed that filial piety of children toward their parents is not only about being able to support and not being disobedient on the level of daily life, but more importantly, the difficulty is with the countenance. Zixia asked what filial piety was. Confucius said, "The difficulty is with the countenance" (*The Analects of Confucius*). This means that the most valuable aspect of filial piety is the attitude. Essentially, filial piety is a *lunli* attitude toward life. Parents are the source of life, and the

---

[1] G. W. E. Hegel, *Phänomenologie des Geistes: The Phenomenology of Spirit*, Chinese version by He Lin and Wang Jiuxing, Beijing: The Commercial Press, 1996, vol. II, p. 14.

lives of children grow up in the withering of the lives of parents. Therefore, the basis of filial piety is not only about repaying debts, but also a compassionate sentiment toward life. Mencius discovered the deeper *lunli* significance of filial piety and proposed a proposition that is difficult to understand for both heterogeneous and modern cultures: "There are three things which are unfilial, and to have no posterity is the greatest of them" (*Mencius*). Why does having no posterity become the greatest thing which is unfilial? It is fundamentally about the ultimate care for life.

The eternal and immortal nature of life is the ultimate pursuit and ultimate care of human beings. In religious cultures, eternal immortality is realized on the other shore of the ultimate substance, while in *lunli* cultures, it is realized in the *dao* of filial piety. The reason why filial piety is the *dao* is fundamentally the recognition and commitment to the eternal and immortal nature of parents' lives. Individual life is finite, but in the generational succession of life, every life will eventually reach eternity. In the continuity of *lun*, the lives of parents and ancestors are perpetuated in their children, which is expressed in modern scientific terms as genetic inheritance, and ethically expressed as eternal immortality. Its social form is the continuous extension of family life. This is why having children in China has never been a personal matter, but a major, even the biggest, *lunli* event concerning the continuity of family life. "Having no posterity" was regarded as the greatest form of filial impiety because it means depriving not only one's parents, but also all ancestors, of eternal life and immortality. It is the severance of the vital bloodline and therefore a serious *lunli* issue and the greatest thing that is unfilial.

Because of this, the issue of filial piety in contemporary China is not only related to social customs, but also to cultural security, as it is a major symptom of cultural disintegration. If people cannot find ultimate care for eternity and immortality in the *lun* of this world, they will inevitably seek other cultural substitutes, with religion being almost the only option. This can explain a phenomenon in modern China where the elderly make up a significant proportion of religious believers. As a result, Chinese *lunli* culture may face significant challenges and cultural security crises may arise.

4   Human Relations Are Based on Natural Relations: The *Lun* World of Humans

The traditional concept of *lun* in China is an organic civilization ecosystem that permeates from the family to society and the country, with strong self-organizing functions and cultural coherence. It not only includes the birth and ultimate care of human life, but also encompasses social life. *Lun* is the inherent color of humans, the way of existence of human life, and also the way of life of humans. More accurately, it is the archetype and ideal form of social life for humans.

The characteristic of Western civilization is a profound rupture between the family and society and the state, as Hegel said in *Elements of the Philosophy of Right*, civil society tears the individual away from family ties. In the family and the state, individuals have two completely different *lunli* roles, namely members of the family and citizens of society. Members of the family are the way individuals exist as natural ethical substances, characterized by not being independent or isolated, and individual behavior is oriented toward the wholeness of the family as a reality. Citizens in ethical sense are new constructions after abandoning the identity of members of the family. They construct the ethical "publicness" of society and the state with a logic completely different from that of the family and its members.

After being torn away from the family, the individual becomes a citizen with independent property relations, and he takes the individual rather than the substance as the starting point. As an abstract individual entity and the lord of the world, he constructs formal universality based on the system of needs. Civil society is a battlefield of individual interests, and therefore the publicness of citizens is only formal universality constructed through judicial means, and has lost the significance of home for the *lunli* substance of the family. Although Hegel believed that the ethical substance entity is ultimately fulfilled in the state, the ethical state he talked about only exists as a kingdom of philosophy in the idea.

On the contrary, Chinese *lunli* establishes a resilient continuity of *lun* between the family and society and the state, making human life and living a world of *lun*. The principle and law of this world can be summarized as human relations are based on natural relations. The family is a natural or inherent *lunli* substance, known as natural relations, while society and the state are also *lunli* substances, extending from the family but different, known as human relations. The difference between the two is what Hegel referred to as the law of man versus the law of God. However, the traditional Chinese concept of *lun* constructs natural relations and human relations and a transition between them, and its essence lies in using the family's natural relations as a model to establish the human relations of society and the state, thereby connecting natural relations and human relations into a coherent whole.

Country in the English-speaking world is translated as *guojia* in China, which not only reflects the different structural elements of the family and state in the early stages of civilization, but also metaphorically represents a pursuit of values and cultural ideals, and even a cultural commitment to turning the country into a family. It also reflects a civilizational law, that is, to construct the country based on the principles of the family. In traditional Chinese society, the concentrated embodiment of the transition from heavenly relationships to human relationships is the so-called Five Cardinal Relationships (between sovereign and minister, father and son, elder brother and younger, friends, and husband and wife) model and the integration of loyalty and filial piety.

The reason why the Five Cardinal Relationships have become the *lunli* model is twofold. On the one hand, they are the most representative five *lunli* relations of Chinese national civilization. The relationship between father and son, and elder brother and younger represent natural relations, the relationship between sovereign and minister represent human relations, and the relationship between husband and wife are intermediaries between natural and human relations, as well as the extension from the family to the nation and state. On the other hand, the internal structure of the Five Cardinal Relationships is even more important. Integrating the family and state with the former coming before the latter, the national civilization establishes all other human relations with the natural relations of family *lunli* as the model. The relationship between father and son serve as a model for the relationship between sovereign and minister, and the relationship between elder brother and younger as a model for the relationship between friends, thus extending from family *lunli* to political *lunli* of society and the state.

From this, we can understand why Chen Wangdao initially translated "Working Men of All Countries, Unite." (the original German text is "Proletarier aller Lnder, vereinigt euch.") as 四海之内皆兄弟 (Within the four seas, all men are brothers.) when translating the *Communist Manifesto*. The expression was later translated as 全世界无产者联合起来 (Proletarians of all countries, unite.). 四海之内皆兄弟 is the most *lunli* translation most adapted to the Chinese context, which makes the political proletarians of all countries brothers based on *lunli* and interprets political ethics in terms of the natural relations of the family, representing a cultural understanding of the Chinese-style thinking based on *lunli*.

In Chinese tradition, filial piety is the core of family *lunli* and the cultural root of all *lunli*. According to *The Analects of Confucius*, "Filial piety and fraternal submission. Are they not the root of all benevolent actions?" Filial piety and fraternal respect are *lunli* requirements in the relationships between son and father and between younger and elder brothers. Because they serve as paradigms for relationships between sovereign and minister and between friends, they are considered the foundation of benevolence, or the fundamental quality needed to be a person. What is the significance of filial piety beyond family *lunli*? Filial piety-based loyalty.

In Western culture, filial piety and loyalty, if any, are considered separate and distinct domains, with a dichotomy between the family and the state. However, in Chinese tradition, filial piety serves as the foundation of loyalty. The cultural premise of filial piety-based loyalty allows for a direct transition between natural relations and human relations. In ancient China, there was a saying that loyal ministers must be selected from among filial sons, and the way of thinking based on *lunli* was meant to construct human relations with natural relations.

The Analects of Confucius further elaborates on this: "The philosopher You said, 'They are few who, being filial and fraternal, are fond of offending against their superiors. There have been none, who, not liking to offend against their superiors, have been fond of stirring up confusion. The superior man bends his attention to what is radical. That being established, all practical courses naturally grow up. Filial piety and fraternal submission. Are they not the root of all benevolent actions?'" Practicing filial piety and fraternal respect in family *lunli* prevents one from disrespecting elders and superiors in national *lunli*, and thus prevents rebellion. In ancient China, loyalty was directly related to the sovereign, but in an abstract sense, it represented the *lunli* substance of the nation symbolized by the sovereign. Loyalty at the beginning of civilization referred to the *lunli* with which the sovereign should treat the people: "The sovereign should often consider how to benefit the people, which is loyalty. Officials in charge of offerings should honestly offer sacrifices to deities, which is faith" (*Zuo's Commentary on the Spring and Autumn Annals*). This also represents an individual's attitude toward *lunli* substances.

The way of reflection based on *lunli* presented by the coherent whole of the Five Cardinal Relationships and the integration of loyalty and filial piety in daily life, and the living *lunli* they present in the world of life, are that in their social life, the Chinese often extend family titles to society. Elderly people are addressed as "grandpa" or "grandma," those who are older are addressed as "uncle" or "aunt," and those who are close to one's age are addressed as "brother" or "sister." In the West, people are usually addressed as "Mr.," "Miss," or "Sir." This is a manifestation of two different *lun* logics. Many of China's major festivals are a training ground for reflection based on *lunli*.

The Qingming Festival, from ancient times to the present, has been one of the most important national holidays in China that combine nature and *lunli*. Sweeping tombs and offering sacrifices to ancestors and going out for spring outings are the two major themed customs of the Qingming Festival. Tomb-sweeping and ancestral worship have become the practices of filial piety for the whole nation. During Qingming, people also go out for spring outings to embrace the new season. These customs contain the collective memory of the integration of loyalty and filial piety. According to legend, during the Spring and Autumn Period, the virtuous statesman Jie Zitui helped Duke Wen of Jin survive 19 years of adversity and eventually helped him establish his rule. However, Jie chose to retire to the mountains with his elderly mother to fulfill his filial duty. Duke Wen was deeply devoted to seeking the talent of Jie and repaying his kindness, so he ordered the mountain to be set on fire. Eventually, under a willow tree, he discovered the bodies of Jie and his mother, who had died while protecting each other from the fire. In order to commemorate Jie's loyalty and filial piety, Duke Wen declared this day as the Cold Food Festival, during which no fire should be lit to cook food. He also designated this day as the Qingming Festival, which later evolved into a holiday for ancestor worship and has continued to this day.

Although modern China has experienced tremendous impact from globalization and modernization, this tradition still exists, indicating that the concept of *lun* as an inherent whole has become a habit of the heart. As Liang Shuming said, "China organizes society with *lunli*." Fundamentally, it organizes society with *lun*.

CHAPTER 8

Being a Person and Staying Together

The *lun* traditional in the *lunli* discourse defines the cultural nature of Chinese culture as *lunli* rather than religious, and it also determines the fundamental difference between *lunli* and ethics. The *li* why humans are human understood by the Chinese civilization based on the *lun* substance is not only the *daode* for being a person but also the *lunli* for staying together. Therefore, Chinese culture is *lunli* rather than *daode*.

1   THE ULTIMATE QUESTION OF CIVILIZATION

The discourse of *lunli* and its tradition pose a significant question: what is the ultimate question of civilization?

It is generally believed that how one should live is the ultimate question of civilization, and of course, it is also the ultimate question of *lunli* and *daode*. It is said to have originated from Socrates. However, textual interpretation shows that Socrates only said, "We cannot live better than in seeking to become better," and there is no concrete evidence to prove that he regarded how one should live as the ultimate question. The narrative of the history of civilization shows that the ultimate question of civilization is not a moral question of how one should live, but a *lunli* question of how 'we' (or humanity) should stay together. This question, expressed in the first person, is: "How can 'I' become 'we'?".

© Foreign Language Teaching and Research Publishing Co., Ltd 2024   103
H. Fan, Lunli *and Confucian Moral Theory*, Key Concepts
in Chinese Thought and Culture,
https://doi.org/10.1007/978-981-99-9105-1_8

The source of Western civilization is the two civilizations of Greece and Hebrew. The two major historical events that express the cultural genes of Western civilization are: Why did Socrates die? Why was God angry?

The most significant event in the history of civilization in ancient Greece is the death of Socrates. As mentioned earlier, Socrates was charged by the Athenian court with the crimes of asebeia (impiety) and the corruption of the youth. Both of these crimes essentially subverted the substance-based civilization of ancient Greece with cultural enlightenment, namely the substance of the God in the spiritual world, and the substance of the city-state in the world of everyday life. This resulted in self-consciousness of individuals toward the gods and individuals toward the polis, thus ending a civilization and opening a new era of civilization, which is the cultural significance of the Socratic turn in the history of civilization.

Socrates tried his best to defend himself in court, proving that he did not commit asebeia and was not a teacher, not just to exonerate himself and escape punishment, but to truly express his cultural consciousness. After being sentenced to death, he died a heroic death not because of the noble morality of obeying the laws of the polis, as commonly interpreted, but because of the ethical pathos. Although Socrates deconstructed a world based on substances through his actions, he still maintained a deep ethical identification with this civilization. In this sense, Socrates must die and could only die. What did he die for? He died for the original substance-based civilization where humans and gods, and humans stayed together. The death of Socrates is a significant ethical event.

The wrath of God is a significant event in Hebrew civilization with profound significance. God created Adam, and then created Eve from Adam's rib. Thus, the world created by God is a substance-based world of staying together. The self-consciousness of this world is the words Adam said to Eve when he woke up: "You are flesh of my flesh and bone of my bone." What caused God's thunderous anger and the expulsion of Adam and Eve from the Garden of Eden for stealing the fruit of wisdom? Assuming there are only two possibilities. One is that God was not merciful enough, but this is blasphemy and cannot be justified. So the only possible explanation is the second one: the consequences of Adam and Eve stealing the fruit of wisdom were too great, even to the extent of committing an original sin.

What are the consequences of stealing the fruit of wisdom? The substance-based world of humanity is divided, and the first and most important difference is the gender difference. This subverted the beautiful ethical world of impersonal substances and split it into Adam as "I," Eve as "you," and the absent God as "he." The first "other" in the history of civilization was born, and it was precisely the Creator Himself.

So, eating the forbidden fruit of wisdom, similar to the enlightenment of Socrates, has a similar significance in the history of civilization. It marked the end of a civilization and amounted to an original sin. What was the fate of humanity after being expelled from the Garden of Eden? It was to embark on a long cultural march in ethics to return to the Garden of Eden based on ethical reversion and God's salvation. The cultural essence of returning to the Garden of Eden was to stay together again.

In contrast to Greek and Hebrew civilizations, the major events in the history of Chinese civilization are Confucius' visit to various states and Laozi's disappearance at Hangu Pass. Both Confucianism and Daoism and both Confucius and Laozi took the Xia, Shang, and Zhou dynasties (2070 BC–256 BC) as an ideal society. What kind of civilization were the three dynasties? It was an ethical world based on substances that corresponds to the pre-Socratic era of the Western world. The chaos of the Spring and Autumn Period deconstructed this state of substance, and Confucius' visit to various states and Laozi's disappearance at Hangu Pass accomplished a *lunli* reversion.

Confucius and his Confucian teachings have two core concepts, namely propriety and benevolence. The former is the *lunli* substance while the latter is the moral subject. As Confucius said, "Benevolence is the distinguishing characteristic of man." Only those who possess the virtue of benevolence can truly be persons in the true sense. What is the essence of benevolence? As Confucius put it, "The benevolent man loves others." The essence of loving others is interpreted by Hegel as not to be an independent person in one's own right, that is, to stay together. Therefore, Confucius interpreted benevolence through propriety, believing that, "To subdue one's self and return to propriety, is perfect virtue. If a man can for one day subdue himself and return to propriety, all under heaven will ascribe perfect virtue to him." The *lunli* substance of propriety is the ultimate goal of the *daode* subject of benevolence. Only by returning to and constructing the *lunli* substance of propriety can one truly be a person and stay together. Returning to propriety means returning to the *lunli* substance of propriety. Confucius said, "If you do not learn the rules of propriety, your character cannot be established." The cultural significance of Confucius' visit to various states is to learn to stay together again.

Similarly, Laozi also affirmed propriety and benevolence, but differed in that he believed that both of them were the results of the deconstruction of substances. According to the *Daodejing*, "Thus it was that when the *dao* was lost, its attributes appeared; when its attributes were lost, benevolence appeared; when benevolence was lost, righteousness appeared; and when righteousness was lost, the proprieties appeared. Now propriety is the attenuated form of leal-heartedness and good faith, and is also the commencement of disorder." Also according to the *Daodejing*, "When the Great *dao* ceased to be observed, benevolence and righteousness came into vogue." The *lunli* of propriety and the *daode* of benevolence are both results of the deconstruction of the substances of the *dao*. Therefore, faced with the chaos and disorder in the Spring and Autumn Period, Laozi chose to disappear. Disappear from what? It is from secular society. Return to where? It is to return to the original state of the *dao*.

From this, we can understand why the slogans of the Western Renaissance and postmodernism were both return to ancient Greece and the ethical state of staying together in ancient Greece. In the early twentieth century, Nietzsche declared, "God is dead," and the Chinese Enlightenment movement called for the overthrow of Confucianism. However, ironically and symbolically, Nietzsche went insane at the age of 44 after declaring God is dead. The madness of Nietzsche is not just a physiological event as neuroscientists concluded that it was due to the genetic inheritance from his father; but rather it should be seen as a cultural event. The connection between the death of God and Nietzsche's madness should not be seen as a mere coincidence, but rather as an inherent spiritual inevitability. The death of God and Nietzsche's madness are significant events in the history of modern Western civilization. God died, substance died, and the atomic world came, and humanity lost its home once again. As a result, Nietzsche went mad, the world went mad, and Nietzsche's madness was essentially an ethical event.

Although traditional Chinese culture, represented by Confucius and Confucianism, has gone through many vicissitudes, Confucianism has always remained standing in the face of storms, and the spiritual world of the Chinese people is still a *lunli* world that cherishes home. The theories of the prophets of the Axial Age provided cultural wisdom for staying together, which is the ultimate question of civilization.

The discourse of *lunli* and its tradition provide a kind of wisdom: being a person and staying together, or more accurately, being a person in staying together. Expressed in Confucius' paradigm, this wisdom is that, "To subdue one's self and return to propriety, is perfect virtue." Returning to propriety is staying together, and having perfect virtue means being a person because as Confucius said, "Benevolence is the distinguishing characteristic of man."

How should humans live is a *daode* question, and how do we stay together is a *lunli* question. Should is what ought to be, and the essence of what ought to be is constantly not yet, and hoping and striving for it to happen is what is called ought to be. Western morality, especially modern morality, starts with individual free will, and individual free will is the fundamental ought to be. However, as Hegel said, this abstract ought to be is subjective moral freedom, and substantive freedom can only be obtained in ethics.

The ultimate question of civilization is how the "I" who pursues freedom of will becomes the "we" of ethical substances. How the "I" becomes "we," and how "we" stay together is the ultimate question of civilization and a challenging issue of modern civilization.

In 2020, as a natural disaster, the global COVID-19 pandemic presented a civilization issue of staying together in an ultimate and severe way. In the face of the global threat posed by the pandemic, how can humans and nature stay together? How can countries stay together? How family members can stay together after isolation? How can members of society stay together? All have been brought urgently back to human attention. COVID has brought humanity to a critical moment: destruction or staying together. Humans must learn to stay together again.

COVID signals a crisis of the atomic society and also tolls the bell for abstract *daode* freedom and atomic civilization. It warns people that they must return to the *lunli* home. Modern society not only needs *daode* freedom but also *lunli* identification, not only free will but also substance consciousness. Francis Fukuyama once said during the pandemic that the pandemic heralded the end of neoliberalism. In fact, it also announced the end of abstract *daode* freedom and the *daode* liberal theory through the power of nature, demanding that the *lunli* of staying together transcend the *daode* of abstract will freedom. It conveyed an urgent call from the depths of civilization to be a person and stay together.

2   THE ESSENCE OF *LUNLI*: BE A PERSON AND STAY TOGETHER

Chinese people have two cultural birthmarks: *lun* and *li*. *Lun* is a birthmark in the sense of existentialism and vitalism. People are born in *lun* and grow in it. *Li* is a birthmark in the sense of consciousness and value. It is a cultural consciousness based on *lun*. *Lun* refers to one's body or the physical aspect, while *li* refers to one's mind or spirit. The *li* of *lunli* is the *li* based on and rooted in *lun*, but not limited to it. *Li* originates from *lun* and extends to the universe and human life. It has become a uniquely Chinese worldview and outlook on life through the construction of a *lunli* culture.

Lun provides roots and a home in the meaning of birth, ultimate care, and world construction. The *li* of *lun* constructs a spiritual temperament that connects the recognition of human nature as inherently good, the rational and emotional structure of the heart, and the self-awareness of conscience, unifying traits of character, mentality, and subjectivity. Both *lun* and *li* revolve around a problem with ultimate significance and construct a unique cultural consciousness and national spirit: being a person and staying together, or more precisely, staying together to be a person.

The common ground of *lunli* and *daode* is to strive to be a person in the spiritual sense. The difference between various cultural traditions lies in what kind of person to be and how to be a person. However, *lunli* conveys a strong concern and serves as a cultural function, which is staying together. Although cultivating virtues can make people stay together better, the cultural mission of *lunli* is fundamentally to make people stay together in the spiritual world and then in the real world. Virtue consists rather in *lunli* ethical virtuosity. Indeed, religion also has a cultural significance in making people stay together, but it is completed through the ultimate substance on the other shore, while Chinese *lunli* is committed to constructing the social roots of staying together and even *lunli* systems on this shore.

After ancient Greece, Western culture replaced ethics with morality and sought to construct social life based on the universality of abstract free will pursuing moral rules. The consequence of losing *lunli* is the contradiction between *daode* freedom and *lunli* identification in modernity, leading to an inherent cultural crisis of staying together. Influenced by Western culture, the problem of modern China without *lunli* also leads to a spiritual crisis of staying together. The discourse of *lunli* and its tradition provides the social roots, cultural consciousness, spiritual home and ideal types of staying together, and modern civilization must return to the spiritual tradition of *lunli* in order to learn to stay together.

The discourse structure of *lun* laid the foundation for being a person and staying together in traditional China. Humans are born from *lun*, not only making individuals persons, but also endowing them with the most important cultural genes and even cultural destiny, that is, staying together. *Lun* is the substance of humans, the essence of life, and the essence of humans, which is staying together. It is not only staying together with the mother who gave birth to him or her, but also with the *lun* that jointly created him or her, or, as Hegel put it, the common personalities of parents. Humans are born from *lun*, grow in *lun* and are persons in *lun*. Birth means that persons stay together with *lun*; staying together with *lun* not only implies a person stays together with others, including, for example, father stays together with mother and children stay together with parents, but also implies they are essentially one.

Birth is the process from conception to delivery, and staying together is its true essence. The true essence of life is staying together, so is the true essence of human life and the world it creates. Perhaps it is the natural genes of staying together during pregnancy that lead to the *lunli* demands for care and concern that infants need after birth, and also give rise to *lunli* feelings of care and concern. It is reasonable to assume that from the *lunli* needs of care and concern in today's adult world to the *lunli* symbols of embracing and other affective life, the *lunli* information of staying together is conveyed, which is related to the genetic code buried in human nature of birth in biology and the science of *lunli*. Pregnancy, holding, embracing and caring and concern is the spiritual journey of staying together from nature to *lunli*, not just a psychological process, but a *lunli* process.

In the process of life growth, China has a nostalgic stage of life called the innocence of childhood boyfriends and girlfriends. What exactly does their innocence mean? The innocent state is the primitive state before Adam and Eve ate the forbidden fruit in the book of Genesis, which is the substance state without distinction of gender after the birth of life. To put in Zhuangzi's words, it is the transition from nothing or something but without any responsive recognition of it on the part of men to recognition without expression of different opinions about it. The birth of life is generating something from nothing, and the single cell is something but without any responsive recognition of it, i.e. without the distinction between male and female. The innocence of childhood boyfriends and girlfriends means no distinction of gender between male and female, i.e. the substance consciousness that does not distinguish between sexes and is rooted in the substance consciousness of staying together based on *lun*.

The developmental history of human life is a history of *lunli* passions for being a person and staying together. Filial piety is the enlightenment and awareness of *lunli* in life. Through filial piety, individuals are not only persons in the substances of *lun*, i.e. persons recognized by *lun*, but also join their parents and ancestors in the *lun* consciousness and behaviors of filial piety, regardless of time and space. It is a recognition and commitment to the eternal life of parents and ancestors, as well as a cultural design and pursuit of eternality. Filial piety is an eternal social chain of life, in which individuals of the same biological species recognize each other and move toward eternity and immortality by staying together.

Lun endows life with the cultural genes of being a person and staying together, the *lunli* law of taking *lun* as home and *li* as the intuitive knowledge and heavenly principle, and the cultural ideal for the *lunli* world. It represents the cultural guardianship of being a person within staying together, and the *lunli* construction of the real world.

Chinese traditional festivals share the same characteristics of natural and *lunli* order, embodying the philosophical concept of the unity of nature and humanity. Many festivals have staying together as their cultural core. The Spring Festival, Dragon Boat Festival, Qingming Festival, and Mid-Autumn Festival are the four major traditional festivals in China, and the Mid-Autumn Festival is often mistaken as a natural festival, but it actually has a profound *lunli* meaning.

Also known as the Moon Festival which originated in ancient times and became popular during the Han Dynasty, the Mid-Autumn Festival falls on the 15th day of the eighth lunar month. On this day, Chinese people have the habit of admiring the moon and eating mooncakes, which represents a *lunli* way of staying together for people in the agrarian era who were separated by mountains and rivers. This can be imagined and restored in terms of *lunli*. In the agrarian era, transportation and communication were not developed, and the saying that a letter from home is worth a thousand pieces of gold illustrates the value and scarcity of family information when people were separated by mountains and rivers. On the night of the Mid-Autumn Festival, people had an agreement to face the bright moon and upload their thoughts to distant relatives and friends, while those far away did the same to download their thoughts, hence the saying the moon represents my heart. The moon became the artificial satellite for Chinese people to stay s together in terms of *lunli* in the agrarian era. There are many works in Chinese culture about the moon, all conveying the *lunli* information of staying together in spite of spatial barriers. The so-called mooncakes are the material carriers of staying together.

The Mid-Autumn Festival is a festival for people who are physically present together, while the Ghost Festival is a festival for both present and absent family members to stay together. The Ghost Festival originated from the ancient worship of ancestral spirits. Legend has it that on the 15th day of the seventh lunar month, the spirits of ancestors will return from the underworld to enjoy the offerings and worship of their descendants, while also undergoing a review of their merits and demerits during their lifetime by the Heavenly Emperor to determine their rewards or punishments. This can be considered a grand reunion for all deceased ancestors and a spiritual reunion for both deceased and living members of the family. Folk customs include lighting lotus-shaped lanterns to guide the deceased ancestors back home.

The Mid-Autumn Festival and the Ghost Festival are *lunli* practices that transcend time and space for present and absent relatives to stay together.

3   THE *LI* WHY A HUMAN BEING COUNTS AS SUCH

In the *lunli* discourse, the *li* is the *li* of *lun* why a human being counts as such and stays together. It is manifested in the *lunli* process from the recognition of the innate goodness of human nature and the rational structure of the mind to how the nature, mind, and subject constructed by *lunli* persons be a person and stays together. It also creates and constructs a *lunli* spirit and temperament of being a person and staying together.

3.1   *The Nature of Being a Person*

Chinese philosophy and culture have a thousands of years of tradition about human nature, with the mainstream being the theory of human nature being naturally good. The reason is simple: it is based on *lunli* and is aimed at revealing the *lun* nature and law of human life and existence.

The saying cutting jade to train people's character conveys a clear cultural message: human nature is inherently good.

What is the essence of the good? The good is the unity of individual will and universal will. Hegel believed that ethics is the living good, stating that, "For the *subjective* will, the good is likewise absolutely essential, and the subjective will has worth and dignity only in so far as its insight and intention are in conformity with the good".[1] The good is the absolute essence of humans, and it is the recognition of one's public nature by one's individual will. Only when the individual consciously and behaviorally conforms to the good, can they have the dignity and value of being persons. Once the individual conforms to the good in terms of their consciousness and behavior, they also recognize each other and stay together.

The essence of the good is not only to be a person but also to stay together in consciousness and behavior. The good is the unity of the individuals and their common essence, so it is to be a person. Because it is the absolute essence of all people, individuals recognize each other in the recognition of the good, so it should also be possible for people to stay together.

In Chinese history, the theories of human nature being inherently good or evil revolve around the core question of how to be a person and why people should stay together.

Mencius advocated for the inherent goodness of human nature, believing that, "That whereby man differs from the lower animals is but small. The mass of people cast it away, while superior men preserve it" (*Mencius*). Human nature is what by which humans differ or are higher or superior to animals. Differing from animals means being persons and makes them good. What is it that makes humans differ from animals? Mencius deduced that, "Therefore I say, Men's mouths agree in having the same relishes; their ears agree in enjoying the same sounds; their eyes agree in recognizing the same beauty—shall their minds alone be without that which the similarly approve? What is it then of which they similarly approve? It is, I say, the principles of our nature, and the determinations of righteousness" (*Mencius*). Human nature is similarly approving, and it is akin to taste, sight, and sound, which are all internal to human nature.

[1] G. W. E. Hegel, *Elements of the Philosophy of Right*, Chinese version by Fan Yang and Zhang Qitai, Beijing: The Commercial Press, 1996, pp. 164, 133.

What is the content of similarly approving? Mencius deduced that it is the four feelings that everyone possesses: commiseration; shame and dislike; modesty and complaisance; and approving and disapproving which are the roots and buds of the Four Virtues of benevolence, righteousness, propriety, and wisdom, respectively. (Mencius) The essence of the four feelings and the Four Virtues they produce is to enable people to be persons and stay together. Why do people stay together? Because they share the four feelings. Why can people stay together? Because of the Four Virtues produced by similarly approving. Individuals are persons and stay together because of their innate goodness.

Chinese *lunli* share a common wisdom: the conclusion of the theories of human nature being inherently good or evil is that everyone can become morally perfect, and the difference lies only in the means to achieve this. Mencius believed that human nature contains the seeds of benevolence, righteousness, propriety, and wisdom, which are the four aspects of the good. Thus, he concluded that, "All things are already complete in us. There is no greater delight than to be conscious of sincerity on self-examination. All that is needed is to seek within oneself, and all men may be Yaos and Shuns (legendary virtuous emperors)." Xunzi's theory of human nature being inherently evil posits that human nature is equivalent to one's innate disposition which requires no effort but is so of itself. He therefore concluded that human nature is inherently evil. According to him, "Thus, if people follow along with their inborn dispositions and obey their nature, they are sure to come to struggle and contention, turn to disrupting social divisions and order, and end up becoming violent" (*Xunzi*). He argued that as long as one "transforms his nature and establishes deliberate effort," "Anyone on the streets can become a Yu (a legendary virtuous emperor)."

The theories of human nature being inherently good or evil convey different perspectives, but both emphasize the belief and confidence in being a person and staying together. The Song-Ming Confucianism established a unified view of human nature that combines the nature of destiny and the nature of temperament, synthesizing dialectically the theories of human nature being inherently good or evil. According to the nature of destiny, humans are persons while the nature of temperament suggests that humans are these persons. Chinese *lunli* is based on the relationship between justice and benefit, as expressed in the saying, "The affairs under Heaven are about nothing but justice and benefit." Chinese *lunli* has *li* and desire, namely, the universal *daode* requirements and individual desires, as its specific content; and ultimately the public and private nature is made the specific content of justice and benefit, *li* and desire. The pursuit of the public nature and the realm that a public and common spirit rules all under Heaven are the *lunli* ideal of staying together for great harmony.

3.2   The Emotion (Qingli) for Staying Together

Qinglism is a mental structure and cultural form that is consistent with *lunli*-based reflection. It can be said that *qingli* is the subjective form of *lunli*. In Chinese tradition, *qingli* constitutes *lunli*. This means that the *li* in *qingli* has the same meaning as the *li* in *lunli*, and vice versa. The value *qingli* expresses and the *lunli* atmosphere it creates are staying together.

Qingli is not the mixture of *qing* and *li*, but the prioritization of emotion in the value ecology of *qing* and *li*, and the prioritization of being reasonable over being justifiable. This is what Li Zehou called the essence of *qing*. However, this expression is not thorough enough. The essence of *qing* is essentially the essence of *lun*. Starting from *lun* and reflection based on *lun* will inevitably require and lead to emotionalism.

The essence of *lun* is inevitably the essence of *qing* because family *lunli* is not only the root of *lunli* but also its paradigm. Family *lunli* relationships are emotional relationships which construct social *lunli* through the Five Cardinal Relationships. The brotherly *lunli* extends to friend *lunli*, and the father-son *lunli* extends to sovereign-minister *lunli*, thereby endowing social and political *lunli* relationships with emotional colors. However, the nature of *lunli* substances is harmony in diversity, and efforts to stay true to *lun* and do one's part with the rectification of names as legitimacy is the basis for the construction of *lunli* and *lunli* substances. Therefore, both *lun* and *lunli* are *li* and must resort to *li*.

Of *qing* and *li*, the former is the basis and essence, and without it, there will be no *lun* to speak of. The concept of *lun* and the *lunli* law of human relations are based on natural relations and determine the priority of *qing* over *li*. In this sense, *lunli* is equivalent to *qingli*. Secular Chinese culture always bases *lunli* on everyday emotional life rather than seeking the ultimate basis of *lunli* in the Heavenly kingdom on the other shore or ontological world. It constructs social *lunli* norms. *Lunli* in Song-Ming Confucianism is elevated to and expressed as Heavenly principles, which is the metaphysical expression of *lunli* norms.

Qingli not only shows the priority of *qing* over *li* but also the subjectivity of emotion over *lunli*. The *li* in *qingli* is essentially the *li* of *qing*. *Qingli* has two semantic interpretation methods and two semantic structures, namely *qing* and *li* and *li* or *qing*. The emphasis on both *qing* and *li* in *qing* and and *li* shows that Chinese *lunli* tradition is neither emotional nor rational, but rather the *qingli* ecology or *qinglism* characterized by a dialectical interaction of *qing* and *li*, and is a third form beyond emotionalism and rationalism. The *li* of *qing* shows that emotion is the subject of *lunli*, and in the mental structure and cultural consciousness, emotion is the subject of reason.

The structure of *qing* and *li* and the *li* of *qing* was constructed in the human nature theory of the Axial Age and has become a consistent tradition. Mencius believed that human nature is the sharing of the four feelings of commiseration; shame and dislike; modesty and complaisance; and approving and disapproving. The first three of these feelings are *qing*, and only the last one is *li*. Therefore, in the human nature structure of the theory of innate goodness, three quarters are *qing*, and only one quarter is *li*. In addition, the feeling of approving and disapproving is only the *li* for approving or disapproving commiseration; shame and dislike; and modesty and complaisance, rather than abstract reasoning, and is, in essence, also *qing*.

The four feelings are the source of the Four Virtues of benevolence, righteousness, propriety, and wisdom. Among the Four Virtues, benevolence, righteousness, and propriety are *qing*, while wisdom is not rationality, but intuitive knowledge. In benevolence and righteousness, "Benevolence is meant to promote harmony while righteousness is designed to define differences." Promoting harmony means staying together; defining differences means act with benevolence and love for others in a reasonable way, following the principle of name rectification. Therefore, in Mencius's view, benevolence is the tranquil habitation of humans, and righteousness is his straight path to benevolence. In this sense, righteousness is also the *li* of love. Because of this, Zhu Xi expressed benevolence, righteousness, propriety, and wisdom as benevolence, righteousness, *zhong*, and *zheng*. According to *Topically Arranged Conversations of Zhu Xi*, "*Zhong* and *zheng* mean propriety and wisdom respectively and properly represent them. *Zhong* is the utmost of propriety, and *zheng* is the essence of wisdom."

Confucius' statement that "To go beyond is as wrong as to fall short" is about the feeling of approving and disapproving. According to *The*

Analects of Confucius, "Zigong asked which of the two, Shi or Shang, was the superior. The Master said, 'Shi goes beyond the due mean, and Shang does not come up to it.' 'Then,' said Zigong, 'The superiority is with Shi, I suppose.' The Master said, 'To go beyond is as wrong as to fall short'." Excessive virtue is as unreasonable as insufficient virtue.

According to *Hanfeizi*, Confucius once recommended a soldier who had repeatedly fled from the battlefield to serve as an official to the ruler of the State of Lu. Confucius asked the soldier why he had done so, and he replied that he had an elderly father at home, and if he died, there would be no one to support his father. Confucius believed that this man not only had filial piety but also was brave, because he risked being executed to fulfill his filial duties.[2] This is the *li* of *qing*.

Wang Yangming directly interpreted Mencius' feeling of approving and disapproving as *qing*, stating that, "Approve and disapprove mean love and hate respectively." Love and hatred represent *qing* because their essence is just as what *The Great Learning* says, "The no self-deception is allowed as when we hate a bad smell and as when we love what is beautiful." This is considered to be the most complete sincerity and is, therefore, *li*. In this sense, all the four feelings are about *qing*. The structure of the mind in Chinese *lunli* is the structure of *li* based on *qing*, the structure of the ontology of *qing* as well as the subject of *qing*.

Qingli is the *li* of *lun*, which has been universalized as a way of thinking and a pursuit of values. It is the core value of reflection based on *lunli*, and its essence is staying together. China has never had a rationalism (*lixing*) in the Western sense. Western rationalism is a philosophical tradition of ontology, scientific culture, and individualistic values. If one must use the Western term rationality to interpret Chinese *lunli*, it is better to say that it is *xingli* or the principle of nature.

Lixing and *xingli* are not simply a reversal of terms but a shift in the focus of values. In *lixing*, *li* comes before *xing* (nature) which is derived from abstract *li*, including the nature of things, human nature, and the *li* of *lun*. In *xingli*, nature comes before *li* and the nature of all things is derived from human nature, including the *li* of *lun*. According to *The*

---

[2] The original text reads, "In the State of Lu, there was a man who followed the sovereign to go to war but repeatedly fled from battles. Confucius asked him about the reason, and he replied, 'I have an elderly father at home. If I die, there will be no one to support him.' Confucius thought this was filial piety and recommended him to be appointed as an official."

Doctrine of the Mean, "It is only he who is possessed of the most complete sincerity that can exist under heaven, who can give its full development to his nature. Able to give its full development to his own nature, he can do the same to the nature of other men. Able to give its full development to the nature of other men, he can give their full development to the natures of animals and things. Able to give their full development to the natures of creatures and things, he can assist the transforming and nourishing powers of Heaven and Earth. Able to assist the transforming and nourishing powers of Heaven and Earth, he may with Heaven and Earth form a ternion." *Xingli* is the connection between one's own nature and the nature of humans and all things, and its highest realm is the harmony between humans and nature. The *lunli* essence of harmony between humans and nature is staying together, where there is harmony between one and oneself, inward and external, and humans and nature.

Lunli is about *qingli*. Its essence is being a person based on staying together. Staying together is the fundamental difference between *qingli lunli* and rational *lunli*. According to Mencius, "Benevolence is the distinguishing characteristic of man." The essence of benevolence and righteousness is *qingli*. Benevolence is love, and righteousness is uprightness and their essence is staying together with people enjoying harmony in diversity. The essence of the harmony between humans and nature, in which one's own nature is connected to the nature of all things, is staying together, in which humans are one with all things in Heaven and Earth, and become great persons enjoying harmony between humans and nature. They are "able to assist the transforming and nourishing powers of Heaven and Earth and may with Heaven and Earth form a ternion."

Why does *qingli* make humans stay together and become persons or make them become persons while staying together?

The core of the *qing* of *qingli* or *lunli* feelings is love. The essence of love is not being alone. Love is a body feeling and dependence developed based on the birth of human *lun*, and its essence is staying together. The *li* of *lunli* or *lunli* rationality are the principle based on *lun* order and represent differences. Emotion and rationality create the dependence and independence of humans. Because of the emotion of *lun*, humans stay together, including humans' *lun* birth and *lun* care. Because of the *li* of *lun*, humans are persons who are content with their lot, do their part and work to fulfil their *lunli* obligations. The "reason" of "rationality" is the reason why we "become human beings" by doing our duty and fulfilling our ethical obligations. However, compared with rationalism, what is highlighted in *qingli* is staying together. This is the philosophical significance and Chinese characteristics of the ontology or the primacy of emotions.

3.3   Conscience of Being a Person and Staying Together

From the three dimensions of human nature identity, spiritual structure, and self-awareness, coherently good human nature, *qingli*, and intuitive knowledge form the *li* of *lunli* in which humans are persons while staying together. Coherently good human nature is the ontology, *qingli* is the application, and intuitive knowledge is the *lunli* subject created by the integration of theory and practice. They strengthen the idea of staying together and being persons from the three dimensions of human nature identity, spiritual structure, and subject construction.

What is conscience? It is the subject of *lunli*. The essence of intuitive knowledge is *lun* knowledge, the knowledge of *lun*. The Ming Dynasty philosopher Wang Yangming regarded intuitive knowledge as the basis of the universe and the heavenly principles and the ability of humans to understand these principles. According to him, "The essence of the mind is the heavenly principles. The ability to understand these principles is intuitive knowledge." Intuitive knowledge is the feeling of approving and disapproving mentioned by Mencius, but this feeling is not a cognitive function in the scientific or philosophical sense, nor is it what is called rationality. It is the knowledge of *lun* based on *ren*, and it is also *lun* knowledge, the knowledge based on and of *lun*. Because it is based on and of *lun*, it is therefore intuitive.

This kind of *lun* knowledge has the following characteristics. First, it is intuitive and natural, not learned but inherent, and it integrates knowledge and action. Second, it is the application of heavenly principles in *lun*, that is, the heavenly principles of *lun*. According to Wang Yangming, "*Li* is the organization of the mind. When *li* is applied to parents, it becomes filial piety. When applied to the sovereign, it becomes loyalty. When applied to friends, it becomes trustworthiness. *Li* can vary infinitely, but its source is always the human heart." Third, intuitive knowledge is a feeling of like and dislike. Conscience is only the heart of right and wrong. According to Wang Yangming, "Intuitive knowledge is merely a discerning mind for right and wrong, while right and wrong are merely matters of preference and aversion. Once one understands preference and aversion, they will understand right and wrong. Once one understands right and wrong, they will be able to grasp the changes of all things." This is because preference and aversion not only pertain to understanding but also to action. It is the unity of knowledge and action.

Intuitive knowledge is a knowledge of *lun*, and therefore is not cognition. Whether in the philosophical or scientific sense, cognition is knowledge and is characterized by objectivity, based on the premise of subject-object duality. On the other hand, intuitive knowledge is an identification that arises from the substance of *lun*. The substance of *lun* and the *lun* of staying together are the premises of knowledge and the locus of intuitiveness. Intuitive knowledge is not cognition but identification. The discussions on human nature in Chinese *lunli*, which lasted for more than two thousand years, are essentially not about the recognition of the good and evil nature of humans, but about the identification of the good and evil in human nature. The aim of the discussion on human nature is to establish the belief and confidence in being a person and staying together, so that the notion that "All men may be Yaos and Shuns" has become a cultural consensus of various schools of thought. Intuitive knowledge not only rejects objectivity, but also abandons it. This is an important characteristic of reflection based on *lunli*.

Intuitive knowledge is not rationality, either. Rationality is based on differentiation, self-affirming cognition and wisdom. On the other hand, intuitive knowledge is based on the unity or substance of *lun*, and ultimately returns to and constructs the substance of *lun*. In the tradition of intuitive knowledge, whether a human is a person depends on whether he or she has the sense of the substance and unity of *lun*, that is, the so-called *lunli* sense. The *lunli* sense is the sense of *lun* and is intuitive knowledge, so intuitive knowledge makes a human become a person and constructs persons in the identification of the substance of *lun*. In cross-cultural dialogues, people often cannot grasp the difference between *lunli* and scientific culture, and they use Western traditions to interpret Chinese traditions, using cognition to dissect, deny, and subvert intuitive knowledge.

In this sense, Aristotle's intellectual virtue and moral virtue are actually the differences between Western and Chinese cultures. People often devalue moral virtue based on Aristotle's assertion that intellectual virtue is superior to moral virtue, and move on to devalue Chinese *lunli* culture. In fact, the intellectual virtue that Aristotle advocated is only a tradition in the West. In *The Nicomachean Ethics*, Aristotle believed that ethics is a branch of politics, that humans are the rational animal and that a political animal. Therefore, it can be assumed that the ethics he talked about was not the ethics in the Chinese sense, but the ethics that is the same as political science in the Western sense.

The Western tradition that equates ethics with political science has continued to this day. John Rawls' *A Theory of Justice* is read and interpreted as an ethics work, but under the questions of Alasdair Chalmers Macintyre—whose justice? which rationality?—Rawls had to retreat step by step and finally declared that the justice he talked about was only political justice, not ethical justice. This reflects the Western tradition that has been passed down from Aristotle to Rawls. In this sense, it can be said that Western ethics is not pure ethics. The excessive negation of ethical virtue, the excessive pursuit of intellectual virtue, and the substitution of cognition for conscience have led to the decline of the ability to reflect ethically, which is the theoretical root of many ethical problems in the West and the dilemma of modern ethics.

What is constructed by intuitive knowledge is not so much a moral subject as a *lunli* subject, because it is the knowledge of *lun*. The personification of a *lunli* subject is the *lunli* person, and the essence of the *lunli* person is to be a person in the context of *lun*, using the substance of *lun* and the *lun* of staying together as the standard and fundamental path of being a person. Wang Yangming's theory that "when it perceives the parents it naturally knows what filial piety is and when it perceives the elder brother it naturally knows what respectfulness is" is a knowledge of and derived from *lun*, and is therefore a knowledge acquired without the exercise of thought and an intuitiveness gained without deliberate learning. Wang described intuitive knowledge as spirit, and said that it is called spirit because of its condensation. Intuitive knowledge is the condensation of the heavenly principles of *lun*, and the *lunli* person it constructs is present in *lun*, and is a person because of *lun*. Therefore, intuitive knowledge is the heavenly principle or the *li* of *lun* of being a person and staying togetherness.

CHAPTER 9

Having a Home and Keeping It

Every culture has its own spiritual homeland, and humans and civilization come from substances, which means they come from their homes. The difference between various civilizations and between *lunli* and ethics is where the homeland is and whether it is on this shore or the other shore. The fundamental issue of modern civilization is whether humans have lost their homeland and whether they have the ability and aspirations to protect their homeland.

Lunli and its traditional spiritual temperament are having a home and keeping it. Because of the substance of *lun* and the spiritual structure and cultural consciousness of *li*, there is a home. Because of the *lun-li* spirit of taking *lun* as home and *li* as the intuitive knowledge and the cultural ideals of the *lunli* world, there is the ability and aspiration to protect the home. The *lunli* person is a person who has a home and protects it.

1 The Road of *Lunli* Spirit to Home

Another spiritual temperament created by the *lunli* discourse and its tradition in the Chinese nation is *lunli* is home. The spiritual home of Chinese culture is a *lunli* home, which is also known as the spiritual home of *lunli*. It takes *lunli* as its home and defends and guards its spiritual home through the continuous creative transformation of *lunli*, constructing and returning to its spiritual home through *lunli* ideals.

© Foreign Language Teaching and Research Publishing Co., Ltd 2024   121
H. Fan, Lunli *and Confucian Moral Theory*, Key Concepts
in Chinese Thought and Culture,
https://doi.org/10.1007/978-981-99-9105-1_9

The history of the development of Chinese *lunli* is a history of the construction, defense and development of the spiritual home through *lunli* spirit. The spiritual home has two basic structures or two settlement bases: the spiritual world and the real world, and the relationship and communication between the two worlds are the basic issues of constructing the *lunli* home. The core of the spiritual home of the inner world is inwardly forming the sage, and the core of the spiritual home of the real world is externally forming the king. The relationship between the two is the relationship between the inward and external, and between the ideal and the reality. Inwardly forming the sage is the path to guarding *lun-li*, while externally forming the king is the way of realizing the ideal of *lunli*. The history of traditional Chinese *lunli* spirit is a history of constantly constructing and developing the spiritual home through the interaction of cultures and mainly based on Confucian *lunli*,.

Chinese culture has its roots in the three dynasties of Xia, Shang, and Zhou, and its spiritual home is summarized by the concept of *li*. Confucius believed that *li* was the unchanging essence of the changing Chinese civilization. He said in *The Analects*, "The Yin Dynasty followed the regulations (*li*) of the Xia; wherein it took from or added to them may be known. The Zhou Dynasty has followed the regulations of Yin; wherein it took from or added to them may be known. Some other may follow the Zhou, but though it should be at the distance of a hundred ages, its affairs may be known." While *li* is commonly understood as a system of governance, in fact, it has always pointed toward the cultural spirit behind the system of rites and ceremonies from the very beginning. *Li* is a *lunli* substance that should be interpreted as a spiritual home constructed with *lunli*. What Confucius meant was that the Shang *li* was inherited from the Xia li, and the Zhou *li* was inherited from the Shang *li* through critical examination and modification. By following this trajectory of critique and modification, the systems and spirits of future generations, even after a thousand years, could be foreseen.

The efforts of the Hundred Schools of Thought in the Spring and Autumn Period had a significance beyond the construction of a social system; it was also the pursuit of a spiritual home. Confucius' visit to various states and Laozi's disappearance at Hangu Pass were two different efforts or directions in search of a spiritual home.

The ultimate goal of Confucius' visit to various states to convince their rulers was to ensure that they subdue their self and repair and return to propriety and make it the fundamental standard for being benevolent, i.e.

being a person. This is why Confucius said, "To subdue one's self and return to propriety, is perfect virtue." Overcoming oneself and returning to propriety is benevolence. For Confucius, propriety was not just a political system, rituals and ceremonies, but more importantly, a *lunli* spirit. He repeatedly asked, "'It is according to the rules of propriety,' they say. 'It is according to the rules of propriety,' they say. Are gems and silk all that is meant by propriety? 'It is music,' they say. 'It is music,' they say. Are bells and drums all that is meant by music?".

Chinese civilization is known as a civilization of propriety and music, and its essence is to increase *lunli* awareness through propriety and music, forming a *lunli* spirit of harmony in diversity. That is the essence of propriety and music. That's why Confucius said that gems and silk are not all that is meant by propriety, and music is not just bells and drums. In *The Analects*, to explain the essence of propriety, Confucius said, "The business of laying on the colors follows the preparation of the plain ground." This is extended to conclude that, "Ceremonies then are a subsequent thing," which means that propriety is not about the form, but about the spirit behind it.

From this, we can also understand why Mencius elevated propriety from *lunli* to *daode* to make it one of the Four Virtues of benevolence, righteousness, propriety, and wisdom, and elevating *daode* to a higher level after benevolence and righteousness. Confucius' visit to various states to restore propriety was not only about reconstructing the social system of propriety, but also about rebuilding a spiritual home in the world of life. The so-called returning to propriety means returning to home with the recognition of the historical existence of the spiritual home of propriety as a premise.

The historical mystery left by the story of Laozi's disappearance is where Laozi went after his disappearance? History and people's attention to this major historical event seems to only focus on the disappearance itself, as well as the timeless classic left by Laozi after his disappearance, the *Daodejing*, without paying much attention to where Laozi went after his disappearance. Laozi's disappearance as a sage master was a historical event with significant symbolic meaning and cultural expression. It was based on the denial of the secular world, believing that the virtues of benevolence, righteousness, propriety, and wisdom in the secular world were all results of the Great *dao* ceasing to be observed. Propriety itself was a sign of the extreme disintegration of the Great *dao* and was needed as a result. According to Laozi, "Now propriety is the attenuated form of leal-heartedness and good faith, and is also the commencement of disorder." In this sense, the fundamental purpose of his disappearance was to seek a spiritual home for oneself and for the world.

Confucius worked to use propriety to rebuild the secular and spiritual homes, while Laozi clearly believed that the upheaval of the secular home ultimately resulted from the loss of the spiritual home. The construction of the *lunli* substance of propriety originated from the overturning of the spiritual home due to the Great *dao* ceasing to be observed. The proposition of establishing a secular home already indicated the loss of the spiritual home. Therefore, Laozi's disappearance is a cultural symbol of seeking and returning to the *dao* as the spiritual home. His disappearance only affirmed the historical fact of losing the home, but also expressed the cultural intention and spiritual direction of seeking home, without pointing out what and where the home was, because it was the *dao*, which could be defined and yet could not be named; because it was the spiritual home, it existed in a small place in a state of emptiness and simplicity which the secular world did not know and found it unnecessary to know. From this, we can conclude that the essence and core of Laozi's disappearance is that over the past thousands of years, people have only known that he disappeared without investigating where he went and found it impossible and unnecessary to know that. This is the wisdom of Chinese culture.

Confucius' visit to various states marked his being in the secular world, while Laozi retreated from the secular world. These two paths of returning to spiritual home may have contained inherent contradictions that would later arise in the protection of China's cultural home. Confucianism, represented by Confucius, emphasizes both the secular home and the spiritual home, but there may be an inherent crisis of secularism obscuring the spiritual and of the both of them splitting from each other. Therefore, Confucius anxiously asked, "Are gems and silk all that is meant by propriety?" After Emperor Wu of Han only venerated the Confucians and expelled all other philosophical schools and Confucianism gained orthodox status, this inherent contradiction gradually became apparent.

The classical Confucianism championed by Confucius emphasizes the need to inwardly form the sage and externally the king. In Confucianism, inwardly forming the sage by studying things, acquiring knowledge, being sincere in thought, and rectifying one's mind constitutes the spiritual home, and externally forming the king by regulating one's family well, governing the state properly, and bringing peace to all under Heaven constitutes the external or secular spiritual home. The integration of inwardly forming the sage and externally the king provides a foundation for people to settle and establish themselves. However, after China began to only venerate the Confucians, the study of Confucian classics in the two Han dynasties one-sidedly emphasized the external function of Confucianism and gradually neglected and lost its inner spiritual home. As a result, Confucianism and the people's spiritual home it constructed faced internal crises during their heyday, and evolved into a cultural crisis under suitable conditions in historical development.

After the Han Dynasty, Chinese society experienced prolonged turbulence from the Three Kingdoms to the Wei and Jin dynasties. The Confucianism of the two Han dynasties, which focused on forming the king externally, could not meet people's needs for spiritual solace, so Daoist teachings began to regain the lost ground when only Confucians were venerated. Unlike Confucianism, the wisdom of Daoist teachings, as depicted in the historical context of Laozi's disappearance, was not interested in external achievements. The lost ground they reclaimed is primarily the human spiritual world or the home of the soul. This formed the unity of Confucianism and Daoism in the Wei and Jin dynasties, known as Wei-Jin metaphysics.

The essence of Wei-Jin metaphysics is assimilating with emptiness, which means using Daoist emptiness to assimilate Confucian propriety and righteousness. The core is the distinction between nature and culture, ultimately leading to the division of Confucianism and Daoism in the spiritual and even everyday world of humans, and this division continued to be passed down to Song and Ming dynasties' neo-Confucianism. The couplet by the Donglin Faction of the Ming Dynasty, "The sound of wind, rain, and reading enters the ears; family affairs, national affairs, and world affairs are all our concern," is the most appropriate interpretation. The first line refers to the Daoist transcendence, pointing to the settlement of the inner world; the second line refers to the Confucian immanence, pointing to the livelihood in the worldly world. In this sense, the spiritual home built by Confucius and Confucianism through *lunli* had already been shaken during the Han Dynasty. Wei-Jin metaphysics did not lack a spiritual home, but rather advocated a diverse or separate spiritual home divided between Confucianism and Daoism.

After the Sui and Tang dynasties, the crisis of the spiritual home became more severe. The journey to the west by Tang Sanzang to obtain the Buddhist scriptures can be seen as a cultural process of searching for a spiritual home.

Sun Wukong, Zhu Bajie, and Sha Wujing in *Journey to the West* are all extraordinary beings in secular life, and the errors they committed led to their expulsion from the "Garden of Eden," symbolizing the loss of a spiritual home. Sun Wukong becoming the Monkey King and Zhu Bajie taking a wife are both comedic expressions of their secular nature, while Tang Sanzang, who seems to lack any worldly abilities, is a personification symbol of persistently searching for a spiritual home in the world. In the end, the four of them all reach the heavenly realm and meet the Buddha, and they all become Buddhas, symbolizing their return to the spiritual home. However, the different levels of achieving Buddhahood also indicate different realms of homecoming, and the scriptures they bring back symbolize the spiritual home regained for all people.

In this sense, *Journey to the West* is both a crisis of the spiritual home and a human drama of seeking a spiritual home on the other shore. The Buddhist studies of the Sui and Tang dynasties marked the emergence of a cultural situation where Confucianism, Daoism, and Buddhism coexisted in the spiritual world.

The neo-Confucianism of the Song and Ming dynasties is, in a sense, a *lunli* defense battle for Confucianism to regain the lost spiritual home. Although the dominant position of Confucian *lunli* in the spiritual home has changed in Wei-Jin metaphysics and Sui-Tang Buddhist studies, both Daoism and Buddhism occupied and divided the spiritual space of Confucianism, transmitting the common will of Chinese culture to guard and continuously construct their own spiritual homes. In the cultural coexistence of Confucianism, Daoism, and Buddhism, there had long been a situation where Buddhism did not actively challenge Confucianism, but mainly regarded Daoism as its opponent or even enemy. The reason is simple: Daoism and Buddhism were not interested in the secular space occupied by Confucianism, but rather it was the spiritual space of humans that they competed for.

Song and Ming neo-Confucianism's formation of Confucianism, Daoism, and Buddhism as a unified system with Confucianism as the main body marked the establishment of a new spiritual home for the Chinese nation. It declared the final victory of the *lunli* spiritual home after facing internal and external challenges. However, at this time, the spiritual home was no longer dominated by Confucianism or *lunli* alone, but rather an ecological home with Confucianism, Daoism, and Buddhism in dialectical interaction and with *lunli* as the main body. The prominent feature of this spiritual home is the incorporation of the rational essence of Daoism and Buddhism by Confucianism, and the construction of the study of the nature of the mind. The neo-Confucianism of the Song and Ming dynasties achieved a dialectical synthesis of traditional Chinese *lunli* spirit through the study of the nature of the mind. The essence of the study of the nature of the mind lies in the construction of an individual's inner spiritual home.

In summary, the spiritual home of Chinese culture is a *lunli* home, with *lunli* as the core. Chinese *lunli* spirituality has evolved from its inception in the pre-Qin period, to abstract development in the Han and Tang dynasties, and to dialectical synthesis in the Song and Ming dynasties, reflecting the dialectical process of the construction, crisis, and return of the *lunli* spiritual home. The long cultural process conveys not only the *lunli* genes and colors of the spiritual home, but also the cultural efforts to uphold and defend the *lunli* spiritual home, as well as the glorious spiritual history of returning to the *lunli* home.

2 FROM FAMILY TO HOME

Chinese *lunli* takes the family as its foundation, which has laid the cultural genes of pursuing and upholding the home. However, the transition from family to home represents a spiritual awakening and *lunli* return. The road from family to home is taking *lun* as home and *li* as the intuitive knowledge and heavenly principle, which is the *lunli* spirit of upholding the home.

The family is a natural *lunli* substance; although it is the cell of society, it is not society itself. Once the family becomes society or is organized according to the logic of society, it will no longer be a family. This is what Confucius meant when he said, "The father conceals the misconduct of the son, and the son conceals the misconduct of the father." In Western discourse, as in Ferdinand Tönnies' book Gemeinschaft und Gesellschaft (*Community and Society*), the family is regarded as a natural and basic community. However, if expressed in Chinese discourse, the essence of the family is polity, but it is difficult to accurately express the term "same," because Chinese culture has the concept of harmony in diversity. The family should be harmonious rather than same. If it is same, it would mean the natural sense of great unity.

In Chinese discourse, the family is a polity of life with temporal and spatial significance. On the one hand, individuals within the same family share a common life source identified by their surname, and they create and extend new lives. On the other hand, individuals within the family occupy different *lunli* positions or sequences. The so-called family titles such as father, son, and brother are symbols of the *lunli* positions in the family, and the *lunli* community of life continues to expand with the inclusion of foreign lives through marriage. This is why in traditional societies, Western civilization bestows the right of surname on women who marry into the family, as a cultural recognition of the contribution of ethical immigrants to the continuation of the family life community, and also as an ethical *lunli* assimilation of new members.

The individuals and their self-awareness within a family are all members, that is, family members. Member is the tangible identification and consciousness of individuals, as well as the *lunli* premise of family existence. Once individuals in a family are granted independent rights, such as forming independent property relationships, the family moves toward society. This is why the *lunli* condition for the existence of a family is called "regulate" in Chinese discourse, which means regulate the family well. To regulate means to create substances. In the substance of a family, individuals in different *lunli* positions and life sequences are only members. To regulate the family means to construct and defend its substance with *lunli* to secure uniformity in this seeming irregularity and make it the source and destination of life for each member. This is the essential meaning of the "regulate" in "regulate the family well."

Jia is the *lunli* extension and abstraction of family. In Chinese discourse, *jia* may have the shadow of a family but not necessarily be a family. It draws on the collective meaning of a family as a natural *lunli* substance and extends it to a broader world of life and living space outside the family. It is a meaning world constructed based on the ideal type of family as a *lunli* concept, which not only points to the spiritual destination of humans, but also points to the place where the spirit originates.

In Chinese culture, *jia* represents the place where parents, who are the common root of life, are located, and it is also the community where wealth, meals, and future are shared. The sayings "wherever parents are, there is home" and "home is where the heart is in daily life of Chinese people" refer to the extended meaning of home derived from the family. The so-called "as close as family" and "being one family under heaven" refer to the ideal type of home constructed by the expansion of the family *lunli* paradigm. The extension from family to home eliminates the spatial meaning of the character *ting* and retains the abstract meaning of home, which is a philosophical elevation in *lunli*.

Jiayuan is the hometown of the family, and hometown, birthplace, etc., are also called *jiayuan*. Both *jiating* and *jiayuan* share a common characteristic, which is to give home the spatial meaning of *ting* or *yuan*, but the *jia* in *jiating* is singular, while the *jia* in *jiayuan* is plural. *Jiayuan* is the base where not just one family but many or even all families can settle. Spiritual home is the dwelling place of the human spirit and the common spiritual home of individuals in the same culture, though each individual may also settle their spirit and life in a special way.

Family, home, and hometown are the settling places for the lives and livelihoods of people who value the ideal of family as their core value. These three concepts represent the continuous expansion and elevation of *lunli* from concrete to abstract to concrete. Clearly, similar concepts exist in every culture, but in Chinese *lunli* culture, family is not only the starting point, but also the prototype, making family the core discourse and ideal type for spiritual settlement.

As the first and foremost of the four traditional Chinese festivals, the Spring Festival year after year embodies the *lunli* pursuit of spiritual guardianship from family to home. The Spring Festival is the beginning of the lunar year in China, evolving from the ancient custom of offering sacrifices to Heaven, Earth and ancestors to pray for a good harvest at the beginning of the year, which reflects the cultural concept that "all things originate from Heaven and man originates from his ancestor." Although it has undergone profound changes in form and content over thousands of years, the Spring Festival's *lunli* connotations and functions are still rich and profound.

The customs of the Spring Festival are diverse and ever-changing, but several *lunli* meanings have been passed down to this day.

Firstly, during the Spring Festival, especially before New Year's Eve, relatives who are separated by up to thousands of miles will return to their parents' homes and hometowns regardless of hardships and costs, reuniting with their families. Even in today's modern China where traditions have greatly faded, family reunion during the Spring Festival is still an irresistible *lunli* force. According to statistics from China's transportation authorities, the passenger volume during the 2019 Spring Festival reached 2.99 billion. The huge flow of people during the Spring Festival is so massive that some people jokingly call it the world's largest animal migration. The annual homecoming movement during the Spring Festival represents a reenactment of family *lunli* warmth, the consolidation of family *lunli* bonds, and a longing for and return to home. Although modern Chinese society is highly open, the Chinese values still hold strong: travel far and wide, but return home for the lunar New Year.

Secondly, during the Spring Festival, people visit relatives and friends. This is an opportunity to revisit and strengthen family *lunli* relationships and friendships, and also an opportunity for the extension of *lunli* home from family to society.

Thirdly, during the Spring Festival, people who have conflicts with each other often use this occasion to communicate and reconcile. Out with the old and in with the new. The Spring Festival is often the most tolerant time for Chinese people in terms of *lunli*, with parents not scolding their children and neighbors reaching reconciliation through mutual New Year's greetings. As a result, the Spring Festival has a strong *lunli* repairing function.

Until today, under the impact of globalization and marketization, although all festivals, including the Spring Festival, have become stages for economic activities and inevitably lost some of their cultural charm, the *lunli* function of the Spring Festival remains resilient and powerful. It can be imagined that when the *lunli* function of the Spring Festival disappears completely, it will mark the end of Chinese cultural traditions.

Chinese culture not only constructs and protects the spiritual home through *lunli* principles, but also provides a cultural paradigm for constructing and safeguarding the spiritual home: take *lun* as home and *li* as the intuitive knowledge and heavenly principle.

Taking *lun* as home and *li* as the intuitive knowledge and heavenly principle not only reveals the cultural laws regarding the relationship between *lun* and *li*, but also expresses the cultural path and paradigm of safeguarding *lunli* and the spiritual home it constructs. Taking *lun* as home means to safeguard the *lun* home and the essence is reflecting based on *lunli*. Taking *li* as the intuitive knowledge and heavenly principle is to reach the state of freedom from the home of *lunli*, and the essence is becoming a person and staying together. *Li* comes from *lun;* without *lun*, there is no *li*, which is the natural and free state of *lunli*. Taking *lun* as home and *li* as the intuitive knowledge and heavenly principle is to safeguard *lun* and *li*.

The cultural laws inherent in the Five Cardinal Relationships and Four Virtues, which are the core of traditional Chinese *lunli* and *daode* are the safeguarding of the spiritual home of *lunli* by taking *lun* as home and *li* as the intuitive knowledge and heavenly principle. The essence of the Five Cardinal Relationships between sovereign and minister, father and son, elder brother and younger, friends, and husband and wife is that human relations are based on natural relations, proceeding from the family *lunli* of father and son, elder brother and younger, and husband and wife to extend the social relationships between sovereign and minister and between friends to become the *lunli* home, ultimately making the whole world a *lunli* home. As the saying goes, "The world is regarded as one family and the country as one person," which is taking *lun* as home and *li* as the intuitive knowledge and heavenly principle.

Among the Four Virtues, which are the core of the traditional moral prototype, benevolence centered on loving others is the home of virtue, and its meaning of home is expressed by Mencius as the tranquil habitation; righteousness is the path of safeguarding the home of benevolence, and its essence is that it is different based on its differences, or, as Mencius put it, the right path. Proceeding from benevolence and following the path of righteousness, one can make progress toward the home of the *lunli* substance based on benevolence that promotes harmony and righteousness which defines differences. This is called the door of propriety. Wisdom is the *lunli* wisdom about the belief in benevolence and righteousness and the relationship between them, and its essence is knowledge which is the spiritual construction of the *lunli home*. Therefore, benevolence is the tranquil habitation of man, righteousness is his straight path, propriety is the substance, and wisdom is the belief. Benevolence is dwelt in and the path of righteousness is pursued. Righteousness is the way, propriety is the door, and benevolence and wisdom should be integrated. The spiritual journey is started from the home to return and safeguard the home by dwelling in benevolence and pursuing the path of righteousness.

The essence of both taking *lun* as home and *li* as the intuitive knowledge and heavenly principle and dwelling in benevolence and pursuing the path of righteousness lies in safeguarding the spiritual home.

3 THE FAMILY-STATE SENTIMENT
AND THE *LUNLI* HOME

The Chinese *lunli* tradition not only emphasizes the creation of a home based on the family, but also upholds the *lun-li* principles of taking *lun* as home and *li* as the intuitive knowledge and heavenly principle to safeguard the family, and constructs the spiritual home of a *lunli* world based on *lunli* ideals.

The so-called *lunli* ideals do not refer to the ideals of *lunli*, but rather the ideals of constructing the entire world as a *lunli* substance, or constructing the real world as a spiritual home based on *lunli*. They are ideals of the *lunli* world or the *lunli* home. The core of these *lunli* ideals is what is known as family-state sentiments.

Family-state sentiments may be one of the most Chinese concepts, embodying the unique spiritual temperament of a *lunli* culture. Essentially, these sentiments are *lunli* sentiments rich in the fullness of Chinese experience. Their essence lies not in the love for one's family or country, but in the unique discourse and special spiritual temperament that arise from the national cultural background. The sentiments are driven by three successive *lunli* structures: the integration of the family and state, the consciousness of all under Heaven, and the substantive spirit.

The *lunli* sentiments generated by the cultural path and social structure of integrating the family and state represent the ideal and sentiments of taking the state as one's family and building the state as one's home. At the origin of civilization history, the Chinese nation chose the path of integrating the family and state with the former coming before the latter. This was not only a historical inevitability, but also a cultural consciousness based on *lunli* norms. In the long process of civilization development, this path has been continuously advanced in two dimensions. One is the political and social mechanisms that integrate the family and state in the real world and the other is the spiritual world that embraces the integration of the family and state.

Family and state sentiments are the spiritual foundation and the spiritual temperament of national civilization. It takes the family as the *lunli* model and ideal type, pledging to construct the social structure between the state and the family-state as a *lunli* home. This integrates the family and the governance of the state. According to *The Great Learning*, "What is meant by 'In order rightly to govern the state, it is necessary first to regulate the family,' is this: It is not possible for one to teach others, while he cannot teach his own family. Therefore, the ruler, without going beyond his family, completes the lessons for the state. There is filial piety—therewith the sovereign should be served. There is fraternal submission—therewith elders and superiors should be served. There is kindness—therewith the multitude should be treated." Although the traditional concept of family and the modern sense of family, especially the core family since the one-child policy was implemented, are vastly different from each other, what is conveyed by the idea that "In order rightly to govern the state, it is necessary first to regulate the family" and the integration of the family and state is no longer just a strategy for governing the state, but a cultural concept and *lunli* ideal, representing the *lunli* ideal of the family contributing to the state and the *lunli* sentiment of taking the state as one's family.

The consciousness of all under Heaven is another structure of the family-state sentiments. The highest ideal of Chinese culture is not merely to regulate the family or to govern the state, but to bring peace to all under Heaven. In terms of *lunli* consciousness and *lunli* ideals, the family and state are both separate structures and interconnected, forming two homes for human life that are connected by *lunli*. They communicate with each other through the "stone of *lunli*." The family and state are not only homologous, but also must be "of the same body" in both spiritual and realistic aspects. This *lunli* concept has been expanded to form the concept of all under Heaven.

"All under Heaven" is not only the *taiji* of the *yin* of the family and the *yang* of the state and represents the same body of the family and country, but also the cultural existence and highest *lunli* entity that transcends family and country boundaries. "*Taiji* comes from *wuji*." In cultural consciousness, the all-under-Heaven concept is neither solely for the family nor solely for the state, but rather a system where the two are interconnected. It is more appropriate to say that all under Heaven is a cultural ideal and ethical sentiment rather than a real existence. It is an ultimate *lunli* substance that has transcendental significance, and a *lunli* existence.

Unlike the family and state, all under Heaven seems to lack a physical presence in the secular world, but it exists in the spiritual world of culture and its subjects, providing ultimate guidance for living. All under Heaven has boundaries but no limits, based on the real world of the family and state but transcending them, and it can constantly expand and extend to the entire world beyond one's own family and state, and even to the natural world. The concept of all under Heaven encourages people to go beyond the confines of the secular home of the family and state, and seek and construct a spiritual home in the whole universe and life. Therefore, the consciousness of all under Heaven or the sentiment of all under Heaven is the highest realm of the family and state sentiment.

The lines from Fang Zhongyan's "Yueyang Pavilion"—"When such men are high in the government or at court, their first concern is for the people; when they retire to distant streams and lakes, their first concern is for their sovereign." and from Du Fu's "My Cottage Unroofed by Autumn Gales"—"Could I get mansions covering ten thousand miles, I'd house all scholars poor and make them beam with smiles."—are often cited as typical expressions of family-state sentiments. In fact, the quotes from Zhang Zai's "Western Inscription"—"All men are my brethren, and all things my companions."—express family-state sentiments. Specifically, he meant to "ordain conscience for Heaven and Earth, to secure life and fortune for the people, to continue the lost teachings of past sages, and to establish peace for all future generations" (Zhang Zai's Discourses of Master Hengqu). From this, we can understand why Chinese intellectuals distinguish between the downfall of a state and that of all under Heaven, where the former is merely a change of dynasty and the transfer of power, while the latter refers to the loss of culture and *lunli*, the collapse of the ultimate home for individuals, and the destruction of civilization.

Therefore, family-state sentiments are essentially sentiments toward *lunli* substances, and their essence lies in taking the family as a model to seek, uphold, and construct a spiritual home that connects the family, state, and all under Heaven as a whole. They are an ideal because they transcend reality. Family-state sentiments revolve around the individual's devotion to their homeland as its essence and symbolize the inseparable unity between the individual and their shared essence, which is the spiritual homeland. They also embody the ideal aspirations and unwavering efforts to return to the spiritual homeland amidst adversity and challenges. Therefore, family-state sentiments are *lunli* sentiments. They are not only a homeland constructed by *lunli* but also a *lunli* homeland, encompassing a *lunli* spirit that transcends the family and state.

The Dragon Boat Festival, one of the four major traditional festivals in China, falls on the fifth day of the fifth month of the lunar calendar and has its origin in ancient totem worship. *The Book of Changes* says that on the fifth day of the fifth moon, "the dragon is on the wing in the sky," so there are customs of dragon worship on this day, such as dragon boat racing and lighting dragon lanterns, which are still popular today. The cultural connotation of the festival revolves around family-state sentiments and includes various legends such as the worship of Jie Zitui and the worship of Qu Yuan, with the latter having the greatest influence.

Qu Yuan was a statesman of the State of Chu during the Spring and Autumn Period, which made great contributions to the country. However, he was exiled due to the slanderous words of corrupt officials, and during his exile, he wrote immortal literary works such as "The Lament" and "Heavenly Questions," which had a profound impact. In 278 BC, when the Qin army captured the capital of Chu, Qu Yuan wrote his last work, "Embracing Sand," on the fifth day of the fifth moon, and then threw himself into the Miluo River for his country. The people of Chu were moved by his patriotism and fed fish and shrimps with rice wrapped in tree leaves to prevent them from eating Qu Yuan's body. This tradition continues to this day as the custom of making and eating rice dumplings during the Dragon Boat Festival in China.

The Dragon Boat Festival conveys and inherits family-state *lunli* sentiments from three dimensions. Firstly, the dragon is a common totem of the Chinese nation, and the Chinese people's belief that they are descendants of the dragon is the *lunli* identification of the Chinese nation, and the custom of dragon worship transcends the family and state. Secondly, Qu Yuan's death for his country spreads the themes of patriotism and family-state sentiments. Thirdly, the continued tradition of making rice dumplings during the festival represents the family-state sentiments of the entire nation.

The essence of family-state sentiments are the *lunli* sentiments and *lunli* spirit of constructing and returning to the substance, and they are also the *lunli* ideal and path to construct a home.

PART III

The Significance of the *Lunli* Discourse for the History of Civilization

Lunli is not just a discourse, but also a concept. Its significance for the history of civilization can be summarized in five points: it is a form of civilization—the discourse of the national civilization, which integrates the family and state with the former coming before the latter; it is a form of culture—the discourse of a *lunli* culture that is secular and transcends the world; it is a form of theory—the spiritual and philosophical form that integrates *lunli* and *daode*, prioritizing the former; it is a worldview—the *lunli* worldview that views the world from a *lunli* perspective; it is a national spirit—the spirit of the Chinese nation of making improvement and embracing things with virtue.

CHAPTER 10

The Ultimate Awakening

If we were to summarize the discourse on *lunli* in China and its traditional significance for the history of civilization in one point, it would be: Learn to reflect based on *lunli*. The essence of learning to reflect based on *lunli* is to learn to stay together.

In the early twentieth century, Chen Duxiu deeply reflected: "The awakening of *lunli* is the ultimate awakening of our ultimate awakening."[1]

In the 1940s, Russell predicted, "But we have reached a moment in human history in which, for the first time, the mere continued existence of the human race has come to depend upon the extent to which human beings can learn to be swayed by ethical considerations."[2]

In the same era, different peoples in different stages of civilization development made the same discovery—the *lunli* (ethical) discovery, and called for the same awakening—the awakening of *lunli* (ethics).

The two *lunli* (ethical) discoveries were made obviously in different historical contexts. The ultimate awakening of the ultimate awakening

---

[1] Chen Duxiu, "Our Ultimate Awakening," Ren Jianshu, Zhang Tongmo, and Wu Xinzhong (ed.), *The Collected Works of Chen Duxiu*, Shanghai: Shanghai People's Publishing House, 1993, vol. 1, p. 179.

[2] Bertrand Arthur William Russell, *Human Society in Ethics and Politics*, Chinese edition, Beijing: China Social Science Press, 1999, p. 159.

© Foreign Language Teaching and Research Publishing Co., Ltd 2024   139
H. Fan, Lunli *and Confucian Moral Theory*, Key Concepts
in Chinese Thought and Culture,
https://doi.org/10.1007/978-981-99-9105-1_10

aimed to awaken the Chinese people from thousands of years of *lunli* traditions, break through the *lunli* shackles, and achieve true and final cultural and social liberation. Russell's discovery is aimed at the unethical modern tradition of Western culture and the destructive disasters brought to the world by organized passions.

Both discoveries are *lunli* (ethical) enlightenments, but Russell's discovery elevated ethical awakening to a higher level of civilization than Chen Duxiu's discovery: it is no longer the awakening of us, a single nation, but the awakening of the entire human race that concerns its continued existence. The two *lunli* enlightenments have different historical connotations: the former is *lunli* liberation, while the latter is ethical construction. The former points to the tradition of Chinese civilization, while the latter points to the modernity of Western civilization. However, whether it is criticism of tradition or reflection on modernity, the ultimate awakening focuses on the same theme: *lunli* (ethics).

Different historical circumstances and their paths of enlightenment shaped the cultural code of *lunli* (ethical) awakening in the twentieth century. As some scholars have pointed out, Western and Chinese societies experienced two completely different enlightenment paths of transformation from tradition to modernity. "Enlightenment had two forms: one is the form of 'liberation through retrogression'; the other is the form of anti-tradition."[3] Liberation through retrogression is the path of the West, and return to ancient Greece is the theme and slogan that ran through the Renaissance and modern and post-modern Western Enlightenment. Anti-tradition for enlightenment is the path of China. Traditional Chinese society, from Confucius to Song-Ming neo-Confucianism, had a tendency to look back, idealizing traditional society. Dai Zhen criticized neo-Confucianism from within for killing people with heavenly principles. The slogan "Down with Confucius" was used during the May 4th Movement. Anti-tradition for enlightenment has been the consistent cultural character of modern and contemporary China. This path of enlightenment is so thorough that "it can be said that there is no other nation in the world that has thoroughly criticized, dismantled, and repeatedly cleansed its traditional culture like us.[4]

---

[3] The Research Bureau of the Chinese Academy of Social Sciences (ed.), *The May 4th Movement and the Construction of Chinese Culture*, Beijing: Social Sciences Academic Press, p. 464.

[4] Ibid., p. 549.

The May 4th Movement marked the beginning of modern Chinese history and in Western discourse, it also heralded the arrival of the adolescent stage of historical development. According to psychological theories, the reason why adolescence rebels in a resolute way to declare independence is not only because of the growth of individuals, but also because of the attachment of individuals to the mother body that gave birth to them. Because the mother body is too powerful for the individual, the ultimate fate is always a return during the period of mature life. In the 1980s, Liang Shuming, during an interview with the renowned American sinologist Guy Salvatore Alitt, posed a famous question that engraved the concerns of family genes and culture, which already foreshadowed this return: *Will the World Be Better?*[5] The English title of this book is translated as *Has Man a Future?* The book extends the cultural concerns from China to all of humanity through reflection on tradition.

In comparison, the historical background of Russell's awakening was the two World Wars in the first half of the twentieth century. He discovered that not only Western civilization, but also the entire civilization, was being destroyed by organized passions. World wars, ecological crises, and all the consequences are caused by the organized passions of nations and peoples. In this context, "the mere continued existence of the human race has come to depend upon the extent to which human beings can learn to be swayed by ethical considerations."

Why does *lunli* awakening become the ultimate awakening of civilization? The ultimate concern of civilization is the loss of morality, which is almost like the beasts. The path to address the loss of morality concern is to teach the relations of humanity. Humanity has a path—educate in human relations. *Lunli* education is the ultimate salvation for the loss of morality, so *lunli* awakening has ultimate significance.

In fact, the ultimate concern for the loss of morality has always existed profoundly in the history of civilization, but different eras have different problematics.

In the early nineteenth century, Goethe already warned the world, "Mankind will become cleverer and more perspicacious, but not better nor happier nor more energetic. I foresee the day when God will no

---

[5] It is recorded that Liang Shuming's father, Liang Ji, asked Liang Shuming before he committed suicide on November 10, 1918, "Will the world be better?".

longer take delight in his creatures, and will once again have to annihilate the world and make a fresh start."[6]

In the 1930s, Karl Jaspers said about the world crisis, "Even those who lack clear knowledge of the subject are becoming decisively aware that they are living in an epoch when the world is undergoing a change so vast as to be hardly comparable to any of the great changes of past millenniums. The mental situation of our day is pregnant with immense dangers and immense possibilities; and it is one which, if we are inadequate to the tasks which await us, will herald the failure of mankind."[7]

A century later today, as civilization once again experiences "a vast change," what kind of "immense dangers" does it face, and how can we discern the "immense possibilities" in the spiritual condition of our times to avoid the failure of humankind?

Contemporary French scholar Alain Touraine has revealed the immense danger facing the human world in his book titled *Can We Live Together?* The question and theme focus on its subtitle: *Equality and Difference*.[8] Confronting the era of globalization where "everything merges into one; space and time have been compressed," Touraine has discovered that the contemporary world is undergoing a profound change "from politics to ethics." He said, "The era of political passion is over. The period to come will be dominated by ethical passions." He argued that behind this is "an upheaval in experience and collective action."[9]

Humanity is entering an era of ethical passions, which will guide people toward collective action or coexistence. This discovery about the ethical passions at the beginning of the twenty-first century by Alain echoes the discovery by Russell half a century ago that humanity has not yet learned to be dominated by reflection based on *lunli*.[10]

---

[6] Karl Jaspers, *Man in the Modern Age*, Chinese version by Wang Defeng, Shanghai: Shanghai Translation Publishing House, 1997, p. 9.

[7] Ibid., p. 19.

[8] Alain Touraine, *Can We Live Together?*, Chinese version by Di Yuming and Lin Ping'ou, Beijing: The Commercial Press, 2003, p. 3.

[9] Ibid., p. 409.

[10] According to Bertrand Russell, the modern world is experiencing a "conflict of passions," and organized passions and their conflicts are destroying the world, bringing the loss of happiness. To put this to an end, it is necessary to dredge the channel from ethics to politics. Russell predicted that, "But we have reached a moment in human history in which, for the first time, the mere continued existence of the human race has

However, the fact of the world of life is that the ethical spirit has come late, and humanity has not learned to be swayed by ethical considerations as Russell had hoped. As a result, not only collective action but also coexistence has become increasingly difficult, and the COVID-19 epidemic in 2019 has once again pushed *lunli* awareness to the ultimate awareness of the "continued existence of the human race," bringing enormous danger to the entire century.

A Western short video with COVID as its master declares, "I was not born to punish you... but to awaken you." Awaken what? Awaken the *lunli* awareness of the world to learn to reflect based on *lunli*.

The COVID crisis has brought the world to the final moment of the continued existence of the human race. Goethe's prophecy "Destroy this world and let everything start anew" and Jaspers' warning of "immense dangers" have now arrived in this world with the COVID virus as its messenger. Faced with the threat of the virus to the entire human world, humanity has once again aroused the terrible and abominable "organized passions" warned by Russell.

To respond to the crisis of the continued existence of the human race, humanity has no choice but to learn to reflect ethically, as Russell advised, and to complete the ultimate awakening of the ultimate awakening advocated by Chen Duxiu. The essence of learning to think ethically is to learn to stay together, and the essence of "equality and difference" is the inherent wisdom of harmony and differentiation in the Chinese concept of *lunli*.

Given the unprecedented "immense dangers" to civilization, "learning to reflect ethically" has once again been endowed with the ultimate significance that concerns the continued existence of the human race.

What can China's discourse on *lunli* and its *lunli* traditions contribute to learning to reflect based on *lunli*? What significance does it hold for the history of civilization? In summary, it contributes a form of civilization, culture, and theory, and a *lunli* worldview.

---

come to depend upon the extent to which human beings can learn to be swayed by ethical considerations." Bertrand Russell, *Human Society in Ethics and Politics*, Chinese version by Xiao Wei, Beijing: China Social Sciences Press, 1992, p. 157.

CHAPTER 11

A Form of Civilization and Culture

The *lunli* discourse and *lunli* traditions are symbolic signs of a form of civilization, namely the national form of civilization. The *lunli* discourse is indicative of a culture, namely a *lunli* culture. The *lunli* discourse and *lunli* traditions are the spiritual genes and cultural imprints of the Chinese nation. They deduce, express, and construct a form of civilization and culture. The concepts of a country of rites and *lunli* culture express the civilization and culture they created.

1 THE *LUNLI* DEDUCTION IN NATIONAL CIVILIZATION

Whether in history or in modern times, the national civilization that integrates the family and state with the former coming before the latter, is undoubtedly a unique form of civilization. From the root of the first and most important transformation of civilization in the human history of the transition from primitive to civilized society, the Chinese nation has opened up a special path of civilization, and has been steadily advancing for more than five thousand years, creating the only uninterrupted form of civilization and cultural tradition in human history.

In the world civilization system, *guojia* is not just a habitual discourse, but a distinct form of civilization that is fundamentally different from the civilizations represented by countries and states. The diversity of civilizations and cultures must first acknowledge the diversity of national

© Foreign Language Teaching and Research Publishing Co., Ltd 2024   145
H. Fan, Lunli *and Confucian Moral Theory*, Key Concepts
in Chinese Thought and Culture,
https://doi.org/10.1007/978-981-99-9105-1_11

civilization in contrast to the civilizations represented by countries and states. Acknowledging the differences between these forms of civilization is a sign of respect and affirmation of human history, as well as mutual recognition and mutual respect among different forms of civilization, and, of course, the self-identification and cultural self-awareness of the Chinese nation.

A question that needs further exploration is what kind of interaction exists between *lunli* and national civilizations and *lunli* culture, and what kind of rationality the interaction possesses in the modern system of civilization.

The essence of the state and the state-family civilization is not only the integration of the family and state, but more importantly, the family contributes to the state. As a chromosome that constitutes the civilization organism, the family has a foundational position in the state. Indeed, the family holds an important position in any civilization system, rooted in the civilization gene that has evolved from the long history of primitive tribal societies. Even this is the similar feature humans share with certain primates such as gorillas. It can be said that the focus on the family is the most basic universal *lunli* of civilization so far. Scholars from both the East and the West acknowledge that the family is a natural *lunli* (ethical) substance and an important source of *lunli* (ethics). However, there is no tradition like in China where the family consistently holds such an important *lunli* position in the entire civilization system.

As this is a form of civilization in which the family contributes to the state, there has been a longstanding misinterpretation that Chinese culture is family-centric. This view has been refuted by Liang Shuming. He believes that family centrism is a characteristic of clan societies, and that any culture values the family, but Chinese culture is centered on *lunli* rather than the family. Why is national civilization *lunli*-centric? It has strong *lunli* demands. In addition, it has abundant *lunli* supply. How can the family and state be integrated as one? What are the cultural conditions and rules for the integration? How can the family contribute to the state? The resolution of these fundamental questions relies on *lunli* and also shapes *lunli*.

Theoretical arguments may be too abstract, but a review of history can provide interpretation. In the history of Chinese civilization, why did Confucianism become the mainstream and orthodox tradition? Why has the Confucian tradition symbolized by Confucius experienced challenges but never been overthrown during China's modern and contemporary transformations? The fundamental reason is that Confucianism has constructed and continuously developed a theoretical and spiritual system centered on *lunli* and *daode* that matches the integration of the family and state, with the former coming before the latter. Confucius' doctrine that "there is government, when the prince is prince, and the minister is minister; when the father is father, and the son is son" is not only a set of principles of rectifying names, but also a personalized *lunli* symbol of the integration of the family and state with the former coming before the latter in terms of discourse style and cultural rules.

During the Axial Age of the Spring and Autumn and Warring States Period in China, among the Hundred Schools of Thought, the most influential were Confucianism, Daoism, Mohism, and Legalism. Among them, Confucianism was neither the most knowledgeable nor the most powerful. Daoism was the most knowledgeable, and Laozi was already the curator of a Western Zhou library when Confucius was tending to his cattle. Confucius, by asking Laozi about matters of etiquette, actually established a teacher-student relationship between them. Legalism was the most powerful, and it was Legalist theory that unified China under the rule of Emperor Qin Shi Huang. Even among the common people, Confucianism was not the most influential, as Mohist thought had once been on par with Confucianism. The reason for establishing their positions was not whether they valued *lunli* and *daode*, but the cultural rules of civilization construction.

If we consider the path of civilization that integrates the family with the state with the former coming before the latter as a fundamental topic, the focus of Legalism is on the state with the state and politics coming before the family and *lunli*, respectively. The focus of Confucianism is on the family, putting the family before the state and stressing the need to be affectionate to parents and lovingly disposed to people generally. The principles of *The Great Learning* that highlight the unity of the self, family, state, and all under Heaven express the *lunli* values of the path of civilization that puts the family before the state. Mohism, is based on society that comes between the family and state, advocating universal love without distinction, and challenging the Confucian concept of benevolence based on familial love. Daoism, rooted in the *Daodejing*, is identified with *daode* in its theory, but its core is a metaphysical doctrine that the laws of nature are also those of humanity or that wisdom should be illuminated to preserve one's life.

As a result, a special historical phenomenon emerged in which Mohism initially split from Confucianism during the Spring and Autumn Period, but then merged with Confucianism during the late Warring States Period. Confucianism suffered a great setback during the late Warring States Period, when the Legalist representative, Emperor Qin Shi Huang, burned books and buried Confucian scholars. But strangely, Emperor Wu of Han abolished the hundred schools of thought and solely honored Confucianism, thus establishing the mainstream position of Confucianism in China, which lasted for over two thousand years.

The fact is simple: Emperor Qin Shi Huang achieved political and economic unification through military means, but when Legalism was used to achieve ideological and cultural unification, his dynasty came to a tragic end during the reign of its second emperor. Although Legalism is highly efficient in governing a country, it does not align with the path of civilization that integrates the family and state with the former coming before the latter. It was Emperor Wu of Han's sole honoring of Confucianism that truly achieved ideological and cultural unification, because Confucianism provided the *lunli* and political theories that integrate the family and state with the former coming before the latter. Later rulers understood this secret and always adopted the strategy of combining Legalism with Confucianism for governance.

In the subsequent process of civilization, Confucianism was challenged many times, such as the challenge from Daoism during the Wei and Jin dynasties resulting in the emergence of Wei-Jin metaphysics, the challenge from Buddhism during the Sui and Tang dynasties resulting in the formation of Sui-Tang Buddhism, and even a period of tripartite competition among Confucianism, Daoism, and Buddhism. However, the ultimate form of Chinese traditional culture is the integration of Confucianism, Daoism, and Buddhism, with Confucianism as the mainstream orthodox belief, known as Song-Ming neo-Confucianism. The phenomenological reduction of history shows that the state-family civilization that integrates the family and state with the former coming before the latter valued *lunli* and created and tenaciously continued the Chinese tradition of *lunli* culture.

Regardless of tradition or modernity, the challenges faced by national civilization always revolve around the relationship between the family and state, both logically and historically. People always affirm the family-state sentiment that arises from this relationship, as well as the enormous *lunli* energy it generates, but they also are deeply worried about and intensely criticize the various civilization problems derived from *lunli* culture that focuses on the family and ranges from the traditional society's hierarchical system to the modern society's wealth disparity and corruption among officials. In fact, from country, state to *guojia*, the challenge of the intrinsic relationship between the family and state exists in any form of civilization, with the difference being in the focus of values and cultural choices when dealing with such relationship.

2   THE CHARACTER AND LAW OF *LUNLI* CULTURE

Lunli culture is the cultural temperament and character of national civilization. China is known as a state of etiquette, presenting the temperament and character of this *lunli* culture. *Lunli* culture does not mean that it is a culture that values *lunli*, as any culture values *lunli*. However, its degree of emphasis on *lunli* is different, and *lunli* has a different position in its cultural and civilizational systems. *Lunli* culture is a culture that places *lunli* as its foundation, according to Liang Shuming. It is a culture that places secular *lunli* as its ultimate concern and is a secular, transcendent and non-religious culture with the family as the sacred *lunli* source.

Lunli culture is a cultural type and character of national civilization, and it is also the cultural law of national civilization. Its cultural character is a state of etiquette; its cultural temperament is social and transcendent; its cultural style is *lunli* but not religious; and its cultural law is to integrate the family and state with the former coming before the latter. This is not only the cultural law of traditional society but also the cultural law of Chinese civilization in modern times.

In his *The Phenomenology of Spirit*, Hegel raised the issue of ethical justice in the relationship between the family and state or peoples, which is the basic problem in the ethical world. The conflict between the two major ethical forces of the family and peoples ultimately leads to the deconstruction of the ethical world. The phenomenological picture of the problem of ethical justice between the family and the state presented by Hegel is that the ethical laws of the state or peoples suppress those of the family and vow to eliminate them, while the ethical laws of the family launch a resistance. The result of the suppression of one law by another is that, "The achievement of public spirit is thereby transformed into its opposite, and the public spirit experiences that its supreme right is supreme wrong and that its victory is to an even greater degree its own downfall"[1] Clearly, this is the phenomenological picture of the history of Western civilization. The civilizational path that separates the family and state in Western society is characterized by the kind of tense conflict caused by the suppression of the ethical forces of the family by the ethical forces of the state, and the path that separates the family and state does not so much resolve the conflict between the two ethical substances as it avoids or evades it in the design of civilization.

The relationship between the family and peoples and between it and the state is not only a question of *lunli* justice in the civilizational system, but also a cultural law of civilizational development, and a fundamental cultural issue in the Chinese civilization that integrates the family and state. The solution of this issue is closely related to the progress of civilization. The 70-year history of the development of the People's Republic of China, including the history of *lunli* and *daode* development, has made a historical and philosophical interpretation of it.

In the nation-building process of the Communist Party of China before 1949, the land reform in the early Agrarian Revolutionary War (1927–1937) and the War of Liberation (1945–1949) was not only about land to the tillers but also about the return of land to the family and the extensive construction of the natural *lunli* substance status of the family in material terms. During the Chinese People's War of Resistance against Japanese Aggression (1931–1945), the great mobilizing force was the feeling of the family and state as sung in songs such as "My Home Is on the Songhua River in the Northeast" and "The Yellow River Cantata."[2] The mobilizing slogan of the War to Resist US aggression and aid Korea (1950–1953) in the early years of the People's Republic of China when

---

[1] G. W. E. Hegel, Phänomenologie des Geistes: *The Phenomenology of Spirit*, Chinese version by He Lin and Wang Jiuxing, Beijing: The Commercial Press, 1996, vol. II, p. 30.

[2] These are two of the most inspiring and mobilizing songs of China's War of Resistance against Japanese Aggression, both of which symbolize the country and family with rivers. "My Home Is on the Songhua River in the Northeast" expresses the ambition of the northeastern anti-Japanese people to fight, recover their home and defend their homeland which was occupied by the Japanese invading army, with the following opening lines: "My home is on the Songhua River in the Northeast... There are my fellow countrymen and my old parents." "The Yellow River Cantata" is a song that mobilized the people of China to resist Japanese aggression after the Japanese occupation of northeast China in 1932, the theme of which is the lyrics "Defend our hometown, defend the Yellow River, defend north China, defend all of China." Both songs link "home, hometown and country" together, with the emotional and cultural logic that defending the country means defending the hometown.

the country was still in need of reconstruction was Mao Zedong's famous call for "resisting US aggression and aiding Korea to defend our homes and our country."[3] Although the Chinese revolution was the most radical in history, respect and affinity for the family was the most important *lunli* factor in its success.

After the establishment of the system of public ownership following the founding of the People's Republic of China in 1949, a series of measures, from cooperatives to people's communes, tried to rebuild the relationship between the family and the state, the essence of which was the *lunli* concession of the family to the state, and the cultural nature of which was, as Hegel put it, to use the ethical power of the state to suppress that of the family. This situation reached its extreme during the Cultural Revolution, which not only worked to make people's communes notable for their size and collective nature, but in the spiritual world also broke down the private, promoted the public and completely undermined the *lunli* legitimacy of the family in the value system. This *lunli* utopia was inevitably met with fierce cultural resistance, resulting in inefficient production and long-term slow economic development.

The entry point and the focus of reform and opening up is the establishment of the household contract responsibility system with remuneration linked to output, whose civilizational core was the re-recognition of the *lunli* status of the family, and the focus was still on the family. By contracting out land to the family, reform and opening up established a new relationship of interests between the family and the state, reassigning *lunli* legitimacy to the family and to individual interests, thus unleashing the productive forces and achieving great success.

The history of 70 years of development of the People's Republic of China exemplifies a historical curve of the *lunli* relationship between the family and state, which not only shows that the relationship or the *lunli* justice between the family and state is the basic issue of Chinese civilization, but also exemplifies the *lunli* cultural law of Chinese civilization under the civilization path that puts the family before the state.

---

[3] The cultural logic behind this slogan that has generated great appeal and mobilization power is: Resisting US aggression and aiding Korea is defending China and defending China is defending one's home. In many military actions throughout Chinese history, the slogan of "defending our homes and our country" was put forward, and the cultural logic behind it is the integration of the family and state with the family coming before the state.

3   *LUNLI* AND CHINESE PEOPLE

Lunli is the *li* of humans, the *li* why humans are persons and why they stay together with others, with themselves, and with communities and the state in Chinese culture. Five thousand years of *lunli* traditions have not only created Chinese civilization and Chinese culture with *lunli* qualities and *lunli* temperament, but also created the *lunli* spirit of the Chinese people in a nation of etiquette. It can be said that one cannot understand Chinese culture, let alone Chinese people, without understanding China's *lunli* concepts and *lunli* traditions.

The formation of China's *lunli* traditions, through a dialectical process of development, has deeply imprinted ancient and modern Chinese people with a *lunli* spirit.

The pre-Qin (the Paleolithic period–221 BC) was a time of gestation and development of China's *lunli* spirit. Prior to 770 BC when the Spring and Autumn Period began, from ancient myths to the Xia, Shang, and Zhou dynasties, China's *lunli* spirit underwent a long period of gestation and growth. During the Spring and Autumn Period (770–476 BCE) of diverse schools of thought and philosophies, China's *lunli* spirit rapidly evolved from a single cell to a higher form, resulting in the emergence of the Hundred Schools of Thought. Among these schools, Confucianism, Daoism, Mohism, and Legalism had the greatest impact on Chinese culture and *lunli*. Confucianism and Daoism, in particular, had the most profound and far-reaching influence.

Confucius (551 BC–479 BC) and the Confucianism he founded later became the mainstream and authentic Chinese cultural traditions, establishing a spiritual and philosophical form that integrates *lunli* and *daode*, with *lunli* being the priority. The founder of Daoism was Laozi (c. 571 BC–date of death unknown). The classic of Confucianism is Confucius' *The Analects*, the main point of which is *lunli*; the classic of Daoism is Laozi's *Daodejing*, the main point of which is *daode*. Confucius and Laozi were contemporaries and produced their *The Analects* and *Daodejing* at the same time, indicating that *lunli* and *daode* in Chinese culture are twins, or a pair of cultural chromosomes in the spiritual life of the Chinese people, laying the foundation for the *lunli* cultural gene of Chinese culture and the Chinese spirit.

The *lunli* spirit of Confucianism is characterized by being engaged with society. Confucius' belief is to do what one knows is impossible. During a time of social and *lunli* disorder, he traveled to different states and persuaded their rulers with the aim of rebuilding a *lunli* order based on propriety. On the other hand, the *lunli* spirit of Daoism is characterized by the concept of withdrawal from society or reclusion. Laozi's belief is to beat peace with what cannot be done and his disappearance became a significant event in Chinese history of civilization because it embodied a philosophy of life that emphasized withdrawing from society and embracing a reclusive and *lunli* wisdom.

The period from the two Han dynasties to the Sui and Tang dynasties (202 BC–907 AD) was a period of abstract development or cultural choice of the Chinese *lunli* spirit. The pre-Qin Dynasty period provided various cultural possibilities for the development of the Chinese *lunli* spirit, i.e. the Spring and Autumn Hundred Schools of Thought. For more than a thousand years from the Han Dynasty to the Tang Dynasty, Chinese history was a long period of cultural experiments and cultural choices, during which explorations were made to determine which cultural theories and civilizational paths were more suitable for China. During the Han dynasties, China only venerated the Confucians and expelled all other philosophical schools, and established a great unification of thought and culture based on Confucian *lunli* and *daode*. During the Wei and Jin dynasties (220–420 AD), attempts were made to combine Confucianism with Daoism, resulting in the so-called Wei-Jin metaphysics. During the Sui and Tang dynasties (581–903 AD), Buddhism became popular, and attempts were made to supplement Confucianism with Buddhism, resulting in a three-pronged cultural domination by Confucianism, Daoism and Buddhism.

The Song and Ming dynasties (960–1644 AD) were a period of dialectical synthesis of the Chinese *lunli* spirit. Having gestated and developed in the pre-Qin Dynasty and been through the cultural selection in the Sui and Tang dynasties, the Chinese *lunli* spirit reached a dialectical synthesis in the Song and Ming dynasties, in which a pluralistic and dialectical structure of the trinity of Confucianism, Daoism and Buddhism was established, with Confucianism as the mainstay. This structure returned to classical Confucianism through the cultural dialogue and dialectical interaction among Confucianism, Daoism and Buddhism, forming neo-Confucianism. Thus, the traditional Chinese *lunli* spirit reached a dialectical synthesis and its mature form.

The Qing Dynasty (1636–1912) was a period of deconstruction of traditional Chinese *lunli* and its transformation into modern *lunli*. The Opium War in 1840 and the May 4th Movement in 1919 marked the beginning of modern and contemporary Chinese history, respectively. Starting from the May 4th Movement, China began a century-long critical reflection on traditional Chinese *lunli* in order to achieve what Chen Duxiu called "the ultimate enlightenment of our ultimate enlightenment."

With five thousand years of tradition, *lunli* culture is not just a tradition or a culture, but the spirit of Chinese people, summarized as the *lunli* spirit. It has not only influenced the daily and spiritual world of the Chinese people, but has also become their cultural gene and cultural code. The Chinese *lunli* tradition is structured with Confucianism, Daoism, and Buddhism as the three dimensions, with Confucianism as the mainstream and Daoism and Buddhism as supplements. In terms of *lunli* orientation, Confucianism is focused on specific life, aiming to achieve the *lunli* ideal in the real world and transcend oneself in the present world; Daoism advocates withdrawal from society or seclusion, providing wisdom for retreating from a secular life in society and its *lunli* relationships when one is not successful or when society is unreasonable; Buddhism emphasizes that all the four elements (earth, water, fire and air of which the world is made) are void, transcending the world and reaching the other shore.

This tradition, which has been refined through thousands of years of trials and tribulations, has become the *lunli* framework and cultural constitution of the Chinese people's spirit and life. Chinese people tend to embrace Confucianism when they are successful and ambitious; Daoism when facing setbacks, believing that "take a little step back, and you will find more space around you"; and Buddhism when feeling despair, believing that all the four elements are void. People tend to follow Confucianism in their youth, unknowingly adopt Daoist principles in middle age, and turn to Buddhism in their later years. This dynamic balance and complementarity ensures that they do not lose the foundation for their existence and livelihood in any circumstances. It is often said that the traditional Chinese economy is a self-sufficient natural economy. In fact, traditional Chinese culture is also a self-sufficient culture. The *lunli* spirit of China is a three-dimensional structure that integrates Confucianism, Taoism, and Buddhism, with Confucianism as the mainstream. It provides a highly elastic foundation for survival and development that is mutually beneficial and complementary.

As Nan Huaijin (1918–2012) once said, Confucianism is like a grain store in Chinese culture, indispensable to anyone at any time; Daoism is like a pharmacy, to be visited when one is sick; and Buddhism is like a department store, where one can always find something useful at any time. Traditional Chinese culture has a saying, "Respect Confucius when successful; read *Zhuangzi* when facing setbacks." This is the power of tradition and the charm of Chinese *lunli* culture.

In summary, the discourse of *lunli* and its tradition represent a form of civilization and culture. As a unique feature of the human world, they stand as a 5,000-year-old monument and cultural Great Wall in the forest of world civilizations. They undoubtedly has a status and significance in the history of world civilization and human civilization. In today's world, they also have a civilizational significance beyond themselves, which is to view the world through *lunli*, construct civilization with *lunli*, and stand among the nations of the world based on *lunli*. To put in a nutshell, it is necessary to strive for self-improvement and embrace virtues for the benefit of all.

CHAPTER 12

A Form of Theory

The *lunli* discourse and its tradition have created a unique form of ethical theory, which is the form of the Chinese theory of *lunli* that integrates *lunli* and *daode*, with the former as the priority.

1 THE *LUN-LI-DAO-DE* DISCOURSE AND THE SPIRITUAL AND PHILOSOPHICAL SYSTEM

Although the term "倫理學" (ethics) was introduced to China from Japan after the May 4th Movement, the naming of ethics has already declared the central position and discourse identification of *lunli* in this discipline. In modern times, ethics is often expressed as moral philosophy, moral science or moral theory in English-speaking countries, and as practical reason or the metaphysics of morals in the Kantian discourse. Although Hegel restored the discourse status of ethics and established a system of dialectical interaction between ethics and morals in his philosophical system, he did not call this discipline ethics. As Engels said, Hegel's ethics is his philosophy of law. This situation may be related to the substitution of moral for ethic during the Roman period. Not only has moral become a substitute concept for ethic in the English-speaking world, but even in theoretical systems, there is only morality and no concept of ethic, as Hegel criticized Kant.

© Foreign Language Teaching and Research Publishing Co., Ltd 2024   157
H. Fan, Lunli *and Confucian Moral Theory*, Key Concepts
in Chinese Thought and Culture,
https://doi.org/10.1007/978-981-99-9105-1_12

In modern China, ethics is still a comprehensive discourse in the disciplinary and theoretical systems. However, in the interpretation of concepts, ethics is often interpreted as the doctrine of studying moral issues, which is a serious misreading and misplacement. In a sense, it is the result of Western theories colonizing China. Ethics does not study ethics but instead focuses on morals, and even in ethics; there is no concept of ethics at all. *Lunli* in ethics is reduced to a discourse shell or even a discourse habit. It has to be said that this is a representation of the loss of tradition in the process of modernization or the alienation of meaning in cultural dialogue.

In traditional Chinese culture, the concepts of *lunli* and *daode* are interconnected in discourse and theory, but they are also strictly distinguished. Xu Shen's *Explanation of Script and Elucidation of Characters* in the Eastern Han Dynasty interprets *lun* as generation (*bei*) and also as way (*dao*): "*Lun* means *bei*…. It also means *dao*." In his note to *The Analects of Confucius*, Duan Yucai of the Qing Dynasty integrated the meaning of *lun, dao,* and *li*: "According to *The Analects of Confucius*, 'Their words corresponded with *lun*.' Bao Xian said in his note, '*Lun* means *dao* and *li*.' In rough terms, it means *dao*, and in refined terms, it means *li*. All the scholars who interpreted *lun* as *li* are not different from those who interpreted it as *dao*." In Chinese culture, *lun, li,* and *dao* can be used interchangeably, but there are also differences. According to *Guanzi*, "*Li* expresses morality through clear understanding of one's own duties and responsibilities." In the sense of expressing morality, *li* is similar in meaning to *lun*, but *dao* and *li* have different priorities in meaning.

There are roughly three theories of the relationship between *dao* and *li* in the interpretation of them. The theories of *li* having priority and *dao* having priority coexisted in the pre-Qin period. According to *Guanzi*, "*Li* is to distinguish between superiors and inferiors and regulate the duties of the sovereign and ministers; *dao* means to follow reason without error."

The separation of right and wrong and the distinction of reason is called *li*, and following *li* without losing it is called *dao*. This is the theory of *li* having priority. According to *Hanfeizi*, "*Dao* is the reason why all things are the way they are, and the sum total of all principles. *Li* is the order that constitutes all things. *Dao* is the basis for their existence. Therefore, it is said that *dao* is something that can bring order to all things." This is the theory of *dao* having priority.

The Confucian scholar Zhu Xi synthesized these two perspectives and used *dao* and *li* interchangeably, with the Five Cardinal Relationships as their specific content: "*Dao* is *li*. When speaking in terms of what people have in common, it is called *dao*; when speaking in terms of their different principles, it is called *li*. Its essence is not beyond the relationships between the sovereign and ministers, father and son, elder brother and younger, husband and wife, and friends. *Dao* and *li* are actually the same thing." *Dao* and *li* are interchangeable and collectively referred to as *daoli*, which is specifically the *lunli* of the Five Cardinal Relationships.

In fact, *lunli* and *daode* formed a spiritual and philosophical system, known as the *lun-li-dao-de* philosophical system, that advanced and developed in Chinese culture. *Lun* is the substance, the home; *li* is to distinguish between superiors and inferiors and regulate the duties of the sovereign and ministers, and means the law of the combination and division of *lun*. *Dao* is to follow *li* without deviation and means the norms and criteria required by *lunli*. "*De* means realization in one self," which is the attainment of *dao*. This is the establishment of the *daode* subject and also represents the return to *lun* or the *lunli* substance to achieve *lunli* virtuosity.

Lunli and *daode* in the Chinese discourse refer to the *lun-li-dao-de* concepts and discourse. *Lun-li-dao-de* are eventually integrated with the interests and realization in the everyday world to form the *lun-li-dao-de*-realization spiritual ecology and philosophical system, which construct the spiritual world of humans in the everyday world, endowing this world with rationality and legitimacy, and endowing the spiritual world with reality.

In this discourse and spiritual ecology, the central relationship is the relationship between *li* and *dao*. In everyday Chinese discourse, there are 道理 (*daoli*) and 知道 (*zhidao*). Chinese people often say "be reasonable" (stress *daoli*), and the term "*daoli*" already includes the structures of *dao* and *li*, placing them side by side, reflecting Zhu Xi's idea of commonality and differentiation of *dao* and *li* when he stated that, "*Dao* is *li*." However, the content of *dao* and *li* is *lun* or the prototype of the Five Cardinal Relationships created by Zhu and the *lunli* substances they created.

Chinese people often say "知道" (*zhidao*), meaning that the object and realm of knowledge are the so-called *dao*, rather than general affairs or the English term "knowledge." According to *The Book of Rites*, "The jade uncut will not form a vessel for use; and if men do not learn, they do not know *dao*." This illustrates that the fundamental purpose of learning is to know *dao*, not to acquire general knowledge. This is why there were schools for the children and adults respectively. However, the first half of the statement, "The jade uncut will not form a vessel for use," is not only a metaphor for the second half, but is directly linked to the meaning of the *li* in statement, "*Li* means to cut jade." "Form a vessel for use" in the statement, "The jade uncut will not form a vessel for use," means "understand *li*," i.e. the *li* of *lun*, which combine to become *lunli*. In the statement, "If men do not learn, they do not know *dao*," *dao* means *daode*.

In the discourse and spiritual ecology of *lun-li-dao-de*, *lun* and *de* are closely connected, with the former being the substance and the latter being the subject, the *daode* subject constructed by respecting *dao* and valuing *de*. The relationship between *lun* and *de* is that, "*De* consists rather in *lunli* virtuosity."

The philosophical essence of *lun-li-dao-de* is what Hegel referred to as the subject or substance. The individual is transformed from a natural individual existence to the universal existence of *lun* or the universal object of *lun* through the construction of *de*.

However, *lunli* and *daode*, or *lun-li-dao-de*, ultimately construct a spiritual world that needs to be restored to the everyday world in order to be realistic. Therefore, the structure of realization is to take *lun* as home and *li* as the intuitive knowledge and heavenly principle, respect *dao* and value *de* while handling the relationship between individuals and substances and between interests and *daode*. Of course, *lun* itself is already a real world. Both natural and human relations are objective existence. What matters is whether one can perceive and grasp their laws, i.e. *li*.

Thus, the *lun-li-dao-de* system and ecology is a dialectical movement that starts from the reality of *lun* and ultimately returns to the real world through the construction of the subject of *de*. This is what Hegel described the dialectical process of negation of negation during which the actual becomes rational. The connection between *de* and realization also conveys the Chinese cultural gene of the law of cause and effect for anything good or bad one does, which has been expressed from ancient mythology as the integration of *de* and realization or the unity of virtue and fortune. This shows that Chinese and Western philosophy are fundamentally compatible, but their discourses and systems are different, with Chinese culture being more concise and mature in the construction of the discourse and spiritual ecology due to its *lunli* nature.

China's *lun-li-dao-de* discourse is significantly different from the Western tradition of moral philosophy. While both have normative content for human behavior (in Chinese discourse, it is *dao*, while in the Western tradition, there are a form of theory of normative ethics), in Chinese tradition, *dao* or moral norms are based on the premise and origin of *lunli*, with Mengzi's Four Virtues matching the Five Cardinal Relationships, generally known as the Five Cardinal Relationships and Four Virtues; Dong Zhongshu's Three Principles matching the Five Constants, generally known as the Three Fundamental Bonds and Five Constant Virtues; and *lunli* being the worldly and sacred source of *daode*. In the Western tradition, either religion serves as the ultimate basis for moral norms, or there are longstanding debates on utilitarianism, and in modern times, there is discourse ethics of Jürgen Habermas, etc. The fundamental difference between the two traditions is over their *lunli* and ethics. In Chinese tradition, *dao* and *de* have *lun* and *li* as their premise, and it is the result of taking *lun* as home and *li* as the intuitive knowledge and heavenly principle. In the modern Western tradition, due to the complete absence of the concept of ethics, the ultimate reality is either sought from the other shore or reason is sought from this shore.

2   HOMELAND OF *LUNLI*

Lunli and *daode* are important components of civilization, and every cultural tradition has its own theories and systems regarding *lunli* and *daode*, but their cultural status and characteristics differ significantly. Liang Shuming once said in his book *Chinese and Western Philosophy and Culture* that there are three cultural orientations in the world's civilization: Western culture, which focuses on the relationship between humans and nature and has contributed science to humanity; Chinese culture, which focuses on the relationship between humans and has contributed *lunli* and *daode* to the world; and Indian culture, which focuses on the relationship between humans and their self and has contributed Buddhism to the human race. He believed that according to the general law of civilization development, the relationship between humans and nature should be explored first, followed by the relationship between humans, and the relationship between humans and their self. Chinese culture and Indian culture have taken their respective paths under the guidance of sages. In this sense, Chinese culture is not only a *lunli* culture, but also an early mature culture. "Chinese culture is the early maturity of human culture."[1]

Indeed, any culture in its development will inevitably pay attention to the relationship between humans and nature, between humans, and between humans and their self, but different cultural traditions do emphasize different things, making the world diverse. As Liang Shuming said, the difference between China and the West is not about advancement or backwardness, but about moving forward on different tracks. *Lunli* and *daode* and their theories are one of the most unique contributions of Chinese culture to civilization.

It is often said that China is a country of etiquette, but in fact, in line with this concept, China is also the home of *lunli*. The statement that China is the home of *lunli* does not only present a fact that *lunli* theories originated in China, but also means that *lunli* and *daode* are the core of traditional Chinese culture. *Lunli* and *daode* have been a consistent core of the 5,000-year Chinese cultural tradition, and it can even be said that they are the spiritual temperament of traditional Chinese philosophy and culture. Over the past 5,000 years, China has established the most comprehensive system of *lunli* and *daode* in the history of civilization, which has constantly transformed and developed in the course of civilization, providing a foundation for the survival of Chinese people, driving the values and spiritual motivation for the development of Chinese civilization, and contributing unique wisdom and cultural charm to world civilization.

Western scholars like Hegel often criticize China for not having philosophy, only *lunli* and *daode* teachings. Some Chinese scholars also criticize China using Western philosophical paradigms, claiming that China lacks philosophy. In fact, what China lacks is only philosophy in the traditional Western sense, but it has its own philosophy. Judging China's tradition using Western paradigms is not only unjust, but it may also be seen as Western-centric and cultural imperialism, displaying a shallow ignorance. From discourse to values, Chinese philosophy often centers around *lunli* and *daode*. For example, in terms of discourse, it does not have the concept analysis tradition pioneered by Socrates' elenctic method. From the *Daodejing* to *The Analects of Confucius*, what is displayed are

---

[1] Liang Shuming, *Essentials of Chinese Culture*, Beijing: Academia Press, 2000, pp. 42, 107.

lunli sentences rather than philosophical sentences. "*De* means realization." "Benevolence is the distinguishing characteristic of man." This does not define *de* and man, but rather interprets *lunli* and *daode* based on principles.

Ancient mythology is the origin of civilization, containing the genetic code of national culture and traditions, as it emerged in the late primitive society and early civilization. It carries remnants of the barbaric era and the beginning of civilized society, conveying a nation's authentic attitude toward the world. The biggest difference between Chinese mythology and Greek mythology is the former's emphasis on virtue over strength. In ancient Greek mythology, there is a world of gods, namely Mount Olympus, where the gods like Zeus, Athena, and Cupid do not have personality or even divinity, but they are the embodiment or personification of various forces, the cultural representation of forces. Zeus is the force of all forces, and Cupid represents the most important force that perpetuates the human world, the force that unites a man and a woman as one, hence being called the god of love, and the arrow of love that symbolizes this force is known as the Cupid's arrow.

Chinese mythology emphasizes virtue. From Pangu creating Heaven and Earth, Nüwa mending Heaven, to the most romantic story of Chang'e flying to the moon, all Chinese myths depict *lunli* rules and *daode* stories, with the theme of good and evil retribution being their eternal. After Chang'e flew to the moon, she transformed from a beautiful fairy into an ugly toad because she selfishly consumed the elixir of immortality that the Queen Mother of the West gave her and her husband Houyi, and as a result, she could only live in loneliness in the Guanghan Palace.[2] In this sense, Chinese mythology is a mature mythology. In the

---

[2] A version of the myth of "Chang'e flying to the moon" goes like this: After Pangu created Heaven and Earth, there were ten suns in the sky, which made it difficult for human beings to survive. The Queen Mother of the West ordered the God of Power, Houyi, to shoot down nine suns with her bow and arrows. When she conveyed this mission, she gave Houyi and her wife a bottle of medicine and instructed them to drink the medicine together after shooting down nine suns. During the long days when Houyi shot down the suns, Chang'e was lonely and could not bear it, so she swallowed the bottle of medicine alone, and then her body swung up and flew to Guanghan Palace in the moon. The Queen Mother of the West asked where Houyi was, Chang'e told her that he was still shooting suns. Just after the words were said, Chang'e's body collapsed straight down, transforming from a wonderful fairy into an ugly toad. The theme of this myth is that Chang'e finally suffered the consequences of good and evil retribution for her own selfish thoughts. So in Chinese culture, the mythical image in the moon is both

childhood of humanity, while ancient Greek mythology was immersed in the world of forces, Chinese mythology had already been depicting the relationship between people and the cause-and-effect of people's good and bad actions, thereby opening up the tradition of Chinese *lunli* culture and the process of *lunli* and *daode* construction.

There is no culture in the world that has shown consistent concern for *lunli* and *daode* for thousands of years from its birth to the present day and established a profound and extensive theoretical system of *lunli* and *daode* like Chinese culture. In this sense, we have every reason to say that the home of *lunli* is in China.

3   The Spiritual and Philosophical Form of the Integration of *Lunli* and *Daode*, with the Former Taking Precedence

The theoretical and spiritual form of Chinese *lunli* and *daode* is characterized by the integration of *lunli* and *daode*, with *lunli* taking precedence. It has three basic characteristics: firstly, unlike the Western form of ethics and morality, it is a spiritual ecology of dialectical interaction between *lunli* and *daode*, with *lunli* being of higher value, and in this sense, it can be said to be a *lunli* and spiritual form; secondly, it is ultimate substance without the need for religion, but it has a form of ultimate concern and is a social and transcendent form of theory; thirdly, it is not only a form of theory but also a form of history and practice. In history, it has not only created a profound theoretical system, but also nurtured a unique spiritual world and national spirit, deeply influencing and guiding the everyday world, thus being the form of theory of *lunli* and *daode* that has exerted the most influence over the spiritual and everyday world.

The cultural genes of Chinese *lunli* and *daode* were already conceived and authentically expressed in ancient myths. During the three dynasties of Xia, Shang, and Zhou, important elements of *lunli* and *daode* such as propriety, virtues, and filial piety were already proposed. During the Spring and Autumn Period, the genes of *lunli* spirit were fully developed, giving rise to various *lunli* schools of thought, among which

Chang'e and the toad, conveying the cultural message of the law of good and evil karma from a beautiful fairy to a toad.

Confucianism and Daoism had the most significant spiritual genetic significance.

In the pre-Qin period, Confucius, Mencius, and Xunzi were the representatives of Confucianism, and they promoted the three development periods of Confucianism. Confucius and his *The Analects* created the spiritual and philosophical paradigm of the integration of *lunli* and *daode*, with *lunli* taking precedence. A leading example is the farmer saying in *The Analects of Confucius*: "Yan Yuan asked about perfect virtue. Confucius said, 'To subdue one's self and return to propriety, is perfect virtue. If a man can for one day subdue himself and return to propriety, all under heaven will ascribe perfect virtue to him'." As the most important proposition in *The Analects*, the statement, "To subdue one's self and return to propriety, is perfect virtue," expresses the Confucian theory and system in a classical way.

In Confucianism, propriety is the concept of the *lunli* substance, and benevolence is the concept of the *daode* subject. This proposition seems to emphasize benevolence, but in fact, it expounds an important assertion that takes the *lunli* substance of propriety as the highest value to define and interpret the *daode* subject of benevolence. The ultimate goal of benevolence is to return to propriety, which means the construction and return of the *lunli* substance. The concept of subduing oneself is the dialectical interaction between the *lunli* substance of propriety and the *daode* subject of benevolence. In the Chinese discourse, to subdue oneself means to surpass oneself to transcend one's individuality and reach universality, and means the same thing as cultivating oneself and cultivating the person.

As a result, the statement, "To subdue one's self and return to propriety, is perfect virtue," fully expresses the three most important elements of Confucianism and the theoretical framework they construct: the *lunli* substance (propriety), *daode* subject (benevolence), and the interaction and harmony between the *lunli* substance and *daode* subject (subduing oneself),[3] thus establishing the spiritual and philosophical paradigm of the integration of *lunli* and *daode*, with *lunli* taking precedence.

---

[3] For the spiritual philosophical paradigm of Confucius' statement, "To subdue one's self and return to propriety, is perfect virtue," see Fan Hao, "The Spiritual Philosophical Interpretation of Confucius' *Lunli* and *Daode* Thought," *Social Sciences in China*, 2014, no. 8.

Mencius developed Confucius' doctrine of benevolence and established the Five Cardinal Relationships of *lunli* (between ruler and subject, father and son, husband and wife, older and younger brothers, and friends) and the Four Virtues (benevolence, righteousness, propriety, and wisdom) based on the ultimate concern and care that, "Men possess a moral nature … and are to be taught the relations of humanity." From then on, the Chinese *lunli* and *daode* tradition based on the Five Cardinal Relationships as the *lunli* model and the Four Virtues as the foundation of virtues was systematically constructed in theory. The Five Cardinal Relationships and the Four Virtues became the classical form of the Confucian system which integrates *lunli* and *daode*, with the former taking precedence. This serves as the foundation for what Tu Wei-ming called spiritual Confucianism, which later developed into the so-called doctrine of Confucius and Mencius.

Xunzi developed Confucius' thought on propriety and elevated the *lunli* substance of propriety to the trinity of heavenly principles, human sentiments, and national laws. This pushed the Confucian *lunli* and *daode* doctrine toward institutionalization to become Confucian norms. This also laid the foundation for what Tu Wei-ming called institutionalized Confucianism.

Daoism does not deny *lunli*, but it emphasizes *daode* more than *lunli*, believing that *daode* freedom is higher than *lunli* consensus. The most illustrative example of Daoist theory and its fate in Chinese culture is the famous fable about fishes keeping one another wet by their slime in *Zhuangzi*: "When the springs are dried up, the fishes collect together on the land. Than that they should moisten one another there by the damp about them, and keep one another wet by their slime, it would be better for them to forget one another in the rivers and lakes."

Zhuangzi designed a special *lunli* situation: "The spring dries up." His fable created a Chinese cultural idiom and value orientation that has been passed down for thousands of years: keep one another wet by their slime in order to stay alive.

If we interpret this from a spiritual and philosophical perspective, keeping one another wet by their slime in order to stay alive can be understood as safeguarding *lunli* in times of adversity, and forgetting one another in the rivers and lakes is the *daode* freedom to avoid the *lunli* substance. The premise of keeping one another wet by their slime is collecting together on the land. In ancient Chinese, collecting together means to stay together, make friends, or form relationships. Collecting together on the land is not only a passive objective result, but also a subjective choice; otherwise there would be no option of forgetting one another in the rivers and lakes. In this fable, Zhuangzi satirizes the *lunli* identification of keeping one another wet by their slime and advocates the *daode* freedom of forgetting one another in the rivers and lakes. However, the historical fact is that for thousands of years, Chinese culture and Chinese people have sought to keep one another wet by their slime in order to survive, and the admonition to one another in the rivers and lakes given by Zhuangzi has long been forgotten. The most tangible evidence of this is that keeping one another wet by their slime in order to survive has become one of the most representative idiomatic expressions in Chinese culture, while forgetting one another in the rivers and lakes may only serve as a side footnote when examining the origin of keeping one another wet by their slime in order to survive.

The fact that forgetting one another in the rivers and lakes has been forgotten, while keeping one another wet by their slime in order to survive has become emblematic of national spirit, reflects the logic and pattern of Chinese culture, which places *lunli* before *daode* and prioritizes *lunli* identification over *daode* freedom. This historical fact also vividly illustrates why, in the history of Chinese culture, Confucianism became the mainstream and orthodox tradition, while Daoism, which provided great wisdom, has failed to achieve mainstream status.

During the two Han dynasties, China achieved unification in thought and culture, and the classical form of the Five Cardinal Relationships and Four Virtues transformed into the official or political form of the Three Fundamental Bonds and Five Constant Virtues through the policy of only venerating the Confucians and expelling all other philosophical schools. The transformation from the Five Cardinal Relationships to the Three Fundamental Bonds is a relatively important *lunli* transformation, and the advancement from the Four Virtues to Five Constant Virtues is only the addition of the virtue of trust, which is designed to construct the belief and faith in benevolence, righteousness, propriety, and wisdom. As the Confucian scholars of the Song Dynasty said, "As distrust existed, the virtue of trust was added."

The transformation of the Five Cardinal Relationships into the Three Fundamental Bonds had its logic and historical inevitability. The Three Fundamental Bonds are the three most structural *lunli* relationships among the Five Cardinal Relationships, namely the relationship between ruler and subject, father and son, and husband and wife, which are the core of the Five Cardinal Relationship. In addition, the Three Fundamental Bonds make relative *lunli* absolute *lunli* in order to sublate the contingency in relative *lunli* and the possibility of *lunli* disruption in the mutual expectations of the kindness of the father, the filial piety of the son, and the love and respect between brothers. However, the Three Fundamental Bonds and Five Constant Virtues are a system that integrates *lunli* and *daode*, with the former taking precedence. The Three Fundamental Bonds come before the Five Constant Virtues.

Until the Song and Ming dynasties, this theoretical system had evolved into a philosophical form of heavenly principles and human desires through the dialectical interaction between Confucianism, Daoism, and Buddhism in their historical development. The Five Cardinal Relationships and the Three Fundamental Bonds became the heavenly principles, so did *lunli*. According to the *Writings of the Cheng Brothers*, "Propriety is *li*.... *Lun* is *li*. Human relations are heavenly principles." "Propriety is a heavenly principle."[4] As human relations and propriety are considered to be heavenly principles, the philosophical and spiritual system of traditional Chinese *lunli* and *daode* has achieved a dialectical synthesis and historical completion based on the return to the classical paradigm of Confucius' theory that "To subdue one's self and return to propriety, is perfect virtue."

Ranging from the theory "To subdue one's self and return to propriety, is perfect virtue" to the Five Cardinal Relationships and Four Virtues, the Three Fundamental Bonds and Five Constant Virtues, the heavenly principles and human desires; assuming the classical form, official form, and philosophical form; and undergoing thousands of years of historical evolution, Chinese culture has constructed and continued a theoretical and spiritual form that integrates *lunli* and *daode*, with the former taking precedence. This is the temperament, style, and character of Chinese *lunli* and *daode* development.

The *lunli* and *daode* theories in China do not advocate, as Aristotle did in his *The Nicomachean Ethics,* that intellectual rational virtue is superior to ethical virtue, nor do they have to, as Kant envisioned in his *Critique of Practical Reason,* to look up at the starry heavens; still less do they need to rely on the absolute spirit of religion, as constructed in Hegel's system. Humanity emerges from substances, and the ethical world

---

[4] Wang Yangming, *The Complete Works of Wang Yangming*, Shanghai: Shanghai Ancient Books Publishing House, 1992, p. 266.

of individuals and substances is the natural world of humanity and individuals. Ethics is home to humanity and humans. However, after ancient Greece, Western modern culture, fascinated by universal rules, constructs individual will and freedom, attempting to replace ethical identification with moral freedom. This rationality-based theoretical system must have a premise in the cultural tradition and discourse, which is the existence of God as the ultimate substance and ultimate concern.

Only with this can we understand why Kant's moral philosophy must rely on the divine existence and the immortality of the human soul as two presuppositions. He expelled God from natural science, but brought him back in moral philosophy in order to achieve the highest good when happiness is distributed in exact proportion to morality. However, even so, he could only express awe for "the moral law within me" by looking up at the starry heavens, because Kant could not find the sacred source of the categorical imperative in the everyday, secular world as in the Chinese *lunli* tradition, where the Kantian categorical imperative and its source lie in the so-called intuitive knowledge and intuitive ability of taking as home and *li* as the intuitive knowledge and heavenly principle. Hegel established a unified spiritual system of the ethical world, the world of cultural maturation, and the moral worldview, but even in the conscience as the moral subject, he could not find a way to reconcile the individual with the universal, or the secular with the heavenly, without relying on the absolute spirit of religion.

The *lunli* tradition of Chinese culture and the system of *lunli* and *daode* it constructs, which integrates *lunli* and *daode* with the former taking precedence, relocates the ultimate concern and sacred source from the heavenly realm to the secular world, and from the belief on the other shore to human relationships and reason, have contributed unique theoretical and spiritual forms to civilization and provided the Chinese people with a reliable spiritual foundation for their livelihoods.

CHAPTER 13

A *Lunli* Worldview

In Chinese culture, *lunli* is not just a concept, but also a philosophy. A philosophy is the reality of a concept; *lunli* is not only a theory, but also a tradition; it is not only a tradition, but also a social reality and social action of the entire nation. The cultural achievements generated by the discourse of *lunli* and its five-thousand-year tradition have formed a special worldview that belongs to the Chinese nation and Chinese culture: the *lunli* worldview.

The essence of the *lunli* worldview is to view the world through the lens of *lunli*; to take the *lunli* world as the cultural belief, cultural faith, and ultimate cultural ideal.

1 A *Lunli* Worldview

The discourse and tradition of *lunli* in China ultimately consist of four structural elements: the tradition of *lun*, the tradition of *li*, the tradition of taking *lun* as home and *li* as the intuitive knowledge and heavenly principle, and the tradition of the *lunli* world.

The tradition of *lun* is a belief in substance, whose essence is staying together. It believes that humanity comes from a substance and possesses the nature, needs, and capabilities of staying together. Returning to the substance is not only the destiny and but also the ideal of staying together. *Li* is the law based on *lun* and the intuitive knowledge of *lun*. Only by

© Foreign Language Teaching and Research Publishing Co., Ltd 2024   171
H. Fan, Lunli *and Confucian Moral Theory*, Key Concepts
in Chinese Thought and Culture,
https://doi.org/10.1007/978-981-99-9105-1_13

taking *lun* as home and *li* as the intuitive knowledge and heavenly principle can humans construct and realize the ideal of the *lunli* world. In Hegel's system, the ethical world is only the primordial state of human spirit and its externalization, but in the discourse and tradition of *lunli*, the *lunli* world is not only the true state of the life of individuals and the human race as a whole, but also the ultimate ideal. *Lunli* is possible, so is the *lunli* world, because it is the true state of the human race; the ultimate mission of *lunli* and *daode* is to express the true genes of human life and civilization, and construct and realize the ultimate ideal of the *lunli* world.

The basic belief of Chinese culture is that humans are integrated with Heaven, Earth, and all things. This cultural gene has been expressed in *The Book of History*: "Humans are the spirit of all things." The world of integration is a world of *lun* that combines unity and differentiation. The world in which humans are the spirit of all things is not constructed by the Western cultural belief that man is the measure of all things. It includes the *lunli* belief that humans are a part of all things, as well as the *lunli* concerns and awareness that "That whereby man differs from the lower animals is but small. The mass of people cast it away, while superior men preserve it" and that "men possess a moral nature; and if they are well fed, warmly clad, and comfortably lodged, without being taught at the same time, they become almost like the beasts." Thus, it nurtures a *lunli* attitude toward the world, rather than a scientific attitude. The essence of this *lunli* attitude is to view the world based on *lunli* and believe that the true state and ideal state of the world are *lunli* states, which are states of integration and encompass the cultural affinity of staying together and the *lunli* concerns and salvation that "men possess a moral nature and should be taught the relations of humanity."

The Four Books, which are considered the classics of Confucianism, systematically point to the path to a *lunli* world. In the interpretation of the classics, people often consider *The Four Books*, namely *The Analects of Confucius, Mencius, The Great Learning*, and *The Doctrine of the Mean*, as the four classic texts of Confucianism. However, they often overlook a question: why did Zhu Xi refer to them as *The Four Books* collectively? What is the inherent necessity for these four classic texts, which are originally not necessarily related, to become *The Four Books* as a whole?

Mencius was not a disciple of Confucius'. Mencius' position in cultural history was discovered more than a thousand years after his death by Han Yu, a scholar from the Tang Dynasty, which led to the concept of the doctrines of of Confucius and Mencius. "The Great Learning" and "The Doctrine of the Mean" are two parts in the classic text *The Book of Rites* from the Qin and Han dynasties. These two essays are short and the authorship is still debated to this day, but why have they achieved a cultural status on par with *The Analects of Confucius* and *Mencius* in cultural history?

From the perspective of systematic significance, *The Analects of Confucius* laid the foundation of Confucianism, creating the *lunli* substance of propriety, the subject of benevolence, and the theoretical paradigm and historical path of achieving the ideal of the *lunli* world that "To subdue one's self and return to propriety, is perfect virtue." Mencius developed Confucius' theory and constructed the Five Cardinal Relationships and Four Virtues, where the former represents *lunli* and the latter represents *daode*, forming the core of Confucian and Chinese tradition of *lunli* and *daode*. Thus, the classical or traditional concept of the doctrine of Confucius and Mencius was established.

The Great Learning summarizes Confucianism theoretically. Its principles, which consist of the three guidelines on illustrating illustrious virtue, renovating the people and resting in the highest excellence and the eight essential principles for studying things, acquiring knowledge, being sincere in thought, rectifying one's mind, cultivating oneself, regulating one's family well, governing the state properly, and bringing peace to all under Heaven, not only reveal the essence of Confucianism, but also construct the system of Confucianism.

In the three guidelines, resting in the highest excellence is the *daode* of illustrating illustrious virtue, and the *lunli* of renovating the people unifies the spiritual world and the everyday world. In the eight essential principles, the so-called all under Heaven represents the *lunli* world constructed by doing as one would be done by others, treating with the reverence due to age the elders in one's own family, so that the elders in the families of others shall be similarly treated and treating with the kindness due to youth the young in one's own family, so that the young in the families of others shall be similarly treated; bringing peace to all under Heaven means to realize the *lunli* world. By what can peace be brought to all under Heaven? By *lunli*. In this sense, what is constructed by the principles of *The Great Learning* or what great men study the learning of the great person constructed by *The Great Learning* is the *lunli* worldview that views the world based on *lunli* and takes *lunli* as the ultimate ideal.

The Doctrine of the Mean incorporates the doctrine of Confucius and Mencius and this *lunli* worldview into a metaphysical realm, and to a considerable extent, forms a metaphysical *lunli* worldview. This *lunli* worldview is expressed in classic form in Chapter 22 of *The Doctrine of the Mean*: "It is only he who is possessed of the most complete sincerity that can exist under Heaven, who can give its full development to his nature. Able to give its full development to his own nature, he can do the same to the nature of other men. Able to give its full development to the nature of other men, he can give their full development to the natures of animals and things. Able to give their full development to the natures of creatures and things, he can assist the transforming and nourishing powers of Heaven and Earth. Able to assist the transforming and nourishing powers of Heaven and Earth, he may with Heaven and Earth form a ternion." Thus, one's own nature, the nature of other men, the nature of things, and the nature of Heaven and Earth are interconnected, forming what is known as the metaphysical realm of harmony between humans and nature. Harmony is the most complete sincerity, which is the nature of the world, and the nature of humans.

Harmony between humans and nature is not only a *lunli* realm, but also a *lunli* world where humans are integrated or stay together with Heaven, Earth, and all things. This *lunli* realm and *lunli* world are still the ideals held by Chinese culture to this day, with their rationality and reality. Tu Wei-ming proposed the concept of spiritual humanism and innovatively developed the tradition of harmony between humans and nature, establishing a new worldview that integrates Heaven, Earth, humans, self, and communities, attempting to transcend anthropocentrism and secular humanism, and its essence can also be seen as a modern effort in constructing a *lunli* world.

Every cultural tradition provides a unique worldview and ultimate ideal. The ultimate ideal of Christianity is the Garden of Eden, that of Buddhism is the Ultimate Bliss, that of ancient Greek city-states is utopia, and that of the Chinese *lunli* tradition is the Great Union. Unlike the Garden of Eden and the Ultimate Bliss, the ideal of Great Union is on the other shore, but here and now; unlike Plato's utopia, Great Union is not only a kingdom of ideas, but also a kingdom of reality.

The ideal of the Great Union is described in *The Book of Rites* as follows: "When the Grand course was pursued, a public and common spirit ruled all under Heaven.... Thus men did not love their parents only, nor treat as children only their own sons." Obviously, this is a *lunli* character, as well as a *lunli* world. Public refers to the substance of *lunli*, and the statement that "a public and common spirit ruled all under" means the realization of the *lunli* substance. The path to its realization is not to treat with the reverence due to age the elders with the kindness due to youth the young only in one's own family. With what can the Great Union be realized? With the *lunli* of not treating with the reverence due to age the elders with the kindness due to youth the young only in one's own family. Why is the Great Union great? It is great because of the *lunli* that a public and common spirit rules all under Heaven, which means the *lunli* substance in which all under Heaven is the *lunli* substance shared and safeguarded by all people under Heaven.

Although the Great Union also has the nature of a utopia, like the implicit message in the traditional Chinese classic *Flowers in the Mirror*, it cannot be denied that the *lunli* path and character described and designed by it do exist in the real world, and as the ideal of Chinese people and Chinese culture, they continue to be respected and pursued. Marxism regards communism as the ultimate ideal, and there are similarities between communism and the ideal of the Great Union. The public ownership system under which the ideal "From each according to his abilities, to each according to his needs" is pursued and the ideal "a public and common spirit rules all under Heaven" can be mutually interpreted and transformed in terms of language and culture. Their biggest difference is that the former is a political ideal, while the latter is a cultural and *lunli* ideal. The Great Union is the cultural expression of the *lunli* worldview and its ultimate ideal. As Liang Shuming said, "The Chinese people have always held a worldview for all under Heaven, which has remained unchanged since ancient times and cannot be more public-oriented and rational. Speaking of national character, this is the Chinese national character."[1]

2   SPIRIT AND THE SPIRITUAL HOME

The *lunli* tradition has established a unique philosophical tradition, i.e. the spiritual tradition or spiritual and philosophical tradition which is different from the rationalism of the West. It has solved a problem of

---

[1] Liang Shuming, *Essentials of Chinese Culture*, Beijing: Academia Press, 2000, p. 330.

modern civilization—the spiritual home. The important core of the *lunli* worldview is that *lunli* is spirit and the spiritual home of the world. The spiritual nature of *lunli* and its significance as a spiritual home are condensed into a concept and philosophy: the *lunli* spirit. The essence of the *lunli* spirit is to affirm the spirit, safeguard the spiritual home, and construct the system of spiritual philosophy.

The discourse and tradition of *lunli* not only symbolize the physicality or public nature of humans but also point to and create a secular and sacred home. Taking *lun* as home and *li* as the intuitive knowledge and heavenly principle is to safeguard and return to the spiritual home. *Lun* is the home, *li* is the spirit, and taking *lun* as home and *li* as the intuitive knowledge and heavenly principle foreshadows the discourse and tradition of *lunli* in China, blazing the path of spirit that is distinctly different from Western rationalism.

When discussing ethics, Hegel once said, "Thus, there are always only two possible viewpoints in the ethical realm: either one starts from substantiality, or one proceeds atomistically and moves upward from the basis of individuality *[Einzelheit]*. This latter viewpoint excludes spirit, because it leads only to an aggregation, whereas spirit is not something individual *[nichts Einzelnes]* but the unity of the individual and the universal."[2] "The unity of the individual and the universal" of "starting from substantiality" and the "aggregation" of "proceeding atomistically" are the two views for examining ethics. These two views on ethics have become the curse of the Hegelian heritage without any other options because Hegel said that "there are always only two possible viewpoints in the ethical realm." "The unity of the individual and the universal" is spirit, and what is "aggregation"? Hegel did not say anything about it, but there is reason to believe that reason and rationalism in modern Western philosophy have this feature.

"Starting from substantiality" and "proceeding atomistically" are two types of ethical concepts and ethical methods. Ethical concepts refer to the concept of ethics, and ethical methods refer to ways of becoming ethical and building ethics. Spirit and reason represent two typical ethical concepts and ethical methods in both Chinese and Western cultures. *Lun* refers to substance and taking *lun* as home refers to staying true to *lun*

---

[2] G. W. E. Hegel, *Elements of the Philosophy of Right*, Chinese version by Fan Yang and Zhang Qitai, Beijing: The Commercial Press, 1996, p. 173.

in terms of the *lunli* attitude and value orientation, which is *lunli* identification; and it "starts from substantiality in terms of the *lunli* concepts and methods. The *li* derived from taking *lun* as home is the spirit of "the unity of the individual and the universal" reached by "starting from substantiality." Taking *lun* as home and *li* as the intuitive knowledge and heavenly principle is to affirm the spirit and return to the spiritual home.

In the Chinese discourse, the *li* derived from taking *lun* as home is called "intuitive knowledge." Why can intuitive knowledge be obtained without study? Because it is a natural reflection of taking *lun* and possessed without study and the exercise of thought. Wang Yangming called intuitive knowledge "natural," as he stated that, "When it perceives the parents it naturally knows what filial piety is; when it perceives the elder brother it naturally knows what respectfulness is."

Although intuitive knowledge can be possessed without the exercise of thought, there must be a *lunli* premise, which is called "perceive" such as "perceive the parents," "perceive the elder brother," and "perceive a child about to fall into a well." "Perceiving" is not just a *lunli* situation, but rather taking *lun* as home, i.e. embodying oneself in the *lunli* substances between the parents and the son and between brothers, where intuitive knowledge has the characteristic of "naturalness." How can intuitive knowledge be gained without external investigation? Perceiving *lun* produces intuitive knowledge which is knowledge acquired naturally by taking *lun* as home.

In daily life in China, individuals often say that they cannot help but do something. Why is that? It is because of *lun*. In *lun*, people's behavior is a natural thing that is not under their control. The difference between the conscious reason of Tu Wei-ming and the cognitive reason in the West is that the former does not require or allow for objectification. *Li* is embedded in *lun*, and intuitive knowledge is a natural understanding of the *li* of *lun* that is gained without external investigation. Any knowledge obtained from external investigation is no longer intuitive knowledge, but cognitive knowledge. This kind of intuitive knowledge is called "spirit."

Wang Yangming directly related intuitive knowledge to spirit. According to his *Instruction for Practical Life,* "With regard to intuitive knowledge, when reference is made to its wonderful use, it is called energy; when reference is made to its natural manifestations, it is called *qi*; when reference is made to its aggregated fulfillment, it is called essence."

"When reference is made to its aggregated fulfillment, it is called essence." What kind of essence is intuitive knowledge? It is the essence of the universal of *lun*. Hegel said that ethics is inherently universal and the universal. This universal is the common nature of human beings and is their home. Individuals are the individual, and to transcend themselves to elevate individuals to the individual, humans need spirit. This is why Hegel said that spirit was "the unity of the individual and the universal." This process has similarities with the return of individuals to ultimate substances such as God and Buddha in religious ethics, which requires the spirit as well. *Lun* is universal, and intuitive knowledge is the condensation of the universal of *lun* in individual consciousness. In the traditional Chinese discourse, any demon is an incarnation, implying "the unity of the individual and the universal." *Dao* refers to the universal, while the physical presence which houses *dao* refers to the individual. In *Journey to the West*, the various demons are all manifestations of the physical presence of *dao*, differing in their *lunli* nature revealed by their behavior.

"When reference is made to intuitive knowledge's wonderful use, it is called energy." What is intuitive knowledge's wonderful use? It is to transcend the individual to become the universal. This is what Wang Yangming meant by "cultivating one's filial piety, fraternal respectfulness, and commiseration," all of which are not just knowledge or *daode*, but are forms of knowing. Their true significance is to obtain the universality of *lun*, to enable the individual to achieve unity with the universal in *lun*, much like how the Christian ethics requires individuals to fulfill obligations to God in their return to the ultimate substance.

"When reference is made to intuitive knowledge's natural manifestations, it is called *qi*." In the Chinese discourse, *qi* refers to both life that is continuous and everlasting, such as the *qi* in *qixi* (breath) and *shengqi* (vitality), and universality, which is represented by *qihualiuxing* (transformation and popularity). *Fengqi* represents the customary language of *lunli* universality, which includes both *liuxing* (popularity) and the resulting widespread behavior patterns.

In conclusion, through the philosophical interpretation of Wang Yangming, intuitive knowledge is energy, *qi*, and essence, which amount to spirit.

Lunli is the intuitive knowledge that derives from taking *lun* as home and *li* as the intuitive knowledge and heavenly principle and is spirit. Therefore, the discourse and tradition of Chinese *lunli* possess a unique cultural temperament that differs from that of Western rationalistic ethics. *Lunli* is spirit, and it must have spirit. Thus, the concept and philosophical construction of *lunli* in China provide a spiritual home for humans, which is called *lun*. Taking *lun* as home is not only a recognition of *lunli* but also the safeguard of the spiritual home. The rationality and legality of human behavior and the sanctity of moral norms can be obtained within the secular taking of *lun* as home without the help of Kant's categorical imperative, the Hegelian absolute spirit, or the ultimate substances of religion such as God or Buddha. From this, a secular yet transcendent, internal yet transcendent *lunli* and spiritual system and tradition are constructed.

However, the fact intuitive knowledge is called spirit and the discourse of China's *lunli* constructed by the spiritual tradition have another important characteristic, which is the unity of knowledge and action.

Unity of knowledge and action is a traditional *lunli* principle in China. Mencius emphasized the importance of both intuitive knowledge and abilities, with the former being acquired without the exercise of thought and the latter being developed without study. These two are interconnected, and intuitive knowledge must be intuitive abilities. Wang Yangming explained the unity of knowledge and action as follows: "unity" refers to intuitive knowledge. Knowledge and action are not two separate processes, but two forms of expression of intuitive knowledge. He explicitly pointed out that the theory of the unity of knowledge and action was aimed at addressing the current problem of the separation of knowledge and action.[3] In his view, "There have never been people who know but do not act." When someone claims to have knowledge of filial piety or brotherly love, it is because they have already acted on these principles, rather than just speaking about them. Prior to Wang Yangming, Lu Jiuyuan had already developed Mencius' concept of intuitive knowledge into the idea of cultivating the heart-mind, stating in *The Complete Work of Lu Hsiang-shan* that, "Collect your spirit. Be your own master. "All things are already complete in oneself." Both conscience and intuitive knowledge are considered as spirit, indicating that spirit is a traditional Chinese *lunli* and Chinese *lunli* discourse.

---

[3] "The concept of the unity of knowledge and action have been proposed to address the issue of modern scholars regarding knowledge and action as two independent matters. These scholars believe that knowledge must be acquired before taking action, which results in a lifetime of inaction. Therefore, the unity of knowledge and action is seen as a corrective measure. These scholars are unable to put their knowledge into practice and are caught up in verbal disputes, becoming further and further removed from the truth." Wang Yangming, "Five Reply Letters to Zhou Chong," *Philosophy in China*, Beijing: SDX Joint Publishing Company, 1979, no. 1.

With the concept of unity of knowledge and action as the nature of its spirit, Wang Yangming's philosophy has similarities with Hegelian philosophy. In his *Elements of the Philosophy of Right*, Hegel stated that spirit is the unity of thought and will, and it is not the case that there are two separate pockets in spirit, one holding thought and the other holding will. Thought and will are simply two different attitudes that spirit takes toward the same thing: "The distinction between thought and will is simply that between theoretical and practical attitudes." Will is the kind of thought that manifests as an impulse to achieve a certain goal.[4] However, Hegel added that there is hypocrisy in conscience as a form of moral subjectivity, which involves only thought without action. Consequently, morality degenerates into an "ethical mood" and ultimately fades away as a "beautiful soul" with no trace left behind.

The problem of the separation between knowledge and action is a major issue in Western ethics, particularly in modern Western ethics *lunli*. Throughout the history of Western ethics, there have always been giants of knowledge alongside small-minded individuals of morality. For example, Rousseau's *Emile* is a classic in education, but his *Confessions* reveals his moral flaws. Bacon coined the slogan "knowledge is power," but his fate, as Wang Yangming pointed out, was to be "lost on a good horse," as his knowledge also led to various moral evils. The phenomenon of the rational fool and sophisticated egoism in contemporary Western society is also related to the separation between knowledge and action. The traditional Chinese *lunli* principle of unity of knowledge and action thus has important implications for modern civilization.

In summary, the discourse of *lunli* and its tradition have shaped the spiritual temperament of Chinese *lunli*, creating a spiritual form and tradition regarding *lunli* and *daode* development that differs from Western rationalism. In this sense, the form of Chinese *lunli* is the form of *lunli* spirituality, which is of great significance in the history of civilization for safeguarding the spiritual home and solving the frontier problem of losing home in the development of modern *lunli* and *daode*.

---

[4] G. W. E. Hegel, *Elements of the Philosophy of Right*, Chinese version by Fan Yang and Zhang Qitai, Beijing: The Commercial Press, 1996, p. 12.

3 *Lunli* Society and Civil Society

Whether in a form of civilization characterized by the integration of the family and state and a cultural form of *lunli*, or a *lunli* perspective and *lunli* way that take *lun* as home and *li* as the intuitive knowledge and heavenly principle, they all convey a Chinese gene of the *lunli* discourse and tradition: viewing the world based on *lunli*. They believe that the world is a *lunli* substance and will restore it to a *lunli* substance. Therefore, it is not only a discourse or a cultural tradition but also constructs and sustains a special worldview, namely, a *lunli* worldview. In contrast to the Western ethical tradition, this *lunli* worldview faces challenges and embodies increasing significance in the history of civilization while addressing responding to the challenges, and its frontier issues are the relationship between a *lunli* society and a civil society.

The spiritual temperament and cultural laws of a *lunli* society are closely related to three issues: the relationship between *lunli* and religion, the relationship between *lunli* and the family, and the organizational structure of society. The most fundamental criticisms of Chinese *lunli* and cultural traditions at home and abroad often focus on two aspects: religion abroad and the family at home.

Many foreign critics believe that China is a country lacking religious faith, and the lack of faith is terrible. This is actually a misreading or even ignorance of Chinese culture. If religion is a necessary structure in any culture and civilization, but a longstanding culture lacks this structure, it can only be said its tradition has its cultural alternative of the structure. Liang Shuming had long argued, "*Lunli* has the use of religion." In addition, as mentioned earlier, the temperament and style of Chinese culture are not without religion but have religion without being religious. The reason for not being religious is that there is *lunli*. *Lunli* and religion create two types of civilization and cultural temperament.

The British classical economist Alfred Marshall pointed out at the beginning of his *Principles of Economics* that the two great forming agencies of the world's history have been the religious and the economic. The former is the core of the everyday world, while the latter is the top-level design of the spiritual world.

However, this is only a law of Western civilization. For China's *lunli* culture, the expression of these two forces is the relationship between righteousness and gain. As the Song and Ming Confucian scholars Cheng

Hao and Cheng Yi put it, "All under Heaven is about nothing but righteousness and gain," which is the fundamental issue of Chinese culture. From Confucius' statement that "The mind of the superior man is conversant with righteousness; the mind of the mean man is conversant with gain" to Zhu Xi's theory that "Righteousness and profit are the foremost concern of Confucianism," this tradition has been passed down through the ages. The secular expression of gain is the same as what Marshall described as the economics, while righteousness is the core of *lunli*. *Lunli* and economics, and religion and economics, respectively constitute the two basic forces of Chinese and Western civilizations. *Lunli* and economics are also fundamental issues that reflect the spiritual temperament of China's *lunli* culture.

The family is the basic structure of Chinese *lunli* and the most distinctive cultural temperament of Chinese *lunli* in the world's civilization. The fundamental reason why China's tradition of *lunli* culture has formed and continued for five thousand years lies in the family's provision of secular and sacred *lunli* roots and ultimate *lunli* concerns. Indeed, in modern and contemporary China and especially since the implementation of the one-child policy during the reform and opening up period, significant and even fundamental changes have occurred in the structure, *lunli* status, and cultural function of the family in China. However, it is not difficult to see that in the interaction between ancient and modern China and between China and the West, the family, as a *lunli* substance, remains resilient and is transforming its form. Yunxiang Yan, a Chinese-American scholar, has found through extensive research that a neo-familyism is emerging in China.

The family's central position creates many challenges for the form of a civilization that integrates the family and the state, but this does not negate its cultural significance. One of the important strategies proposed by Daniel Bell in *The Cultural Contradictions of Capitalism* to overcome the contradictions of Western capitalist culture is to establish a public household or second household. The *lunli* and cultural forms rooted in the family as a secular and sacred source have nurtured the *lunli* worldview of viewing the world from a *lunli* perspective. The notions that people should be as close as family and that all under Heaven are one family and other *lunli* ideals or sentiments are cultural expressions of this *lunli* worldview.

The greatest challenge to the *lunli* worldview is the so-called civil society. Many people believe that the family's central position makes it difficult for China to develop a modern civil society and therefore to embark on the path of modernization. In fact, this is a typical manifestation of Western civilization-centrism or Western cultural colonization. Civil society is a theory proposed by Hegel in *Elements of the Philosophy of Right*. It is worth noting that it has two characteristics as a theoretical source.

Firstly, civil society is a speculative structure and serves as an intermediary between the natural *lunli* substance of the family and the *lunli* substance of the state. Therefore, there is a contradiction in Hegel's discussion of civil society, especially in the relationship between civil society and the state. He believes that, "Civil society is the [stage of] difference [*Differenz*] which intervenes between the family and the state, even if its full development [Ausbildung] occurs later than that of the state.... the creation of civil society belongs to the modern world."[5] Since civil society appeared later than the state and is created only in the modern world, why does it become a stage of difference between the family and the state in philosophy? Hegel did not explain this clearly, and current research on civil society lacks convincing discussions on this. If this problem cannot be truly resolved, civil society is only philosophical speculation, not a reality of civilization.

Secondly, as an intermediary between the family and the state, civil society is a *lunli* substance, but what it constructs is only a form of universality. According to Hegel's theory, civil society, as the system of needs, has two principles. One focuses on individuals and is "a mixture of natural necessity and arbitrariness," and the other is that each person asserts himself through universality and gains satisfaction through the others.[6] Therefore, civil society has a profound civilizational defect that it is the field of conflict in which the private interest of each individual comes up against that of everyone else. "Just as civil society is the field of conflict in which the private interest of each individual comes up against that of everyone else, so do we here encounter the conflict between private interests and particular concerns of the community, and between both of these together and the higher viewpoints and ordinances of the state."[7] As an ethical substance, civil society is only a form of universality, and

[5] Ibid., p. 197.

[6] Ibid.

[7] Ibid., p. 309.

its essence is "the field of conflict in which the private interest of each individual comes up against that of everyone else." Therefore, at least in the Hegelian theory, the reality and rationality of civil society should be questioned.

The concept and reality of the *lunli* worldview are not civil society, but *lunli* society. In his *Community and Society*, Ferdinand Tönnie distinguishes between community and society. Community refers to ethical substances such as families and villages, while society is a product constructed by rationality. Both community and society are broad societies, and the former is an ethical society, while the latter may refer specifically to civil society. People often criticize China for having only family and state but not society, and the so-called society is limited to the *lunli* circle of acquaintances, thus only having the *lunli* of an acquaintance society. In fact, this is also the result of excessive reference to Western civilization, especially the civil society theory.

Liang Shuming believed that a major feature of Chinese civilization is organizing society based on *lunli*, and a *lunli* society is a society of emotions and friendships, which originates and is nurtured in the family.[8] Liang Qichao once said that China only has members of ethnic groups but not members of civil society. The traditional culture of *lunli* looks at the world from a *lunli* perspective. The characteristic of an ethical society is that after the individual is torn away from the family as Hegel said, society is constructed as an ethical substance rather than the kind of society that is based on formal universality and an individualistic perspective.

Lunli society is different from civil society that is seen as "the field of conflict in which the private interest of each individual comes up against that of everyone else." It is a social and *lunli* substance with warmth. It does not have the huge gap between the family and society, and the transition from family members to members of society is not like what Hegel said: "Civil society tears the individual [individuum] away from family ties." Family members carry the *lunli* warmth and care of the family on their way to society, and in the continuous return to the family after entering society, they strengthen both the *lunli* status of the family and the cultural ability of family *lunli* to construct social *lunli*.

Many of China's major festivals revolve around the theme of family reunion, which is a reflection of the cultural design of *lunli* society. As

---

[8] Liang Shuming, *Essentials of Chinese Culture*, Beijing: Academia Press, 2000, p. 88.

mentioned earlier, important traditional Chinese festivals have *lunli* as their theme, with the philosophy of harmony between humans and nature as their foundation. The Qingming Festival is about honoring ancestors and respecting the past; the Dragon Boat Festival expresses family and national feelings; the Mid-Autumn Festival is about family reunions crossing time and space with loved ones; the Ghost Festival is about reunions between family members and ancestors and loved ones across time and space; and the Spring Festival is a nationwide reunion of family members across mountains and rivers.

Lunli society establishes *lunli* relationships between individuals and between them and society and constructs the *lunli* substance of society by considering others in one's own place. Treating with the reverence due to age the elders in your own family is not just a *daode* principle, or even not a moral principle, but a *lunli* principle and a way of constructing *lunli* and *lunli* substances. Specifically, it is a way of constructing social *lunli* with individual and family *lunli*, making it a *lunli* view and approach. It is the way of constructing *lunli* society that corresponds to Western civil society in the context of the *lunli* discourse and its traditional background, and it is also the model for constructing the *lunli* society in a civilization that integrates the family and state, with the former coming before the latter.

There are two existing realities that make society a *lunli* substance: wealth and state power. The universality of wealth and the public nature of power are the cultural conditions for society to exist as a *lunli* substance. As Hegel said, state power is a direct good because it must achieve the unity of individual and universal will; while wealth is a reverse good that can only be realized in consumption. However, the *lunli* nature of wealth is that selfishness is just an imaginary thing. The *lunli* nature of wealth encounters the paradox of the logic of the philosophy of right and economics. The logic of the philosophy of right is about equality, while that of economics is about efficiency, which creates the problem of unfair distribution. Chinese *lunli* culture provides special wisdom to address this issue.

The statement in *The Analects of Confucius*, "He is not concerned lest they should be few, but only lest what they have should be ill-apportioned; he is not concerned lest his people should be poor, but only lest they should be divided against one another," has been misinterpreted in regards to China's *lunli* culture. It is evident that Confucius' concept of apportionment refers to the philosophical or *lunli* logic of the distribution of wealth, while division is the embodiment of the *lunli* principle of giving rest to others. Choosing between "few" and "apportioned" and between "poverty" and "division" is a *lunli* choice made between two values and an expression of *lunli* culture. It cannot be simply interpreted as the so-called egalitarianism of economics. The statement, "He is not concerned lest they should be few, but only lest what they have should be ill-apportioned," is obviously a wealth value of *lunli* society. In today's world, unequal distribution and polarization have become a global problem. To overcome this civilization's problem, we must go beyond the one-dimensional logic of economics and use a *lunli* worldview and the ideas of a *lunli* society to avoid "the field of conflict in which the private interest of each individual comes up against that of everyone else."

Certainly, considering others in one's own place and transitioning from family *lunli* substances to social *lunli* substances is not only idealistic, even utopian, but the family's genes may also limit the *lunli* society constructed by it to the realm of considering others in one's own place or even carry the disease of blood relationship. The prevalence of nepotism in social life is a manifestation of its shortcomings. However, the charm of *lunli* ideals lies in the tough efforts described by Confucius in the statement, "In moments of haste, he cleaves to it. In seasons of danger, he cleaves to it." Any cultural gene expresses its powerful vitality while inevitably possessing some internal defects. In the historical process of traditional continuity, perhaps the most important thing for each generation is the cultural attitude toward it.

The world is a substance of *lunli*. *Lunli* spirit is possible, so is *lunli* society provided that there is a belief and faith: to see the world from a *lunli* perspective. Perhaps this is the significance of China's *lunli* discourse and its tradition for the history of civilization.

Epilogue

During the Mid-Autumn Festival of 2018, Mr. Xuejun Yan, a former classmate and good friend of mine, and Ms. LinWang, senior editor of Foreign Language Teaching and Research Press, came to visit me in Nanjing and asked me to write a book, to introduce the basic discourse of ethical studies in China to the Western world. Previously, I had usually followed my plan in research and never deviated from it. However, this time I decided to embrace the change and take the offer—Mr. Yan was my best friend in college, and decades of friendship have acquainted me with his lofty pursuit and acumen. Yet, I didn't start the project for a while, partly because of the heavy research workload involved, partly because I needed time to think it through before including it into my research plan.

The establishment of Chinese discourse had not yet been a national strategy at that time, but after a period of deliberation, I decided that it would benefit the dialogue and exchange between Chinese and Western civilizations to introduce the basic academic discourse embodying the Chinese cultural genes to the West. Since its reform and opening up launched decades ago, China has introduced a plethora of concepts and theories from the West, but on the whole the academic exchange has been not on an equal footing. Acquainting the West with China and contributing Chinese wisdom to the world should be made a historic undertaking, and the conditions are already ripe. The humanities and social sciences are different from the natural sciences in that their discourse theories, especially their basic concepts, have been deeply rooted

© Foreign Language Teaching and Research Publishing Co., Ltd 2024   187
H. Fan, Lunli *and Confucian Moral Theory*, Key Concepts
in Chinese Thought and Culture,
https://doi.org/10.1007/978-981-99-9105-1

in tradition, and have "grown" from the life of cultural subjects spanning millennia. In exchanges and dialogues, they follow the law of "transplantation" like human organs, and simple information conversion tends to incur academic risks, namely loss of meaning and alienation of value. The introduction of basic concepts in a comprehensible and readily acceptable manner to other cultures is actually a difficult academic topic.

Lunli and *daode* are the two fundamental concepts in Chinese ethics and even traditional Chinese culture and are the two most misunderstood discourses in academic dialogues between China and the West. In teachers' lectures to graduate theses, they are often deemed the equivalents of "ethics" and "morality," respectively, despite their much richer connotations. The ethics and morality of the Western culture featuring "withdrawal from secular affairs" do not carry the important civilization mission as the *Lunli* and *daode* of the Chinese culture advocating "engagement in secular affairs"; they also follow completely different cultural principles. After much thought, I decided to make *Lunli* the first Chinese discourse in ethics. Firstly, the Chinese culture is called an ethic-oriented culture rather than a moral culture just because ethics has a higher philosophical status than morality in the theoretical system and in historical development. Secondly, ethics has a greater academic dialectical significance than morality in the dialogue between Chinese and Western civilizations. Mr. Yuelin Jin once noted that the greatest enlightenment of human beings in the Axial Age was the proposal of some "noblest concepts," such as "logos" by the Greek, "God" by the Hebrews, "Buddha" by the Indians, and "Dao" by the Chinese. The discovery of the "noblest concepts" bespeaks Mr. Jin's keen insight. However, in Chinese culture the "noblest concepts" include not only the metaphysical ontological "Dao," but also the overarch ethical concept "Lun." Dao and *Lun* jointly constitute the yin and yang structure of the "noblest concepts" of the Chinese culture. Compared with Western culture, a prominent feature of the Chinese *lunli-daode* tradition and its spiritual and philosophical form is the integration of *lunli* and *daode*, with priority given to lunli, in contrast to the Western-style moralism. Therefore, China is not only a country of propriety and righteousness, but also the hometown of ethical studies. *Lunli* has become the most important discourse of Chinese ethics and the Chinese ethical and moral tradition. Of course, if this work is to be moved forward, *daode* should be the second most important basic discourse.

Eventually, the project saw a dramatic start. At the end of December 2019, I completed my tenure as Vice President of the Jiangsu Provincial Academy of Social Sciences and returned to Southeast University. In mid-January 2020, I paid an academic visit to Nanyang Technological University in Singapore. Less than a week after my arrival, the outbreak of the COVID-19 epidemic in Wuhan and the ensuing worldwide flight cutoff left me stranded in Singapore for eight months. At the international faculty residence of the National University of Singapore, I started my research and writing for this project. I studied during the day, and in the evening, I went to join my daughter, who teaches at the National University of Singapore. In her house, I sought spiritual peace beside the cradle of my newly born grandson. Outside the window, occasionally a car would drive by, down the originally hustling and bustling road, its lonely silhouette setting off the desolation of the world. Standing on the balcony and looking at the huge and harshly bright moon above, I no longer felt the awe of the starry sky overhead like Kant had felt. Instead, I was filled with fright, because the moon—so transparent, so round and so close—seemed to have blurred the boundary between day and night, or rather that between "the law of day" and "the law of night" in Hegel's term. It eroded the distance between the world of facts and the world of meaning, depriving everything of their shelter. A tiny virus cell has stalled the entire planet, almost bringing the world to a standstill. As a result, the ethical essence of the relationships between humans and nature, humans and each other, and humans and themselves has become seemingly simple and clear. The true ethical nature of civilization seems within reach. The *Lunli* resonating from the depths of China's five-thousand-year history appear to be faintly captured by Einstein's "big ears." Although I had to face an unprecedented fear of uncertainty, I had abundant time since I was free from temptations or distractions of the daily world in this abnormal world. Before I knew it, the originally planned manuscript of 50,000 characters expanded to one of 100,000 characters. With unease, I wrote to Ms. Wang Lin and told her about the excessive length, and Ms. Wang promptly replied that there would be no limit on length.

At the end of July, I returned to China, revised the manuscript in two weeks, and then submitted it to Ms. Wang. In the meantime, I serialized it in four theses, which were favorably accepted. When I came to Singapore again this summer, my grandson was already attending the kindergarten for the second year. The toddler who was carried to my bedside every morning to dry his butt could now take me through the winding paths of the residential compound, and volunteer to interpret for me and his playmates from other countries. As this angel has grown, it is time for the messenger of Chinese ethics born about the same time to set on its path toward the world.

I would like to thank my old friend Xuejun Yan, the kind and mission-filled editor Ms. Lin Wang, and the senior translators Mr. Xiaohua Tong and Ms. Yanan Shao. This is not my first work to be translated, but it is a work that I anticipate most. I hope that it will have soulmates in foreign lands and will not be too lonely.

June 2024   Hao Fan
                              The National University of Singapore

BIBLIOGRAPHY

Alain Touraine, *Can We Live Together?* Chinese version by Di Yuming and Lin Ping'ou, Beijing: The Commercial Press, 2003.

Bertrand Arthur William Russell, *Human Society in Ethics and Politics*, Chinese edition, Beijing: China Social Science Press, 1999.

Cf. To Cho Yee (Ed.), *Transplantation and Application of Western Social Sciences Theories*, The Chinese University of Hong Kong Press, 1993.

Chen Lai, "Feng Youlan's 'Ethical Concept'," *Journal of Tsinghua University, Humanities and Social Sciences*, 2016.

Guo Qingfan, *Interpreting Zhuangzi*, Vol. I (1), punctuated and collated by Wang Xiaoyu, Beijing: Zhonghua Book Company, 1961.

G. W. E. Hegel, *Elements of the Philosophy of Right*, Chinese version by Fang Yang and Zhang Qitai, Beijing: The Commercial Press, 1996.

Karl Jaspers, *Man in the Modern Age*, Chinese version by Wang Defeng, Shanghai: Shanghai Translation Publishing House, 1997.

Karl Jaspers, *The Origin and Goal of History*, New Haven, CT: Yale University Press, 1953.

Karl Jaspers, *The Origin and Goal of History*, Beijing: Huaxia Publishing House, 1989.

Liang Shuming, *Essentials of Chinese Culture*, Beijing: Academia Press, 2000.

Wang Yangming, *The Complete Works of Wang Yangming*, Shanghai: Shanghai Ancient Books Publishing House, 1992.

Yang Xiong, *Notes on Supreme Mystery*, Vol. 9, annotated by Sima Guang, Beijing: Zhonghua Book Company, 1998.

© Foreign Language Teaching and Research Publishing Co., Ltd 2024   191
H. Fan, *Lunli and Confucian Moral Theory*, Key Concepts
in Chinese Thought and Culture,
https://doi.org/10.1007/978-981-99-9105-1

GPSR Compliance

The European Union's (EU) General Product Safety Regulation (GPSR) is a set of rules that requires consumer products to be safe and our obligations to ensure this.

If you have any concerns about our products, you can contact us on ProductSafety@springernature.com

In case Publisher is established outside the EU, the EU authorized representative is:

Springer Nature Customer Service Center GmbH
Europaplatz 3
69115 Heidelberg, Germany

The manufacturer's authorised representative in the EU is Springer
Nature Customer Service Centre GmbH, Europaplatz 3, 69115 Heidelberg,
Germany. If you have any concerns regarding our products, please
contact ProductSafety@springernature.com

Printed and bound by CPI Group (UK) Ltd, Croydon, CR0 4YY
29/04/2026
02099545-0001